Global Pressure, National System

A volume in the series

Cornell Studies in Political Economy
edited by Peter J. Katzenstein

For a list of titles in the series, see www.cornellpress.cornell.edu.

Global Pressure, National System

How German Corporate Governance Is Changing

Alexander Börsch

Cornell University Press
Ithaca and London

First published 2007 by Cornell University Press

Printed in the United States of America

Library of Congress Cataloging-in-Publication Data

Börsch, Alexander.
   Global pressure, national system : how German corporate governance is changing / Alexander Börsch.
      p.   cm. — (Cornell studies in political economy)
   Includes bibliographical references and index.
   ISBN-13: 978-0-8014-4536-1 (cloth : alk. paper)
   1. Corporate governance—Germany.   2. Globalization—Germany.   I. Title.   II. Series.
   HD2741.B65 2007
   658.40943—dc22

                                                    2006035549

Cornell University Press strives to use environmentally responsible suppliers and materials to the fullest extent possible in the publishing of its books. Such materials include vegetable-based, low-VOC inks and acid-free papers that are recycled, totally chlorine-free, or partly composed of nonwood fibers. For further information, visit our website at www.cornellpress.cornell.edu.

Cloth printing   10 9 8 7 6 5 4 3 2 1

To my parents and my grandmother

Contents

Figures and Tables

Acknowledgments

This book was made possible by the many people who contributed in numerous ways to the ideas developed here. The project began at the European University Institute (EUI) in Florence. At the EUI, my thanks first and foremost go to Martin Rhodes for his support and encouragement. I am greatly indebted to him. Throughout the project, he supported me in every conceivable way, generously providing ideas, contacts, and suggestions, and kept me on track. I am also most grateful to Fritz Kratochwil, who introduced me to the field of political economy and international relations, guided me through my years of study in Munich, and had a major impact on my ideas over the years.

A number of people gave me feedback on parts or all of the book and provided constructive advice, suggestions, and criticisms. I thank Colin Crouch, Markus Lederer, Mary O'Sullivan, Falk Reckling, and Winfried Ruigrok for their valuable input. Many other people provided helpful suggestions when I presented the book's underlying ideas. I am indebted to the participants of the three European Political Economy Infrastructure Consortium (EPIC) workshops in Corfu as well as the seminar participants at the EUI and the University of Warwick. Comments on related work from Michel Goyer, Wyn Grant, Peter Hall, Bob Hancké, and David Soskice helped me a lot in revising.

Over the course of the work, I enjoyed the hospitality of several institutions. My thanks go to the London School of Economics and Political

Science, the Wissenschaftszentrum Berlin (WZB), the University of Warwick, and INSEAD, where Jonathan Story made my stay possible. I am particularly grateful to the Deutsche Akademische Austauschdienst (DAAD) and the European University Institute for funding the study. I am also grateful for grants from the European Union that paid for my stays at LSE and Warwick.

Special thanks go to Bob Hancké. He not only facilitated my stays at LSE and the WZB and supervised me during the EPIC workshops but also provided continuous invaluable input at various stages on content and research design questions.

The final shape of the book owes much to Peter Katzenstein. He was sometimes tough, but always enormously helpful and constructive. His comments helped me a lot in shaping my argument. I also profited from the comments by an anonymous reviewer. Katherine Tobin provided valuable linguistic support. I am grateful to all these people, but the errors that might remain in the book are of course mine.

Finally, I am thankful to my parents, Rita and Joseph Börsch, and my grandmother, Anna-Lina Metzdorf, for their unconditional support and encouragement over the years. I am also grateful to my partner, Alexandra Storck, for her support and her understanding. I thank her and my daughter Lara for insisting that there is a life beyond corporate governance and much, much more.

Global Pressure, National System

Chapter 1

Theory and Practice of Corporate Governance

Corporate governance is a core element in the institutional setup of political economies. How firms are directed and controlled, and how national economic and political institutions shape the governance patterns of corporations, has become one of the main issues in comparative political economy and public policy. Not only are there strong differences in the governance of states; traditionally firms have also displayed marked diversity in the way they govern themselves. Continental European and Japanese firms have not had much in common with their Anglo-Saxon counterparts in areas such as business policy, finance, organization, and employee influence. Corporate governance systems in the Anglo-Saxon countries, termed *outsider* or *shareholder* systems, have been fairly close to the market ideal. On the other hand, corporate governance in Continental Europe and Japan relied to a much higher degree on coordination through relationships and negotiations between the key actors within the firm; hence the label *insider* or *stakeholder* systems best applies to these systems.[1] A large part of the differences between these two systems has been grounded in different national institutions and their impact on firm behavior.

Ironically, the academic discussion about differences of corporate governance systems became more visible at a time when these differ-

[1] The notions *insider/stakeholder* and *outsider/shareholder* systems will be used interchangeably.

ences were widely thought to be disappearing. German corporate governance in particular has had a fairly volatile standing in academic research over the last twenty years. When corporate governance became a topic of serious academic investigation in the 1980s, the German version of stakeholder corporate governance was considered exemplary, in line with the then superior growth performance of the German economy. In the 1990s the German model lost this role and became associated with low economic growth rates, inflexibility, and backwardness.

Why this change in public perception? The main reason has to do with the global integration of financial and product markets. Globalization threatens the diversity of corporate governance systems, because it seems to reward market-oriented systems. The rise of institutional investors, the growing importance of stock markets, the new economy bubble, the ideological predominance of neoliberalism, and the competition on global product markets all seem to favor shareholder-oriented systems and make the stakeholder model appear outdated. In this context, the viability of different sorts of corporate governance and capitalism more generally, as well as institutional change and continuity within national models, have become pressing questions of academic and practical interest.

Globalization and Corporate Governance

Scholars are deeply divided over the question: How does globalization affect stakeholder systems in general and the German variant in particular? The key question has been whether globalization pressures force stakeholder systems to abandon their institutional trajectories and transform themselves into shareholder systems. Basically, two schools of thought emerged. Convergence theory suggests that transformation is inevitable. It starts from the assumption that market governance is superior in terms of efficiency to other forms of economic governance. Globalization leads to increased competition for capital and customers in international markets. Since only those firms that satisfy investors' demands for high profits and share prices will get the necessary sums of capital, firms from stakeholder systems have to surrender to the norms of the capital markets and to investor preferences. Similarly, in order to confront increased price competition on the product markets, firms from stakeholder systems will have to adopt market-oriented corporate governance structures to lower costs and increase efficiency, which requires the introduction of shareholder system–type institutions. Otherwise, they will be driven out of the market.[2] This imitation will spill over to decision-making structures and firm behavior. Eventually, the competition between corporate governance systems will lead to the demise of the stakeholder variant and the formerly different systems will converge into a single, market-based standard.

The second school of thought, broadly associated with the "varieties of capitalism" approach, rejects the assumption that a "one best way" exists. It argues that there is not only one, but that there are multiple equilibria for corporate governance and economic systems as a whole. Firms face different institutions in different countries, which provide incentives to pursue different strategies with different structures. Therefore, national institutions give rise to different corporate governance systems and enable firms to excel in different activities and markets within the global economy.[3] There is a close fit between national institutions, the competitive advantages of firms, and the comparative advantages of political economies. These institutions are interdependent and complementary, and together form a coherent system of economic organization. Consequently, globalization will not destroy the structures of the stakeholder systems, but will reinforce the prevailing patterns of corporate strategy and governance. Firms are expected to deepen their product market specializations; since these specializations are dependent on their corporate governance system and the wider institutional infrastructure, the diversity of corporate governance will be reinforced. Globalization will therefore not result in a transformation of corporate governance, but in institutional reproduction and stability. In this view, globalization is not about becoming more alike, but becoming more diverse by leveraging different competitive advantages.

Empirically, scholars have focused on the paradigm case of a stakeholder system: Germany. The main reason for the attention German corporate governance has attracted is that German firms managed to achieve a high degree of competitiveness in the postwar era despite or because of—depending on the perspective—its stakeholder-oriented governance structures. So far, the ongoing changes in German corporate governance and other stakeholder systems have been mainly studied on the aggregate level. But looking mainly at quantitative indicators on the whole system can only uncover broad tendencies that are underway. However, globalization affects some firms more than others. In this way, aggregate data may obscure the relationship between economic integration and its effects on corporate governance.

[2] See Bratton, McCahery (2000), 18.
[3] See Hall, Soskice (2001).

The Centrality of Firms

The purpose of this book is therefore to complement the literature on the effects of globalization on corporate governance by concentrating on the firm level and by disaggregating firm behavior into its various components. Investigating and disaggregating the behavior of firms allows a more subtle understanding of the effects of globalization. Convergence theory and the varieties of capitalism approach do theorize about firm behavior under the pressures of globalization but hardly ever investigate the adjustment paths of single firms. Both approaches adhere to an *equilibrium conception* of corporate governance systems, in which either one equilibrium replaces another, or the existing equilibrium does not change substantially. In line with standard microeconomic reasoning, convergence theory treats firms as black boxes that immediately adjust to changing environments and to changes in relative prices. The mechanisms of this adjustment, however, are rarely considered. Institutional approaches, such as varieties of capitalism, focus on the effects of national institutions on corporate governance. However, institutions cannot force firms to follow a certain pattern of behavior; they allow a variety of adjustment paths.[4] Institutional frameworks may exclude certain adjustment paths but cannot prescribe which ones are chosen. How firms adjust to a new environment is therefore not deducible from the institutional framework.

In this sense, the behavior and strategies of firms are critical variables that mediate between globalization and its effects on corporate governance. There is no lockstep relationship between globalization pressures and outcomes on the firm–level, nor between institutions and firm strategies. Firms have a toolbox of choices to adjust to globalization, and the empirical part of this study will explore which tools they chose for this adjustment. Another advantage of doing firm-level research is that the link between corporate governance and product market strategy, one of the key causal relationships in the varieties approach, is best studied on the firm level.

I will use case studies to investigate German "flagship firms," which are most affected by financial and/or product market pressures and whose behavior is likely to affect the behavior of other firms in the economy more generally through demonstration effects.[5] After all, firms that are especially exposed to globalization feel its effects the deepest. If these firms reproduce their traditional corporate governance patterns, then this should also hold for firms that are affected to a lesser degree. In

[4]Hancké, Goyer (2005).
[5]Lane (2000a), 210.

this sense, I have constructed a "double" critical case research design. Because of the stakeholder character of the system, German corporate governance in general should be highly affected by globalization, and the most exposed firms should be the most affected subunits within the system. I will disaggregate firm behavior into several dimensions in order to gain a more subtle understanding of the adjustment paths of German firms. The puzzle of the study is therefore the following: To what extent does adjustment transform the distinct characteristics of corporate governance on the firm level, and are there differences in the degree of change in the various elements—and why?

The firms investigated are Siemens, Deutsche Telekom, and Bosch. Siemens and Deutsche Telekom both decided to list on the New York Stock Exchange (NYSE). Hence, new investors must be targeted in competition with American and international companies that are likely to be more shareholder value oriented, so the demand for a change in the corporate governance arrangement increases and should have a major impact.[6] Moreover, listing on the NYSE implies—according to convergence theory—compliance with American standards of corporate governance.[7] In both cases, the firms have had additional incentives for substantial change in their strategies and structures. Deutsche Telekom, as a former state enterprise, has had to signal its commitment to shareholder value in order to win investors. Because of deregulation, Siemens has had to confront the challenge of the loss of its quasi-monopolist position in several markets. Despite these similarities, there is a major difference: Siemens's ownership is widely dispersed, whereas Deutsche Telekom's ownership structure is highly concentrated. Since the effects of ownership structure play a prominent role in the corporate governance discussion, this difference allows us to investigate whether ownership concentration has significant effects on adjustment paths. Moreover, Siemens is heavily exposed to capital market pressures not only because of its dispersed ownership structure but also because of its wide-ranging activities, which the stock markets tend to punish with the so-called *conglomerate discount*.[8]

Bosch is highly internationalized in terms of product markets, but it is an unlisted firm. Therefore, the case of Bosch enables us to disentangle the effects of financial and product market globalization. Since financial and product market globalization affect most large firms, these two factors are hard to separate, and the relative influence of each is hard to assess. Therefore they are mostly presented as an interwoven challenge

---

[6]See Maher, Andersson (1999), 30. See also Davis, Useem (2002), 252.

[7]See Coffee (1999).

[8]Conglomerate discount means that conglomerates as a whole have a lower value on the stock exchange than their parts. This is due to their lower transparency compared to single product firms and investors' fears of cross-subsidization.

that demands changes in the behavior of firms and leads in the same direction. Moreover, as an unlisted but highly internationalized firm, Bosch is representative of many of the medium-sized companies that are widely considered to be the backbone of the German economy.

I will investigate the main structural areas in which German firms have behaved differently compared to their counterparts from shareholder systems. The American system of corporate governance will be used as a benchmark for assessing changes in German corporate governance. Although the American corporate governance system is a moving target, the American economy is the "closest approximation to the Walrasian equilibrium model. . . . Only under this system is there so much mobility in the labor market, and is the market for corporate control rights, or takeover mechanisms, so highly developed. It is its resemblance to the model of perfect competition that is believed to lend the Anglo-American system a high degree of rationality and legitimacy."[9]

Working on the level of the firm, the concept of restructuring will be used. *Restructuring* is defined as a "significant and rapid change along one or more of three dimensions: assets, capital structure or management."[10] *Financial restructuring* involves changes in the debt/equity mix, greater payments to shareholders or stock buybacks, changes in firms' governance structure, and its relationships to shareholders and the capital market. *Portfolio restructuring* refers to asset divestment, diversification, acquisitions, and downsizing. Lastly, *organizational restructuring* involves changes in the structure, systems, and/or people of the company.[11] Along all these dimensions, German firms have differed structurally from their Anglo-Saxon counterparts. If the integration of financial and product markets transforms the German corporate governance system, we should see changes in all of these dimensions as the outcome of restructuring; and these changes should point toward Anglo-Saxon patterns. Therefore, wherever possible, the findings of the case studies will be compared to developments among the direct Anglo-Saxon competitors of Siemens, Deutsche Telekom, and Bosch in order to see whether the firms are taking similar paths of adjustment.

Thus the research questions are whether the firms under investigation have restructured toward shareholder value patterns; how they restructured; whether the restructuring efforts have led to significant changes in the firms' governance structure in response to capital market pressures; and to what extent they have introduced shareholder value-related instruments, and if so how these are designed? In order to judge the developments, some benchmarks will prove helpful. The convergence

[9] Aoki (2000), 3.

[10] Ruigrok, Pettigrew, Peck, Whittington (1999), 42–43.

[11] See Bühner, Rasheed, Rosenstein (1997), 321–26, as well as Ruigrok, Pettigrew, Peck, Whittington (1999), 42–43.

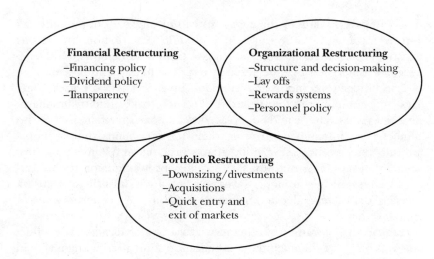

Financial Restructuring
–Financing policy
–Dividend policy
–Transparency

Organizational Restructuring
–Structure and decision-making
–Lay offs
–Rewards systems
–Personnel policy

Portfolio Restructuring
–Downsizing/divestments
–Acquisitions
–Quick entry and
  exit of markets

Figure 1: Dimensions of restructuring

model, which argues for changes along all of the restructuring dimensions, provides the benchmark case. The direction of changes, as envisaged by convergence theory, is as follows.

In the area of ownership structure and financing policy we should see a move toward more dispersed ownership structures, a greater role for foreign and institutional investors, as well as a higher dependency on financial markets in terms of corporate finance. Additionally, and as a consequence, we should see more investor-friendly dividend and information policies, and generally higher transparency.

In the realm of organizational restructuring and employment policy, we should see changes in the incentives of managers and employees toward capital-market-oriented performance measures, employment policies according to market swings, as well as changes in managerial compensation patterns and career paths. In terms of incentives, we should see the introduction of the main instruments for managers to focus on share prices in shareholder systems: profit goals for divisions, discounted cash flow principles for investment decisions, and stock options for management. Also codetermination itself should be under pressure, because shareholder value policies are antithetical to management-labor cooperation: they require quick reactions by management concerning employment levels, and a lower commitment to markets, the basis of long-term tenure of managers and employees. The search for higher flexibility might therefore lead to a weakening of codetermination, a more hire-and-fire oriented approach to employment policy, and a more open market for managers instead of internal recruitment and long tenure.

Concerning portfolio restructuring and product market policy, convergence theory lets us expect that in response to the central demand of a shareholder value approach—the concentration on core competencies—the commitment to product markets and corresponding long-term strategies will decrease and be replaced by an active portfolio policy with a quick entry into and exit from markets. If this happens, the traditional product market policy, diversified quality production (DQP) should also change, because its institutional preconditions would erode. In general terms, we should see a higher investor orientation, implying a focus on shareholder value, and a "downsize and distribute" approach in terms of general strategy.

Besides the pressure from financial markets, globalization of product markets may also change internationalization strategies. Changes should be in the direction of networklike transnational companies with only loose connections to their homebase and globally dispersed strategic functions instead of the traditional strategies of German companies to internationalization. The traditional internationalization strategies are a consequence of the German production model and are characterized by centralized decision making, centralized control, and a general approach to internationalization, which sees international operations as appendages to a central domestic corporation—the so-called multidomestic strategy—which results in a high embeddedness in the home base.[12]

The Path of Corporate Adjustment

The main message of this book is that globalization affects not all elements of corporate governance equally. Its impact varies significantly and institutional change is limited to certain areas of corporate governance. The firms discussed in this book introduced some institutional changes in confined areas, but preserved the main elements of their preexisting corporate governance arrangements and their fundamental structures, especially with regard to decision-making structures. Adaptation is partial, most pronounced in the area of information policy, but does not spill over to other elements of corporate governance, such as industrial relations and corporate strategy.

The pressure of financial markets prompts, above all, accurate information about the financial situation of enterprises. Since there is no corresponding move toward a market for corporate control on the macro

---

[12]See Lane (1998).

level, the higher transparency does not translate to deeper strategic issues. Therefore, financial and product market globalization do not result in a transformation of German corporate governance, as convergence theory would expect. The restructuring efforts differ from Anglo-Saxon patterns and practices of corporate restructuring in kind and in character. On the other hand, the findings also contradict the notion of strong complementarities in German corporate governance, which would imply a snowball effect to other institutions and the whole institutional ensemble once "alien" institutions are put in place.

Why is it that institutional change affects only some elements of corporate governance and leaves others intact? Building on institutional theories and research in the discipline of strategic management, I suggest that the explanation has three elements. First, preexisting institutions mediate financial market pressures and shareholder value demands; stakeholders subject these pressures and demands to negotiation. Thus, the concrete measures will be watered down in the process of decision making, adjusted to the institutional environment, and will therefore be less far-reaching than in shareholder systems.

Second, the shareholder value concept has several components. Some of these are much harder to introduce, because their conflict potential is high and they meet resistance on the part of the involved stakeholders. This implies that the introduction of the shareholder value concept in its entirety is highly unlikely, whereas selective adaptation is quite possible. Third, several institutional preconditions are the basis for upmarket product market strategies—especially DQP and system strategies. Thus it is not in the interest of management to change these preconditions, given that the most likely response to higher competition is the leveraging of existing assets and competitive advantages. Also, investors can be expected to accept these requirements of product markets and support the existing strategy. Therefore, core institutions that are crucial for the product market strategy are unlikely to change.

In sum, the process and outcome of restructuring in German firms are different from the patterns found in shareholder systems. Consistent with this, the firms under investigation followed similar paths despite their different ownership structures and characteristics. Their restructuring efforts generally emphasized cooperation with employees and have not resulted in a weakening of codetermination. Financial restructuring did not change their basic financing patterns; they have tried to avoid dependency on banks and financial markets. However, there is significant change in the information policies and a move toward higher transparency, especially at Siemens.

Organizational restructuring brought the introduction of some shareholder value instruments. Siemens and DT introduced stock options, but the designs of the schemes differ significantly from Anglo-Saxon practices and do not provide management with strong incentives to focus on share price as the exclusive goal of business policy. Siemens also introduced a management system that is supposed to govern the company according to financial market expectations. However, this instrument has been accommodated to its environment; the financial goals are much lower than those of its international competitors, and the concept did not actually result in an active portfolio policy, which the management system actually implies. Patterns of management recruitment and tenure remain largely unchanged.

In the realm of portfolio restructuring, Siemens, DT, and Bosch show a strong commitment to the markets in which they are active. Siemens and Bosch divested business lines, but these spin-offs were motivated more by a lack of competitiveness in fast-moving high-tech markets than by financial market demands to concentrate on core competencies in order to promote share price. In both cases, businesses were spun off that are based on radical innovation, an innovation pattern for which there is little institutional support in the German political economy.[13] Despite the spin-offs, expansion has been the main principle of the firms' business policies. The product market strategy of all three firms has been deepening with a focus on diversified quality production and systems solutions. An active portfolio policy would not fit this product market policy.

In terms of their internationalization strategy, all three firms internationalized aggressively. This internationalization, which has been fully supported by the work councils, follows the traditional patterns of a multidomestic strategy: it does not lead to the development of network structures within the enterprises and consequently to no disembedding from the homebase. The companies remain firmly anchored in the German corporate governance system, and all three have kept all of their strategic functions in Germany.

Overall, adjustment strategies have combined continuity in the basic strategies and structures with the introduction of some shareholder value instruments, which—in line with the institutional framework and the product market strategies pursued—are designed differently compared to shareholder system practices. The outcome is not convergence or imitation of the shareholder value model in all or even most of its aspects, but partial and selective adaptation without a fundamental change in the structures and strategies of German corporate governance.

[13]See Casper, Lehrer, Soskice (1999).

The book deals first with international differences in corporate governance and why they have emerged. Following this, I will present theoretical approaches dealing with the impact of globalization on corporate governance and explain why stakeholder systems should be under considerably more pressure to change than others. Following that, I will establish what a shareholder value policy implies for firms, what its elements are, and how these relate to corporate strategy. Finally, I will elaborate the argument about why German firms cannot be expected to adopt all elements of the shareholder value concept and why restructuring is likely to differ according to the issue area under investigation. In Chapter 3 I examine the properties of the German corporate governance system as the prototype of a stakeholder system, recent regulatory reforms in the financial system and business law, and aggregate changes in the relevant indicators of corporate governance during the 1990s. The indicators for assessing change are the main dimensions of corporate governance on the system level—corporate finance, ownership, merger and takeover activity, accounting standards, the role of institutional investors, the attitudes of management, and management remuneration patterns. Chapters 4–6 contain company case studies, while in chapter 7 I summarize the case studies, broaden the argument by presenting case study material on a wider sample of German firms, and draw out the theoretical implications of the study.

Chapter 2

Corporate Governance and Globalization

In the most basic sense, corporate governance refers to the way companies are controlled and operated. It captures the various rules and practices that impact the governance of firms. In other words, corporate governance is the study of the range of mechanisms and arrangements that affect decision making in corporations.[1] The notion of national systems of corporate governance implies that these rules and practices are not randomly distributed but shaped by the national environment in which firms operate. The governance arrangements of firms depend to a large degree on national structures, be they formal rules and regulations or more informal structures and practices. In this sense, corporate governance encompasses the institutional and legal arrangements that influence the behavior of firms.[2] Management literature emphasizes four basic forces that shape corporate governance systems: ownership structures, the relative importance of financial markets and banks, internal decision making, and regulatory environment; figure 2 illustrates this.[3] These are the main ways in which national systems of corporate governance differ and which influence governance practices, as well as the choice of strategies. Differences in these institutions give rise to different

---

[1] See Schmidt (2004), 388.

[2] See Dufey, Hommel, Riemer-Hommel (1998), 46.

[3] Based on Bühner, Rasheed, Rosenstein, Yoshikawa (1998), 123, with permission from Elsevier.

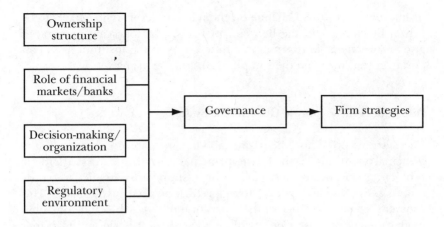

Figure 2: Shaping factors for corporate governance systems

relationships of firms with their environment, especially concerning the influence stakeholders and shareholders can exercise.

Nonetheless, there is no wholly deterministic relationship between the national environment and the governance of firms. Institutions are "the formal rules, compliance procedures, and standard operating practices that structure the relationship between individuals in various units of the polity and economy."[4] In the realm of corporate governance, practices and informal structures are at the heart of cross-national differences. Apart from laws and regulations to which firms must comply and which contribute to a certain uniformity of firms in a given country, most of the institutions that govern corporate governance are informal in nature and have developed historically. For example, close relationships between banks and firms or concentrated ownership structures are informal institutions that are possibly supported by certain regulations, but certainly not determined by them.

National systems of corporate governance provide a set of incentives and constraints to firms, but firms have significant degrees of freedom to respond to the institutional setup. Hence, it is crucial to distinguish two levels of corporate governance. The first level concerns the national environment; the second level encompasses the firm. On the firm level, companies decide how to structure their corporate governance arrangements within the national framework. They possibly even decide to pursue strategies that stand in contradiction to the national framework, which then puts pressure on the national framework itself. Therefore, institutional change can take place on the national level as well as on the

[4]Hall (1986), 19.

firm level. Institutional change on the national level is most likely to be driven by changes in the behavior of firms. The following paragraphs give an overview of cross-national differences in the institutions of corporate governance and their implications on the firm level.

Differences in Corporate Governance Systems

The starting point for theorizing about corporate governance is the principal-agent approach. In the principal-agent framework, the basic problem of corporate governance is how "suppliers of finance to corporations assure themselves of getting a return on their investment."[5] This problem is a consequence of the separation of ownership and control in modern corporations, a point first made by Adolf Berle and Gardiner Means in 1932.[6] The principal-agent problem arises in situations characterized by asymmetric information between the principal and the agent—or owner and manager—and differential risk aversion. The agent is normally better informed than the principal and therefore has an incentive to cheat and to maximize only his personal utility, thereby possibly damaging the principal.[7]

Perfect monitoring by the owners/principals is not feasible, because they are not qualified or informed enough to assess management's actions and its consequences. This is the very reason they hired the manager in the first place: they need the manager's human capital to generate returns on their funds.[8] The economic problem now is how to make sure that the agent acts in the interest of the owner. The shareholder is considered to be the owner, because he bears the risk of the company's performance and is thus the "residual claimant," while the other stakeholders receive returns according to their contract.[9] The solution to the principal-agent problem, therefore, is to design a contract that gives the agent highly powered incentives so that his interests are the same as those of the principal, so that the manager acts as if he were the owner. Owners therefore need to design monitoring mechanisms that ensure that the manager acts in a profit maximizing manner, which is assumed to be the only interest of the owner and to be a precondition for an efficient allocation of the firm's resources.

[5] See Shleifer, Vishny (1997), 737.
[6] See Berle, Means (1932).
[7] On the contractual nature of the firm, the position of the owner in this nexus of contracts, and the problems of team production see Alchian, Demsetz (1972).
[8] Ibid.
[9] Due to its view that the corporation exists primarily for the benefit of its shareholders, the principal-agent approach has been also named the finance model of corporate governance.

However, the principal-agent approach leaves out critical dimensions of corporate governance. Its results depend on the prior assumption that the main problem of corporate governance is the relationship between owners and managers. But there are other actors involved in the governance of the firm who are not considered in the principal-agent framework: for example, employees, creditors, suppliers, other firms, and the larger public, whose influence impacts on the way corporations are governed. In reality, most organizations and firms are multilayered hierarchies.[10] Thus, in many settings it is not clear who is the principal and who is the agent. Even though it is possible to introduce models with multiple principals and multiple agents, the results are not as clear-cut as in the basic principal-agent model. Consequently, the application of the principal-agent approach is only fruitful in quite limited settings; its focus on one incentive problem gives "much too limited a view of the nature of the firm, and one that is potentially misleading."[11]

Related to this is the exclusion of national institutions and their consequences for the principal-agent problem from the analysis. National institutions are either left out of the principal-agent analysis or are treated as a drag on efficiency when they do not conform to the recommendations of the theory. However, the importance of the principal-agent problem is dependent on the way in which corporate governance systems are organized. In systems in which ownership is concentrated, the principal-agent problem is less urgent than in systems with dispersed ownership, because majority owners have powerful devices to monitor and control management as opposed to dispersed investors, who suffer from the free-riding problem in monitoring management. The institutions of ownership therefore lie at the heart of differences in corporate governance systems, which will be dealt with next.

Shareholder versus Stakeholder Systems

The corporate governance systems of the advanced economies can be broadly categorized into stakeholder/insider and shareholder/outsider systems. These distinctions are based on the mechanisms of control and the relative influence of stakeholders and shareholders on decision making within the firm. The most important differences between stakeholder and shareholder systems are the following:

---

[10]See Aoki (1996), 5. It can also be argued that other groups, particularly workers, also make investments in terms of firm-specific human capital, which should give them voice in the management of the firm. For an argument along these lines see Blair (1995).

[11]See Holmström, Roberts (1998), 75.

- Ownership Concentration: In shareholder systems we find dispersed ownership; the main actors on the financial markets are institutional investors, which diversify their holdings as much as possible to minimize portfolio risks. In stakeholder systems, ownership is concentrated with nonfinancial firms, individuals, and banks being the main shareholders. The importance of institutional investors is therefore much lower.
- Financial Systems: The main distinction here is between capital-market-based and bank-based financial systems, which differ in the role they assign to markets and financial institutions in channeling savings to investment. Shareholder systems of corporate governance go with market-based financial systems and stakeholder systems with bank-based financial systems. In the former, firms rely for financing on the financial markets, which contributes to a high market capitalization and implies a minor role for banks. The legal framework emphasizes full information through strict disclosure requirements and strong legal protection for minority investors. In bank-based systems, financial intermediation is largely done by banks; capital markets are therefore underdeveloped and regulations tend to favor debtors over shareholders. Firms and banks have a long-term relationship, and banks have access to firm-specific information. This allows banks to provide long-term credits—or "patient capital"—that are not necessarily based purely on market criteria. Banks try to maximize the returns from the relationship as whole, not from single projects. Due to the information advantage of banks and their prominent role in company financing, stakeholder systems provide less publicly available information and less legal protection for minority investors.[12]
- Mechanisms of Control: Owing to the different ownership and financial market institutions, control is exercised very differently. In shareholder systems, the core control mechanism of the monitoring structure is the market for corporate control, which is supposed to encourage managers to act in the interest of the investors because an underperforming firm runs the risk of becoming the target of a hostile takeover. Hence, the main goal of managers should be to maximize the share price in order to prevent a takeover, which would cost management its job. Control is of an external character and works through market mechanisms. On the other end of the spectrum, concentration of ownership leads to internal control in stakeholder systems. Concentrated ownership with its consequences of underdeveloped financial markets and an absence of markets for corporate control discriminates against market control. Insiders or stakeholders with a privileged position and superior information control the firm.[13]
- Coordination mechanisms: These institutional differences affect the capacities for coordination of firms in different corporate governance sys-

[12]Steinherr (1998), 185.
[13]Schmidt (1999), 14.

tems. In shareholder systems, market-based relations between the economic actors prevail. The minority and institutional investors very rarely
have strategic interests in the firms they are investing in; they want to
maximize returns on their capital and are not interested in direct control of the company. Owing to the free-rider problem, monitoring of
firms is difficult for dispersed investors, and the costs of monitoring are
too high for the single investor. "Exit," the selling of shares, is the dominant reaction when firms run into trouble. In stakeholder systems, the
large investors tend to pursue "voice" strategies within the company, because "exit" is costly. The agency problem is mitigated, because insiders
can confront management on the basis of long-term commitments and
relations and force a strategic change, a form of behavior unavailable to
dispersed investors. Insiders are also less affected by shareholder pressures and short-term share performance.[14]

These distinguishing characteristics have significant implications for
other areas of corporate behavior, especially for corporate strategy.[15]

Corporate Governance and Corporate Strategy

The different features of financial market organization and control
mechanisms shape the strategy of firms, since they limit the range of options that are available to a firm and create incentives to behave in a certain way. In stakeholder systems, the long-term nature of relationships
between various stakeholders encourages long-term strategies and specific investments on behalf of the firm. There is a high degree of commitment and trust between stakeholders, enabled by concentrated ownership, which facilitates stability in company development. Reliance on
bank finance ensures that firms can afford to neglect their own share
prices, because they are largely independent from the financial markets
in raising capital, which is mainly provided by banks. A hostile takeover is
unlikely to succeed because the controlling owners can be expected to
support incumbent management owing to their insider position. Thus,
shareholder value maximization is not the top management priority in
stakeholder systems. Instead, a stakeholder orientation prevails, in which
the claims of the various stakeholder groups are balanced. This allows a
longer time horizon and the consideration of the concerns of nonshare-
holder constituencies. The prevalence of long-term investment has the

[14]See OECD (1998a), 20.
[15]For econometric evidence on the relationship between labor relations, firm strategy,
and corporate governance in different systems see Hall, Gingerich (2001). See also Bassanini, Ernst (2002).

consequence that firms from stakeholder systems often pursue growth in market share at the cost of lower rates of return on equity investment.[16]

The institutional setup and the central role of insiders also shape the adjustment strategy of the firm. Since strategic decisions must be coordinated between several actors, a strategy of "small steps" seems likely to be taken by firms in stakeholder systems.[17] Changing a strategy involves bargaining, is information intensive, and requires patience on part of the stakeholders. Patience is needed because a strategy of small steps may lead initially to performance deterioration en route to the proposed aim. The advantage of this strategy is that the end result is more precisely targeted, but on the other hand it is more time consuming. However, once decisions are taken, they are likely to be implemented without further conflict.

The properties of shareholder systems encourage different strategies. Market-based relations between the relevant actors and the dependence of firms on the stock markets give firms a high flexibility in adapting to change. Firms from shareholder systems tend to rely on "big leaps." This strategy seems appropriate because although big leaps may be inexact, they do not need much time to complete and in the case of success, they pay off. They also do not require patience on the part of the shareholders: they are free to exercise the exit option if they disagree with the goals of the big leaps, that is, the general strategy. And if they do so, they are easily replaceable. Thus, coordination between the actors is not needed, which facilitates the big leap strategy and more generally greater flexibility. Owing to capital market pressures and an active market for corporate control, corporate governance in shareholder systems primarily "refers to the defence of shareholder's interest."[18]

This means, in terms of strategy, that firms in shareholder systems have a higher flexibility at the price of limited capacity for long-term strategic planning, again a mirror image of stakeholder systems. In sum, the basic strategic orientation of firms is to a high degree dependent on the prevalent corporate governance structure, which sets up incentives for different strategies and different patterns of change.

The structures of corporate governance also impact the formation of human capital, internal labor markets, and the career paths of employees. In principle, firms want their employees to invest in firm-specific human capital, because this enhances productivity, especially if the acquired skills or knowledge are tacit. Whether employees will do so depends to a large degree on the incentives they encounter. If they are to

[16]See Bratton, McCahery (2000), 9.
[17]For the distinction between "small steps" and "big leaps" strategies see Hackethal, Schmidt (2000), 23–26.
[18]Tirole (2001), 1.

invest in firm-specific human capital, which is difficult to transfer to other firms, they need to ensure that their investment will be worthwhile. Thus a mechanism is needed that guarantees that they are not easily fired and that they can influence the strategy of the firm. In other words, employees need a credible commitment on part of the management that their investment will not be lost.

One way to provide such a commitment is long average job tenure, increasing salaries linked to qualifications or the practice of recruiting managers from inside the firm, and the provision of "voice" to employees. This creates incentives to accumulate firm-specific human capital. To facilitate that accumulation, management must be able to ensure long-term financing; otherwise, its commitment would not be credible, because laying off employees would be unavoidable in difficult market situations. Hence, long-term financing, facilitated by the bank-firm relationship, can be seen as a precondition for credible commitments that facilitate the accumulation of human capital. And since human capital is often firm-specific, employees must have opportunities for the exercise of internal influence within the firm.[19] This pattern of human capital formation is congruent with stakeholder systems.

In shareholder systems, employees face a different set of incentives. The management does not have the institutional capacities to provide a credible commitment because its strategy is dependent on the reactions of the stock market. Thus management needs the option to restructure the firm quickly and fundamentally in order to increase share price. Furthermore, a long-term planning horizon is made difficult by the possibility of a hostile takeover, which may render implicit contracts and firm-specific human capital worthless. Therefore, inside influence is quite limited because management needs to be free to maneuver. It enables management to react more flexibly to new market opportunities. This freedom to maneuver, however, makes credible commitments with stakeholders less likely.

Knowing this, employees will invest in transferable assets that are valuable to many firms.[20] Acquiring firm-specific assets would be of limited utility because these assets could become sunk costs. Hence employees are not interested in inside influence, their relationship with their employer is more market-based, and they try to preserve their outside opportunities. Therefore, the job fluctuation in shareholder systems is higher and tenure is shorter. An important feature of this labor market is that pay is more incentive-based. The wage differentials within the firm are higher and career paths do not favor employees within the firm.

---

[19] See Hall, Soskice (2001), 25, and Hackethal, Schmidt (2000), 20.
[20] See Hall, Soskice (2001), 30.

TABLE 2.1
Differences between stakeholder and shareholder systems

	Stakeholder system	Shareholder system
Ownership concentration	Concentrated shareholdings	Dispersed shareholdings
Type of financial system	Bank-based / Relationship banking with control orientation	Capital market-based with liquidity orientation
Monitoring	Strong monitoring function for banks and other non-financial enterprises	Monitoring function fulfilled by the market for corporate control
Mode of coordination	Relationship-based with various stakeholders	Market-based with arm's length relationships between actors
Transparency	Privileged information for insiders	High disclosure to outside investors
Human capital formation	Incentive to build up firm-specific human capital; long tenure	Incentive to acquire general human capital; short tenure
Strategy of firms	Long-term oriented, "small steps" strategies, and market share orientation	Short-term oriented, "big leap" strategies, and shareholder value orientation

Management positions are often filled by outside candidates and management's compensation is linked to share price through stock options.

The same mechanism works also in the market for managers. Shareholder systems have a well-developed market for managers; thus managers are primarily interested in their own marketability. This again leads, as in the case of "normal" employees, to the acquisition of generally applicable knowledge, because of a need to develop a professional reputation and to be ready to change jobs quickly. Since stakeholder systems recruit the bulk of their managers from internal labor markets, short-term trends do not matter significantly to managers, because they can rely on long-term employment and a slower career path within the same firm. However, they are risk-averse, because they need to minimize employment risks.[21]

Table 2.1 summarizes the most important differences between corporate governance systems. In sum, the differences in financial and corporate governance systems lead to substantially different outcomes in firm strategies. If we assume that neither of these systems is—in its pure form—generally superior to the other in terms of efficiency,[22] the ques-

[21] See Hoskisson, Yiu, Kim (2000), 140.
[22] See Shleifer, Vishny (1997), 773; Maher, Andersson (1999), 44, as well as La Porta, Lopez-de-Silanes, Shleifer (1998).

tion is why systems with such different features may be functionally equivalent.

Complementarities in Corporate Governance

The existence of complementarities is crucial for the fit of economic institutions. Basically, complementarity means that one institution functions better if certain other institutions are also present. These institutions are therefore interdependent and together they form a specific sort of economic organization that is coherent and varies from country to country. Put differently, each institution "permits or facilitates the existence of the others,"[23] that is, they form what Douglass North calls an "institutional matrix."[24] This central role of complementarities implies, in turn, that changing one institution has consequences for the whole system, because it may threaten "a certain pattern of complementarity."[25]

In the context of corporate governance the "institutional matrix" structures relations between owners, boards, top managers, and employees; and it shapes the goals of the corporation. Complementarity is a precondition for consistency: "Complementarity is an attribute of elements of a given system, and consistency is the corresponding attribute for entire systems. Elements of a system are complementary (to each other) if they 'fit together,' i.e. mutually increase their 'benefit' in terms of whatever the objective function or the standard for evaluating the system may be, and/or mutually reduce their disadvantages or 'costs.' "[26]

Hence, complementarities can explain why very different corporate governance systems can be equally efficient: the contrary values for the elements within stakeholder and shareholder systems complement each other in different ways, which results in two consistent systems. Generally, the fit between the institutional elements leads to an institutional logic or an institutional path of corporate governance. Institutional logic is characterized by "a distinct pattern of constraints and incentives [that] generate typical *strategies*, routine approaches to problems and shared decision rules that produce predictable patterns of behavior by actors. When actors are confronted with new situations they will resort to these strategies, routines, and decision rules."[27]

The presence of complementarities makes it hard to import elements from another system. If the single elements are not separable, but part of a larger institutional structure and logic, best practice aspirations become useless. For example, if elements of shareholder systems are intro-

---

[23] See Amable (1999), 8–9, and Aoki (1996).
[24] North (1994), 361.
[25] Amable (1999), 10.
[26] Schmidt, Spindler (1999), 9.
[27] Deeg (2001), 14.

duced into stakeholder systems, the overall coherence of a system may be distorted. This may lead to two different outcomes. The change can have no effect, because it does not lead to adjustments in actors' incentives and the system works as it used to. Alternatively, reforms may lead to an unworkable blend of the two systems with efficiency losses. These efficiency losses are due to the distortion of the local optimum, that is, the equilibrium the system had achieved. And since there are, in the complementarity perspective, only local optima, and not global ones, efficiency decreases. The old system may be destroyed without the emergence of a superior system, because the supporting institutions are lacking. A mixture of systems that tries to achieve the "best of both worlds" might be incoherent and dysfunctional, because the components are not divisible.[28] The result would be an inconsistent patchwork of different systems.

Hence, according to the complementarity concept, corporate governance systems tend to be stable, and if change happens, it is likely to happen in an abrupt manner.[29] However, in the presence of complementarities, predictions about change become indeterminate. Either reforms have no effect on the working of the system, or even small changes can destabilize the system, because institutions no longer fit together.

Why Do Corporate Governance Systems Differ?

Market economies can match up with widely varying corporate governance systems. There is more to corporate governance than the principal-agent problem. The preceding sections have established how institutions influence corporate governance. This, however, opens up the question of how and why these institutional differences developed in the first place, and how they are sustained.

Political Underpinnings of Corporate Governance

Political approaches to corporate governance start from the premise that political institutions are related to corporate governance institutions and may even determine them.[30] The degree of separation of ownership from control and the degree of labor influence in particular mirror the macrostructure of a nation on the microstructure of a firm. The key players of corporate governance—owners, managers, and employees—have to adapt to different political settlements and environments, which shapes the structure of firms.

[28] See Schmidt, Spindler (1999), 16.
[29] Hackethal, Schmidt (2000), 31.
[30] See Roe (2004).

Mark Roe was the first to develop a political theory of corporate governance. He stresses the ideological opposition between left and right for ownership concentration and labor influence. According to this variant of the politics approach, the development of corporate governance systems is dependent on the dominant political orientation of a country, ingrained in its party systems, political institutions, orientation of government, interest groups, and ideologies. The more social democratic a country is in its general political orientation, the more likely it is to have concentrated ownership and high labor influence. Social democracies are characterized by governments with a strong role in the economy, an emphasis on distributional policies, and a tendency to favor employees' interests.[31]

The political constraints in social democracies oppose coalitions between shareholders and managers and instead induce coalitions between managers and employees. Managers as well as employees have a preference to avoid downsizing, high-risk strategies, and rapid change; both prefer expansion, because expansion increases managers' prestige and workers' job security.[32] Unprofitable expansion, however, runs against the interest of investors who primarily seek profit maximization. Through this coalition of managers and employees, enabled through social democratic politics, the managerial agency costs for owners increase and, if ownership is dispersed, tight shareholder control is nearly impossible. Therefore, social democratic countries promote concentrated ownership. Concentrated ownership is the only possibility to control management in social democracies for owners. Ownership concentration is reinforced by the underdevelopment of shareholders' tools to discipline management in social democracies, such as transparent accounting, incentive compensation for management, or hostile takeovers.[33] Liquid financial markets and dispersed shareholdings do not fit social democracies and are therefore prevalent in the Anglo-Saxon countries. Hence, firms in social democratic countries will be much less committed to maximizing shareholder value than U.S. firms.

Generally, according to Roe's variant of the politics school, there are two "packages" of corporate governance in the rich democracies: "(1) competitive product markets, dispersed ownership, and conservative results for labor; and (2) concentrated product markets, concentrated ownership, and prolabor results. If social democracy is strong, product market competition will be weak and prolabor politics will prevail. Managers will side with employees and ownership will be concentrated to reduce managerial agency costs. If social democracy is weak, the op-

---

[31] Roe (2003), 24.
[32] Ibid., 37.
[33] Ibid., chapter 5.

posite applies. The elements in each package mutually reinforce one another."[34]

Since these elements are complementary, politics can determine the
structure of one of the elements and the others follow. Once the institutions are in place, change in one institution is difficult. It would require
a change in the other institutions and change across various institutional
spheres is difficult to coordinate, which is a severe obstacle to major
changes in corporate governance.[35] Path dependency characterizes corporate governance systems, even if the initial conditions have changed.
In this variant of the political approach, complementarities stabilize corporate governance because political reforms in all relevant areas are too
complex to yield significant results. However, it remains unclear what
happens to an institutional configuration if one element is changed and
the others are not, the common problem with the concept of complementarities.

A second strand of the "politics school" builds on Roe's insights and
agrees that corporate governance structures are the result of political decisions. But it enlarges the coalitional possibilities beyond the left versus
right scheme and explicitly incorporates political institutions into the
analysis. Peter Gourevitch and James Shinn combine the preferences of
the actors in corporate governance—management, labor, and investors—with the political institutions of a country in order to explain
the variance of corporate governance systems. Corporate governance systems, in their account, are shaped by the interaction of economic preferences and political institutions. Each group has preferences for a corporate governance regime that fits their interests best. These
preferences can be combined in a variety of ways, which makes different
coalitions between investors, managers, and workers possible.

Because the choice for a particular corporate governance regime is
determined in the political arena, coalitions are necessary. Which
group(s) wins depends to a high degree on political institutions that
shape the patterns of interest aggregation, and thereby the chances of
success for the different coalitions. Political institutions can enable or
hinder specific coalitions between owners, managers, and workers. The
resulting policies generate rules and regulations that affect the incentives of actors and consequently corporate governance outcomes, and
are a reflection of the preferences and power of the actors, mediated by
political institutions.[36] Different coalitions and the structure of political
systems determine whether countries operate block holder or diffused

---

[34] Ibid., 140.
[35] Ibid., 5–6.
[36] See Gourevitch, Shinn (2005), chapter 4.

ownership systems of corporate governance. The main divide between political systems is whether they are majoritarian or consensus systems. Majoritarian systems allow sharp swings in public policy and tend to support policies that work in favor of diffused ownership. Consensus systems are built on greater policy continuity and favor stable governance forms of block holding.[37]

Depending on the type of dominant cleavage or conflict—class, sectoral, or property—different coalitions can emerge with two groups forming a coalition against the third. However, preferences within these broad groups are not monolithic and can vary with sometimes diverging goals, which enlarges the coalitional possibilities. While the corporate governance outcome is either diffused or concentrated ownership, the political mechanisms leading to these results can be quite different. There are six possible political coalitions, two coalitions on each cleavage, which can lead to either diffused or concentrated ownership. Six models emerge from these coalitions: the investor, labor, corporatist compromise, oligarchy, transparency, and managerism models.[38]

Change in these models is less constrained by path dependency than in Roe's account. Change can happen when either the economic preferences shift or the political institutions are transformed. Since political institutions are fairly stable over time, change in corporate governance is most likely to be grounded in changing economic preferences. The most likely scenario for the latter case is change in the overall economic conditions. These may lead to new policy incentives and to changing policy positions of the actors, new coalitions, and new political regulations for corporate governance. However, which new equilibrium will be reached, in other words into which of the six models the corporate governance system develops, depends on political institutions.[39]

Social Underpinnings of Corporate Governance

Sociological approaches focus on the institutional embeddedness of corporate governance systems. They stress the structures in which firms are embedded and the relationships between actors, rather than the agency of firms or the political institutions. This perspective is based on the premise that all economic action is socially grounded. Social rules define social relationships and provide interpretative frameworks for actors, which organize interests. Once organized, these institutions tend to be

[37] Ibid., 16.
[38] See ibid., 116.
[39] Ibid., 525.

stable and also structure the shape of newly emerging firms and industries.[40]

According to sociologists, corporate governance, like all social institutions, is shaped by culture, ideology, and the values of society. It interacts
in myriad and complex ways with the institutional features of a country's
political economy. Hence, due to the diversity of national institutional
traditions and trajectories, many different corporate governance models
emerge. These are adapted to local circumstances and to the variety of
political, social, and economic actors involved in corporate governance.
Because of repeated interaction and because the internal structures of
firms reflect social processes, the governance structures within firms as
well as the social relations between firms and other actors tend to be
stable.[41]

The organizing logic of economic action differs from country to
country; institutions create a path-dependent context for economic action. These logics of economic and corporate governance systems are
held to be "repositories of distinctive capabilities that allow firms . . . to
pursue some activities in the global economy more successfully than others."[42] Efficiency stems not from the adherence to an abstract market
ideal, but from the match between the social organization of societies
and the opportunities of the global economy.[43] For example, traditions
influence the emergence of corporate networks, in terms of personal and
capital networks. These networks, in turn, enable firms to coordinate
their behavior and regulate competition. The industrialized countries
differ widely in terms of the significance of corporate networks, which
gives rise to more organized and more "spontaneous" market orders.[44]
Therefore, corporate governance systems are made up of different actors
with different relationships, which make universal principles, such as the
principal-agent approach, irrelevant.

Owing to institutional embeddedness, corporate governance is characterized by path dependency, because "history and accident play some
role in the origins of economic modes of organizing. At these originat-
ing moments, there may be several ways to organize production, none of
which has any obvious advantages. . . . Over time, institutions grow up
around a certain organization, and they tend to reinforce that organization's advantage."[45] Put simply, there are many ways to organize markets
and firms; which kind of organization is chosen depends on the institu-

---

[40] Ibid., 176.
[41] See Fligstein (2001), 7.
[42] Biggart, Guillen (1999).
[43] Ibid.
[44] See Windolf, Nollert (2001).
[45] Fligstein (2001), 175.

tional context. Foreign models that are perceived to threaten preexisting institutional arrangements thus tend to be rejected. Learning from other actors and other countries takes place only selectively.[46] Overall, economic sociology points to the fact that corporate governance systems do not emerge and evolve in a vacuum, but are shaped by nationally specific norms, values, and cultures. These broad institutions are not constraints for action, but resources. Countries focus on their different strengths, thereby producing not homogeneity, but diversity and renewal.[47] Thus the variety of corporate governance systems is not surprising or a drag on efficiency; it is an expression of different social environments. Whether this is still the case under conditions of globalization has been the main topic of the corporate governance debate in the social sciences in recent years.

Globalization and Corporate Governance: Convergence or Divergence?

Economic globalization refers to rapidly expanding international trade, investment, and capital flows. Financial and product market globalization are the most advanced aspects of globalization. Although there is considerable disagreement among scholars as to whether this process has created a truly unified market, it constitutes, without doubt, a new level of economic integration in the postwar era. That globalization is likely to affect corporate governance systems in an asymmetric manner results from the fact that corporate governance systems differ in their modes of coordination. Shareholder systems are based on the capital market, whereas stakeholder systems rely mainly on nonmarket coordination between several actors. The evolution of global finance essentially means a strengthening of the capital markets, and if global capital markets force corporations to pursue shareholder value maximization as their prime goal, this only reinforces existing properties of shareholder systems. Hence, globalization of finance does not require much change for shareholder systems.

This is different for countries with stakeholder systems. Their governance arrangements seem inconsistent with capital markets and shareholder value demands. Actors in stakeholder systems mainly coordinate through long-term relational contracting, which presupposes the presence of social networks, trust, and mutual consistent expectations. These conditions develop historically over decades, and dismantling them is much easier than developing them: "The ownership and governance features of insider systems encourage co-operative arrangements between

---

[46]Guillen (2000b), 8–9.
[47]See Guillen (2003), 228.

firms and between managers and employees. As with any co-operative arrangement they are vulnerable to exploitation of self-interest by particular parties."[48]

Globalization and Convergence

Proponents of the convergence thesis argue that economic globalization removes formerly relatively closed economies from the influence of national institutions and leads to the transformation of different capitalisms towards one, market-conforming model. The strong selection mechanism of markets will lead to the erosion of inefficient arrangements and to the emergence of a single, optimal equilibrium. In the field of corporate governance, the supposed mechanism, based on neoclassical economics, is as follows. Financial globalization facilitates capital mobility. Therefore, enterprises, wherever they are located, have to ensure that investing in their shares offers a competitive rate of return to investors.

If they do not, capital will move elsewhere. Investors will not provide firms with money that do not maximize shareholder value. Firms from stakeholder systems have to adopt an Anglo-Saxon style of corporate governance, because U.S. and British corporations provide higher returns to shareholders. They must ensure that arm's length investors get a comparable, risk-adjusted return. Hence, in order to stay competitive, firms will have to change their corporate governance structures to develop institutions similar to those typical of firms in shareholder systems, which give investors confidence that management's priority is shareholder value.

According to convergence theory, two mechanisms drive the process of convergence, whether induced by the market or investors. The first mechanism works through changes in relative prices. In global capital markets, the cost of capital should change for firms from stakeholder systems, which are then expected to reform their corporate governance structures. However, empirical research has not found evidence for lower capital costs in outsider systems.[49] A second mechanism is more actor-centered and assigns the role of "change agents" to institutional investors, such as insurance companies, pension funds, and investment companies, which dominate the share markets in shareholder systems.[50] Their growing role in stakeholder systems can be regarded as the "most

---

[48]Jenkinson, Mayer (1992), 9.
[49]See Becht, Bolton, Röell (2003), 43.
[50]For this reason, outsider systems are sometimes identified with "investor capitalism." For an extensive treatment on the influence of institutional investors in the U.S., see Useem (1996).

important factor in changing the financial structure and behavior in the OECD area."[51]

Furthermore, Anglo-Saxon institutional investors are investing increasingly in firms in stakeholder systems in order to diversify their portfolios. Institutional investors are expected to force firms to prioritize share price, because their sole business mission is to maximize the capital of their clients, and international investors must match the rates of return in their home market. These pressures will magnify with a growing stock of institutional investors.[52] Because the major institutional investors are mainly of Anglo-Saxon origin, they are likely to aim at changing the corporate governance structures in the firms in which they invest toward the Anglo-Saxon pattern of corporate governance. This may occur either via direct influence or via the selling of shares, which means problems for firms seeking to raise capital. Furthermore, on a more political level, institutional investors are likely to lobby for changes in the laws and regulations governing companies, such as adequate public disclosure standards, a market-oriented accounting system, and a generally transparent legal framework for the financial and institutional sectors.[53]

In sum, according to what can be called the *strong convergence thesis,* the outcome of financial globalization is that corporate governance systems must converge toward the market-oriented model of corporate governance, whose shareholder orientation fits better into the new financial environment: it constitutes a best practice to be imitated, because it is closer to the market-ideal. This holds for all enterprises, regardless of the institutional context.

The complete neglect of institutions and initial conditions is obviously a serious weakness of this approach. There is no consideration of how different institutions mediate between external shocks and domestic outcomes and how existing institutional matrices filter the external pressures in different systems. A refined globalization thesis acknowledges that institutions are difficult to change, but argues that this does not matter much for firm behavior. It starts out from the observation that the proposition of a complete convergence in forms of corporate governance underestimates the functional adaptivity of corporate governance systems as well as their persistence in form.[54] Formal convergence is too costly and therefore unlikely; the creation of new institutions requires new investments and the old institutions are backed by interest groups.

---

[51]Blommestein (1998), 41–42. For example, the total assets of the institutional investors in the OECD area rose from 36 percent of GDP in 1981 to 102 percent of GDP in 1995.

[52]Some institutional investors have already issued guidelines for corporate governance practices in different countries.

[53]See Blommestein (1998), 47.

[54]Gilson (2000).

Moreover, introducing new institutions may hurt the whole system of interdependent and complementary institutions.

Thus, it is not formal convergence, but functional convergence, that is expected to emerge if the existing institutions are flexible enough to accommodate the new demands of altered environments. Functional convergence implies an actor–centered perspective; despite the institutional infrastructure firms will act in the same way in different contexts. An example for this is provided by a study of CEO turnover in times of poor performance. Indeed, the reactions of firms and the tenure of the CEOs are by and large the same in the United States, Japan, and Germany.[55] The main point is that institutional structure does not determine the firms' courses of action. Firms can introduce strategies that are characteristic of other systems or they can try to find functional equivalents. Formal structural changes may not be necessary to bring competing corporate governance systems into relative parity.[56] The measures can be chosen by the firms, and formal institutional changes with high transaction costs are unnecessary. The prediction is that under globalization pressures, firms will imitate their most successful competitors, yet still within their own institutional framework. Therefore, at least on the firm level, convergence should be observable, due to globalization pressures.

Essentially, the approach acknowledges the existence of institutions but denies any serious institutional effects on firm behavior. Irrespective of the institutional framework, companies can choose the most efficient strategies.

"Varieties of Capitalism" and Divergence

That convergence and adherence to shareholder value is inevitable or efficient is denied by theories of divergence, especially the varieties of capitalism approach. On the contrary, advocates of this approach expect institutional reproduction and continued divergence in economic and corporate governance systems because national institutions and their different incentive structures continue to shape the behavior of firms and their possibilities to coordinate.

Crucial to the varieties perspective is the issue of coordination. The coordination problems of firms can be dealt with by market or by non-market coordination. The type of coordination that will be prevalent is dependent on national institutions, which are interdependent and complementary; hence political economies develop institutions in different areas, which all support one type of coordination, either market or non-market based.[57] These differences in coordination give rise to liberal

---

[55] See Kaplan (1994a,b).
[56] See Coffee (1999), 82.
[57] See Hall, Soskice (2001), 17–21.

market economies (LMEs), such as the United Kingdom or the United States, and coordinated market economies (CMEs), with Germany being the prime example. The wide range of nonmarket institutions in CMEs in areas such as finance, education and training, industrial relations, and intercompany relations provides actors with capacities for negotiating, monitoring, and enforcing agreements, thereby rendering nonmarket coordination possible.[58]

The differences in economic organization will lead to different specializations between countries because they facilitate or hinder the development of organizational competencies in firms that are necessary in order to compete in different markets. Therefore, firms have competitive advantages in different sectors and markets, which translates into "comparative institutional advantages" on the national level. Hence, CME and LME frameworks generate competitive firms but in different industries and with a different organizational structure.[59]

The mechanism through which specialization patterns are reinforced is the influence of institutions on innovation processes.[60] Incremental innovation—the continuous, but small scale, upgrading of established products or production processes—is best suited for CMEs, because it requires commitment and long-term relationships among the relevant actors as well as cooperative industrial relations, long-term finance, and a highly educated workforce. Radical innovation—the development of new products and processes—is prevalent in LMEs, because it involves large uncertainties and risks. Therefore, it requires room for management to maneuver, short-term finance, highly powered incentives for the workforce and generally a high degree of flexibility in order to react adequately to new and volatile markets. The differences between CMEs and LMEs are further amplified by the presence of institutional complementarities. Consequently, there is not a single efficient equilibrium but several, depending on the prevalent institutions and how these influence coordination between the actors.

The institutions of corporate governance determine in which competencies firms will invest and they interact to maximize coherence; in the case of CMEs:

A starting point is the conditions for an effective system of initial vocational training in company-specific and industry technology skills and in which companies make serious investments. This requires: long-run finance, since the return on the investment is a long-term one; coordinated wage setting, to minimise the risk of poaching, and cooperative company-level industrial relations to ensure cooperation from highly skilled and hence powerful employees; and cooperation between companies in tech-

---

[58] See Hall (1997), 297.
[59] Soskice (2000), 179.
[60] The following section builds on Soskice (1997) and on Casper (1999).

nology transfer and standard setting. . . . Long-run finance requires the
ability on the part of owners (or their delegated monitors) to have good information about the potential performance of companies and their competencies. . . . Cooperative industrial relations within companies require
that companies can credibly commit to long-run relations with employees,
which in turn requires long-term finance; it also requires highly skilled
employees, so that companies will be concerned not to lose them. Each element of the institutional framework thus reinforces the others.[61]

Owing to the institutional foundations of firm strategies, the varieties of
capitalism approach also expects institutional stability in corporate governance systems under conditions of globalization. Since firms derive
their competitive advantage from national institutions, they will try to
preserve them under conditions of globalization as well.

Furthermore, complementarities discriminate against radical change
in corporate governance, because actors try to preserve complementary
institutional arrangements in different spheres of the economy that are
of value to them.[62] Firms will try to sustain their institutional advantages
by leveraging their traditional competitive advantages that are dependent on the institutional frameworks.[63] Hence globalization will not transform economic and corporate governance systems, but reinforce their
characteristics. Therefore, adjustment paths and strategic behavior of
firms will remain distinctive, depending on the national institutional
context.[64] For stakeholder systems, this implies that we should not expect
a major transformation, but a continuing or even increasing reliance on
their traditional features.

Nevertheless, the greatest danger for stakeholder systems is seen in international financial deregulation, because if stakeholder firms raise a
sizable portion of their capital on international financial markets, they
become exposed to shareholder value demands and the necessity to
focus on shareholder value may destroy the long-term employment patterns, long-term relationships, and production strategies.[65] Thus
changes in one element of corporate governance may destabilize the
whole system. In the end, the prediction that the diversity of capitalisms
will persist and possibly even deepen stands on shaky ground. The role of
complementarities remains undertheorized because if complementarities can be responsible for both stability and transformation, then convergence is equally likely.

[61] See Soskice (2000), 172.
[62] See Hall, Soskice (2001), 64.
[63] See Guillen (2000a), 200.
[64] See Hall (1999) 161.
[65] Hall, Soskice (2001), 61.

Institutions, Shareholder Value, and Corporate Adjustment

The preceding discussion leaves us with two possible outcomes regarding the impact of globalization on stakeholder systems of corporate governance: either a transformation of stakeholder systems of corporate governance into shareholder systems or their continuing persistence. Both convergence theory and the varieties of capitalism approach focus on the level of whole corporate governance systems. This structural perspective cannot readily accommodate adjustment and change.

First, it allows only for dichotomous outcomes, because if there are only two coherent systems, then there can only be complete transformation or complete divergence. Both approaches suggest an equilibrium perspective on corporate governance systems. As commonly occurs in the analysis of comparative statics, convergence theory suggests that one equilibrium will be replaced by another due to exogenous factors.[66] The varieties approach assumes that these exogenous factors are not necessarily damaging to the existing equilibrium or not powerful enough to transform the ex-ante local equilibrium. In the first case, the mechanisms of transition between the equilibria are left open, whereas in the second it is hard to incorporate change at all. Conceptualizing change in a purely equilibrium perspective will therefore miss the more nuanced changes going on inside the models of corporate governance and especially on the firm level.

Second, both approaches play down the agency of firms. Convergence theory states that the globalization pressures force firms to adopt shareholder value strategies to avoid being driven out of the market. In this sense, firms do not have real options in their strategic behavior; it is dictated by market forces, which allow only one efficient course of action. In the varieties approach, firms are largely objects of their institutional environments. Choosing strategies that contradict the institutional framework is inefficient and will therefore not be pursued. However, firms do not mechanically adjust as the black box perspective of convergence theory suggests, nor are they simple institutions takers. Large firms in particular can be considered to be partly autonomous from their national corporate governance system, because their resources and their international engagement allow them to recombine national and international practices.[67]

Third, looking only on the systemic level will miss important dynamic elements of economic change. Firms are exposed to globalization pressures in different ways, so their strategies of adjustment will appear in the aggregate data only after a considerable time lag. Differences in their

[66] See Rathe, Witt (2001), 334.
[67] See Mayer, Whittington (1999), 936.

vulnerability will not enter aggregate data at all and different adjustment strategies will go unnoticed in aggregate analyses.

Hence, in order to study processes of adjustment and the effects of globalization on corporate governance, a move from the systemic level to the firm level seems inevitable. On the firm level, adjustment pressures should have an immediate impact. Conversely, adjustment strategies of leading companies will have an effect on the working and the institutional logic of the corporate governance system.

Elements of a Shareholder Value Strategy

What exactly do globalization and the pressures from financial markets imply for company strategies? In this context, the concept of shareholder value is central, because it is the expression of capital market preferences and the assumed outcome in convergence reasoning on the level of the firm. It is the link between capital market pressures and firm strategy. The shareholder value concept is derived from agency theory and consequently puts the shareholder at the center of attention. The shareholder is supposed to maximize his portfolio and to do so primarily by focusing on future cash flows. Thus, investors need transparency about the value and the strategy of the firms they want to invest in.

The fundamental purpose of the corporation is seen to be generating economic value for its shareholders, that is, the market value on the stock exchange. Traditional accounting measures do not necessarily reflect economic value for shareholders and are therefore seen as misleading. They are oriented toward the past and the linkage between these indicators and shareholder returns is uncertain.[68] Instead, the focus should be on net present values of investment projects. This means that estimated cash flows in the future should be discounted by the cost of capital.[69] These cash flows are the basis for shareholder returns and only those projects should be realized which show a positive net present value.[70]

The idea behind this concept is that cash flow is the sum that really is available for investment projects or, alternatively, for distribution to shareholders.[71] The free cash flow is the money that remains in the firm after all projects with a positive net present value have been realized; it should be distributed to the shareholders and not retained.[72] Businesses

[68] See Rappaport (1986), chapter 2.
[69] The measure for the return on capital is usually the after-tax profit of a company or division, which is related to the after-tax profit required by the capital invested, which is the product of capital employed and the weighted average cost of capital. See Holmström, Kaplan (2001), 17.
[70] For an elaboration of the concept see Rappaport (1986), chapter 3.
[71] See Sablowski, Rupp (2001), 58
[72] See Jensen (1989), 66.

that do not deliver a positive net present value should be divested. Thus, the value of an enterprise is not determined by its actual or past profits, but only by its expected earnings and cash flows in the future.

The shareholder value concept evolved into the main principle of American corporate governance, helped by the rise of institutional investors.[73] The main implication for corporate strategy has been pressure to deliver higher returns on their stocks. Simultaneously, the "commitment of financial resources to corporate strategies came under considerable pressure."[74] The until then dominating "retain and reinvest" strategy, which means the retention of revenues for reinvesting them in physical and human resources, did not serve the investors' demands for high returns. Shareholder value changed the incentives for management. A high share price was the only means to prevent a hostile takeover, and via the use of stock options, pursuit of shareholder value became a very lucrative approach for management. Hence, the "retain and reinvest" strategy was replaced in the course of the 1980s by a strategic orientation that has been focusing on the principle "downsize and distribute," which manifested itself in restructurings, downsizings, rising dividends, and an explosion in share buybacks.

These strategies followed the logic that if a firm is not able to create shareholder value, then it should distribute the free cash flow to its shareholders; they can then decide how to maximize their portfolios. Thus, the ultimate say over the free cash flow should be given to the shareholders in order to enable them to diversify their portfolios according to their preferences, which would not be possible when earnings are retained. Downsizing thus allowed the shareholders to gain from previously undervalued assets.[75] Shareholders and their interests were prioritized in the strategic consideration of companies.

The main strategic implications of a shareholder value policy include the following:[76]

- All matters relevant to investors should be transparent and communicated clearly to them. This includes quarterly reports, accounting according to United States Generally Accepted Accounting Principles (U.S.-GAAP) or to International Accounting Standards (IAS), and regular meetings with analysts. Generally, a high degree of transparency concerning the firm's strategic and financial decisions is required;

---

[73] See O'Sullivan (2000), 7–8 and 155, as well as Lazonick, O'Sullivan (2000b), 27. See also Holmström, Kaplan (2001).

[74] O'Sullivan (2000), 146.

[75] A development that contributed to the breakthrough of the shareholder value concept was the leveraged buyout, in which investors, often including managers from the target company, acquire the equity of a company and finance the purchase by credits for which assets of the target company serve as collateral. See Jensen (1989), 65.

[76] The listing is based on Vitols (2000), 3. See also Streeck (2001), 10.

- Free cash flow should be distributed to shareholders, implying high dividend payments as well as stock buybacks;
- The remuneration of managers and employees should be linked to stock performance;
- Minimum profit goals should be set for all business units and the firm as a whole. Underperforming units should be sanctioned and, if there are no performance improvements, sold or shut down;
- A form of value management should be introduced, which is deduced from the shareholder value approach and serves to divide the company organizationally into parts with each part maximizing individual value contribution.[77]
- A firm should define a core set of markets which offer above-average growth potential. Subsidiaries and business units not belonging to this set of markets should be sold; acquisitions in the core areas should be undertaken.

These requirements of a shareholder value strategy affect different levels of corporate behavior and should be clearly distinguished. Transparency and shareholder-oriented accounting concern the information given by the company to the public. Stock-based remuneration patterns, minimum profit goals, and value management are elements that affect the organizational incentives within firms. The most far-reaching strategic step is the concentration on core competencies, which is linked with the introduction of value management and minimum profit goals, because they determine on which activities a firm should concentrate. The implication is the downsizing of firms, which is likely to result in serious conflicts with the workforce.

It is important to note that on a theoretical level the shareholder value concept does not necessarily lead to improved economic performance or to higher share prices for firms that implement it. Rather, the link between the shareholder value concept and stock price reactions is uncertain. This stems from several problems of the concept. First, it is hard to predict future cash flows as well as to determine the correct—risk-adjusted—discount factor for investment projects. Moreover, it is not clear whether investors really make their decisions according to future cash flow criteria.[78]

Second, whether a shareholder value policy is efficient from an economic viewpoint depends on the validity of the strong form of the efficient market hypothesis, which assumes that even information that is only available to company insiders, such as executives, is fully reflected in stock market prices. When this is not correct and the firm's own executives have superior information about the value of various alternatives

---

[77] See Schmidt, Maßmann (1999), 7, 11.
[78] See Sablowski, Rupp (2001), 60–61.

than do investors, then it is more efficient if the executives take the decision no matter the market reactions.[79]

Third, even if the strong form of the efficient market hypothesis is correct and all relevant information is reflected in share prices, then superior stock price performance can only be expected for the period in which a firm changes from a nonshareholder-oriented to a shareholder value policy. In information-efficient capital markets, the valuation of shareholder-value-oriented firms might be comparatively high. But there is no above-average yield for investors, because the valuation must have already been high in the beginning of the period. Hence, a change to a shareholder value policy can have positive short-term effects on the share price, but is not enough to push share price in the long-term.[80]

Fourth, management according to shareholder value principles does not account for economies of scope, because the value contribution of each division and department should be covered separately.[81] If these economies of scope are destroyed by the introduction of value management, then performance on the product markets is likely to deteriorate and so will share price. To sum up, a shareholder value strategy is not unambiguous, and more important, its requirements differ markedly in their impact on firm behavior and therefore in the ease of implementation.

Corporate Governance, Competitive Advantage of German Firms, and Shareholder Value

The key characteristic of the institutional structure of German corporate governance has been that various stakeholders, such as employees, banks, and other firms, have a voice in corporate decision making. Therefore firms can coordinate policy with relative ease. The institutional constellations provided firms with stable finances and facilitated long-term employment policies and investment horizons. The institutional arrangements were fairly sheltered from market forces, because a high degree of cross-ownership and codetermination prevented the emergence of a market for corporate control. Consensual decision making hindered rapid restructuring in times of financial distress, which prevents asset-stripping and discriminates against an active portfolio policy. The result is a high commitment to markets, which is a precondition for long-term strategies and incremental innovation. The outcome of this distinct institutional structure in strategic terms has been that the strategy of German firms has been production-oriented, focused more on in-

[79] See Milgrom, Roberts (1992), 471.
[80] See Schmidt, Maßmann (1999), 4.
[81] See Ibid., 7.

vestment and sales growth than on profitability. Product quality, market share, and employment have been seen as equally legitimate goals as return on shareholder investment.

These structures and strategies are the basis for competitive advantages, especially in products with complex production processes and long product cycles, and in industries that require cumulative learning and highly skilled employees. The emphasis on technology results in diversification of a technological kind, not unrelated diversification. The dominant strategy is to compete on differentiation and not cost, and to move into more sophisticated segments. This has been made possible by a strong commitment to the respective industries as well as investment decisions based on technical criteria in order to secure technological leadership.[82]

This last point is especially at odds with the shareholder value concept and its core requirement, namely investment decisions strictly according to financial criteria. But also the tendency of technological diversification contradicts the main strategic implication of shareholder value, the concentration on core competencies. The strategy of technological diversification is essentially incompatible with a shareholder value concept that only assesses the contribution of single divisions and investments. Hence, there are certain trade-offs between financial-market and product-market requirements.[83]

However, it is important to note that heightened transparency does not necessarily interfere with the German corporate governance model. Transparency in shareholder systems is of crucial importance because it complements the market for corporate control by providing investors with relevant information about the financial situation of a company. But in systems where a market for corporate control is virtually absent and where outsiders do not aim at performing a governance role within corporations, transparency as such has no immediate consequences for firm behavior. In this sense, it is a secondary element in corporate governance systems. Nevertheless, transparency is the top priority of institutional investors. Even without a market for corporate control, they aim at obtaining as much information as possible and companies are therefore judged according to their information policy, because this minimizes their risk of being exploited by insiders.[84]

Structures and Strategies

How companies perform on the product market is dependent on a wide range of factors. According to the "dynamic capabilities approach" in

[82]See Porter (1990), 375–80.
[83]For this general point see Prahalad (1994), 47.
[84]See the contributions in Deutsches Aktieninstitut (2001).

strategic management, technological, financial, reputational, structural, institutional, and market assets, as well as organizational boundaries, determine the performance of firms by constituting resources on which the firm can draw.[85] Strategic choice is guided by the exploitation of these firm-specific resources, which must be bound together through a high degree of organizational coherence.[86] The competitive situation of a firm depends on the firm's routines, on its firm-specific resources, and on the strategic alternatives it can choose from. In order to build up capabilities, firms have to make long-term commitments to certain areas of competence. Hence, strategic choice is shaped by past choices and firms follow certain trajectories in their development.

A firm's position and its development path shape its options and what it can do. Thus past commitments to markets and capabilities are decisive for future choices, and thus a variety of strategic options is excluded. Firms face a limited choice set, and therefore firm behavior is characterized by path dependency.[87] It follows that strategic change is generally incremental, because new capabilities must be built on existing capabilities and internal processes in a cumulative manner.[88]

This implies that firms cannot adjust to the changing international environment by a far-reaching transformation of their strategies and structures. They are bound to their existing assets and experiences, which constrain the types of markets in which they can gain a competitive advantage. Hence, adjustment is likely to take place by leveraging existing assets and product market strategies. In other words, when firms have pursued differentiation strategies that depend on cumulative investments, they will adjust by deepening these strategies. Deepening them requires that the institutional preconditions stay in place. If long tenure of specialized employees, management-labor cooperation, and high investments are the basis for a firm's competitive advantages, management will not have an interest in changing these practices nor will investors. As Kathleen Thelen has shown, German employers have been unwilling to dismantle centralized bargaining structures because they play an essential role in the production model.[89] This reasoning is valid not only for wage bargaining, but also for other dimensions of company behavior.

Institutions, Restructuring, and Adjustment Strategies

What does this mean for the process of adjustment and restructuring of firms? First, the restructuring efforts will be mediated by the institu-

[85] See Teece, Pisano, Shuen (1997), 522.
[86] Ibid., 519.
[87] See for an introduction to the dynamic capabilities approach Teece, Pisano (1994).
[88] Lazonick, O'Sullivan (2000a), 103, as well as Rugman, Verbeke (2000), 378.
[89] Thelen (1999).

tional context. In the case of German firms, this implies that the pressure from financial markets is subject to a negotiation process among the participating stakeholders. Since various actors are involved in decision making, their diverging interests must be to a large degree reflected in the final outcome; otherwise they will not agree. Neither the introduction of shareholder value strategies nor the broad goal to generate shareholder value is excluded by the institutional context, but the concrete measures will hardly be identical to the ones in shareholder systems. This means that they will be not as far-reaching, because they will be watered down in the process of restructuring and adjusted to the institutional environment.

Second, the various measures will not be introduced in their entirety. The stakeholder groups, especially labor, are affected differently by the various elements of the shareholder value concept, so some common ground must be found, which makes it unlikely that all elements will be introduced. For example, it has been shown that labor is not necessarily hostile to increased transparency, so that coalition building with institutional investors against management is possible on that issue.[90] Regarding downsizing, a coalition between labor and institutional investors is highly unlikely. Here, coalition-building between management and labor is much more likely, because both have a preference for expansion. Even if there are attempts to downsize, labor must be compensated by a soft approach to downsizing, which cushions the social consequences of downsizing, or by concessions in other areas of business policy. Hence, when the hurdles for a complete transformation of corporate governance are very high, selective adaptation on the contrary is quite possible.

Third, apart from the interests of the actors involved, selective adaptation cannot take place randomly. Given that product market strategies are built on various enabling preconditions, the willingness of management of abandon them should be low from a business economics perspective. For example, a hire-and-fire approach in firms that operate in industries in which the main success factor is cumulative knowledge and specialized skills of the employees is inappropriate. The least we can expect in such a setting is that the company tries to shelter its core set of workers and acts with consent of labor. Conversely, rational investors can be expected to accept these requirements of product markets, so that they do not push for a change of strategy or for downsizing. In these circumstances they should rather support the existing strategy or its deepening, as long as transparency is provided. Therefore, change should be limited to those elements that do not destroy the prevailing product market strategies.

[90]See Höpner (2001).

Consequently, restructuring in a stakeholder system such as Germany differs from shareholder systems. The process of restructuring is lengthy, consensus-oriented, and the measures implemented are less far-reaching than in shareholder systems. More important, stemming from these characteristics of restructuring, the outcomes are also different. Not all dimensions of restructuring—financial, organizational, and portfolio measures—will be implemented to the same degree. While there are certain aspects that can be implemented quite easily in the realm of financial and organizational restructuring, such as a higher transparency, better investor relations, or changes in management compensation, the more fundamental elements that concern the basic strategies are much more resistant to change. Therefore, the willingness of firms to adopt restructuring measures that point in the direction of shareholder value strategies varies with the characteristics and the consequences of these measures.

In this chapter I have examined the differences between shareholder and stakeholder systems of corporate governance, explanations for these differences, the possible impact of globalization, and obstacles for the implementation of shareholder value policies in a stakeholder system such as Germany's. It turns out that on the firm level the institutional properties of German corporate governance discriminate against the core elements of shareholder value strategies. Moreover, the introduction of these strategy-related elements are likely to hurt the competitive advantages of German firms, so that none of the actors involved—management, investors, workers—is likely to develop a pronounced interest in implementing them rigorously. Thus, the impact of globalization will vary according to the area of restructuring.

We can expect implementation of those features that are relatively easy to implement, such as higher transparency, but a much more contested and sluggish implementation of the core features of the shareholder value concept. Moreover, because of the institutional setup, the process of restructuring will be lengthy, bargained, and consensus-oriented; thus institutions moderate the outcome of restructuring. Therefore, we can expect that the elements of the shareholder concept will be incorporated only selectively, and those elements incorporated will have a different form and therefore different incentives than in the system from which they originated. The next chapter is concerned with Germany's system of corporate governance and the aggregate changes therein.

Chapter 3

German Corporate Governance, Regulatory Reforms, and Aggregate Changes

Traditionally, scholarship on German corporate governance has concentrated on the relationship between firms and banks—the *Hausbank* relationship—the role of the banks in Germany's industrialization,[1] and the role of negotiated agreements between private economic actors and the state in economic adjustment.[2] Whether the role of German banks is still that special, or has ever been that special, has been subject to considerable controversy, even before the advent of globalization.[3] The relationship between banks and firms is certainly an important element of German corporate governance, but corporate behavior is, as has been argued by the more recent literature on corporate governance, influenced by a variety of institutions, such as the organization of capital markets, ownership patterns, industrial relations, or education and training systems. Thus, the following sections briefly analyze the institutional setup of German corporate governance and the consequences for innovation and economic specialization. Then, I will investigate regulatory reforms in the field of corporate governance and aggregate changes within the system.

[1] See Hilferding (1981) and Gerschenkron (1962). An often overlooked corollary in Gerschenkron's argument is that the *Hausbank* relationship is seen as a temporary phenomenon. After the initial phase enterprises would emancipate themselves from the banks and finance themselves by retained earnings.

[2] See Shonfield (1965) and Zysman (1983).

[3] See Vitols (1995a), Vitols (1995b), Edwards, Fischer (1994), Deeg (1999).

A Brief Overview of the German Corporate Governance System

The most important traditional aspects of German corporate governance are concentrated ownership, bank-based finance, internal control mechanisms, a two-tier board system with codetermination by the employees in the supervisory board (*Aufsichtsrat*), and a legal order that promotes the view of the firm "as constitutional construction for structuring a process of ongoing negotiation among different groups within the firm."[4]

Banks, Capital Markets, Corporate Finance, and Ownership

German banks are universal banks and face almost no legal and regulatory constraints on their activities; they can offer all financial services either within the structure of the parent bank or by subsidiaries. The historical roots of the universal banking system and the close *Hausbank* relationships with firms lie in the capital shortage of the 1870s, when neither developed capital markets nor sufficient savings existed, so that banks facilitated Germany's industrialization by financing the then new industries and the transformation of family firms into industrial enterprises. The banks' influence on firms has stemmed from four sources: credits, supervisory board representation, proxy voting, and direct ownership.

Credit provision is at the core of the *Hausbank* relationship: the providing of "patient capital," that is, long-term, low-interest credit, "enabled management to take the long view."[5] The long-term nature of credit and the access to credits in financial crises have also been seen as the distinguishing features of the *Hausbank* relationship. For example, in 1989, the share of long-term bank lending to firms was 57 percent of total lending. In the United Kingdom, the pattern was reversed: two-thirds of bank lending, according to one estimate, was of a short-term character.[6]

The predominance of credit financing is also reflected in the traditional accounting rules. These are lender-oriented: the main goal is to serve the firm's credits, not to provide investors with transparent figures. This has not only been beneficial for the banks as lenders, but also for management by giving it considerable freedom to manipulate accounting figures. Under the traditional accounting rules, management tended to undervalue assets and overvalue liabilities; this leads to the building up of hidden reserves, which can be used to absorb economic shocks. The result is that "there is enough liable capital available, whether it is

[4] Ziegler (1999), 1.
[5] Streeck (1997), 41–42.
[6] Edwards, Fischer (1994), 268.

shown in the balance sheet or not."[7] Outside investors, however, have had a hard time obtaining reliable figures on the financial state of a firm.

The reason why banks have been able to provide credits partly irrespective of market conditions lies in their informational advantages through supervisory board representation. In 1996, for instance, the big three banks were represented on the supervisory boards of twenty-one of the twenty-four nonfinancial DAX companies, and they provided eleven chairmen.[8] The Deutsche Bank had representatives in nineteen of these firms, Dresdner Bank ten, and the Commerzbank six.[9] The banks' presence has been concentrated in the large firms, especially the DAX firms. Bank representation on the supervisory board is correlated with their equity holdings and their exercise of proxy votes. But even in firms in which banks had no equity voting rights at all, banks were represented in half of the cases on the board and in a few they also had the chairman seat.[10] Thus, thanks to their informational advantage, banks are better informed about the risks of their loans and have the capacity to help to reorganize a firm when it runs into serious trouble.

Banks are in principle unrestrained in their corporate ownership, and they have held considerable portions of shares in German listed companies. Their ownership rights and voting rights are multiplied in the proxy voting system. Banks can cast proxy votes on behalf of the shares of clients they hold on deposit after having solicited permission for voting on their behalf. Many small shareholders grant this permission and agree with the preannounced voting proposals of the banks. In 1992, 84 percent of shares were associated with a bank. Sixty-one percent consisted of proxy votes, 13 percent of bank equity ownership, and 10 percent of dependent investment companies. Eighty-seven percent of German domestic investment funds are majority-owned by a bank, and the largest investment funds are fully owned by banks.[11] Thus, at the annual shareholder meetings banks are the dominant players.

Hence, in the traditional picture of German corporate governance, the dual functions of providing capital and managing the enterprise have been to a certain degree integrated, with banks exercising some of the functions normally attributed to owners. The incentive to monitor management and to collect relevant information stems from their interest to secure their credits. In other words, banks have been an important actor in the internal monitoring of firms and in their financing.

[7] Prigge (1998), 999.
[8] See ibid., 959.
[9] See Matthes (2000), 50, figures from 1996.
[10] See Edwards, Nibler (1999), 13–14.
[11] See Prigge (1998), 982.

The strong position of the banks and the reliance on credits has come at the expense of capital markets. German capital markets have been relatively underdeveloped, and a market for corporate control—the main mechanism of external control—has been virtually nonexistent. For example, during the 1980s the number of mergers in Germany was roughly half of that in the United Kingdom. Moreover, there had only been four cases of successful hostile takeovers in Germany between World War II and 1993.[12] The reason for this lack of a market for corporate control lies in institutional impediments, such as the two-tier board structure, ownership concentration, codetermination, legal impediments, capital protection rules, interlocking share holdings, the proxy voting system, shares with different voting rights, and a market structure with a small number of listed firms.[13]

However, the notion of a bank-based system should not obscure the fact that management autonomy is high, especially with regard to corporate finance. In international comparisons of corporate finance, it is evident that internal finance dominates by far all other sorts of finance, regardless of the corporate governance system.[14] According to the "pecking order" of finance, new investments are financed first by retained earnings, then by loans, and only in the last instance by equity issues. Financing by retained earnings guarantees management the greatest autonomy and independence from any sort of control, and it may even be that internal finance has, assuming information asymmetries between managers and investors, lower agency costs than external finance.[15] Hence, the differences between corporate finance systems are less in the aggregate finance figures, but more in the residual external finance patterns. According to the Bundesbank, "The patterns of financing of large corporations . . . are characterized by a high level of provisions and a broad capital base, which ensure extensive financial autonomy and adaptability."[16]

Ownership structures are highly concentrated in Germany. Two-thirds of the 650 largest companies have an owner holding more than 25 percent of the equity stock;[17] 51 percent have a majority owner. In comparison, none of the largest firms in the United States has a majority

[12]Three of these takeovers happened in the period 1988–93. See Franks, Mayer (1995), 187.

[13]See Prigge (1998), 992.

[14]See Corbett, Jenkinson (1998), 107, and Hackethal (2000), 128–35.

[15]See Hellwig (2000a), 101–14, as well as Hellwig (2000b), 3.

[16]Deutsche Bundesbank (1999), 45.

[17]The 25 percent threshold is important because it confers veto power to the block holder in important decisions. Key decisions often require changes in the corporate bylaws, which requires a consent of more than 75 percent of the votes.

TABLE 3.1
Median size of largest voting block, mid
1990s

	Largest voting block
Germany	57.0
United Kingdom	9.9
United States	
NYSE	5.4
NASDAQ	8.6

Source: Becht, Mayer (2001), 19, table 1.1. By
permission of Oxford University Press.

owner with more than 50 percent, 0.1 percent have an owner with a stake
of more than 25 percent, and 95 percent of all shareholdings in firms are
smaller than 5 percent.[18] The concentrated ownership structures are
also visible in the median size of the voting block of the largest shareholder, which table 3.1 illustrates for the mid 1990s. The most important
owners are nonfinancial companies, insurance companies, investment
funds, and banks. Ownership concentration creates a network of these
actors, which own and control each other. This network "allows relations
involving commitment on the part of investors to be sustained . . . concentrated ownership is required where investment by other stakeholders
is important and cannot be promoted contractually."[19]

Codetermination and Decision-Making

Germany runs the most extensive formal system of employee representation worldwide. Codetermination is intended to institutionalize employee participation. There are two levels of codetermination. The first
level concerns the supervisory board. Large companies are obliged to include employee representatives on their supervisory boards. The most
important law in this context is the Codetermination Act (*Mitbestim-
mungsgesetz*) of 1976. It applies to almost all companies with two thousand or more employees.[20] The crucial provision of this law is that employees must have 50 percent representation on the supervisory board,
while the other 50 percent are shareholders. In case of a deadlock be-

[18] See Windolf (2002) 38.

[19] Franks, Mayer (1995), 193.

[20] A stronger form of codetermination applies for companies mainly involved in steel
and coal mining, whereas a weaker form applies to most companies between five hundred
and two thousand employees.

tween these two blocks, the chairperson, who is elected by the share-holders, has a deciding vote.

Employee participation is not limited to the supervisory board in large firms, but also exists on the plant level. Every plant with at least five full-time employees is entitled under the Works Constitution Act of 1952 (*Betriebsverfassungsgesetz*) to elect a works council. The work councils are entitled to participate in issues such as the hiring of new employees, introduction of new technologies, and use of overtime and short-working time; in case of mass redundancies they have the right to bargain with management about social plans covering redeployment, severance payments, and early retirement. Management has to bargain with the work councils over most issues that are of immediate concern for the workers. Furthermore, there is usually a personal interdependence between plant and supervisory level codetermination since the head employee representative is typically a leading works council member. There is a ban on strikes to enforce workplace demands, and works councils are legally required to act in the overall interest of the enterprise.

The involvement of employees and other stakeholders has ramifications for corporate decision-making. Several actors are able to act as veto players. In most key decisions, managers must consider the interests of these veto players and must consult them in order to reach a decision. This institutional mechanism requires "mobilization of consent."[21] Agreement must exist before decisions are taken and implemented. Owing to the coordination and consultation processes, decision making takes longer; however, once decisions are taken, they are easier to implement, simply because all important stakeholders have agreed.[22] If all actors agree, and since there is little reason to expect one of them to subsequently deviate, long-term planning becomes possible. Moreover, institutionalized employee involvement has one important side effect for strategic behavior: "The participation of labor on the supervisory boards of German corporations is a key mechanism compelling firms to look for smart ways of employing the skills of their expensive though extremely productive and sophisticated workers."[23]

Management's Incentives and Orientation

The stakeholder setup of the governance system is also visible in the attitudes of German managers. In the mid 1990s, 83 percent of German managers agreed to the statement that the firm should be run for the in-

[21] Hall (1997), 304.
[22] See Streeck (1997), 37.
[23] Guillen (2000a), 181–82.

terest of all stakeholders, whereas 71 percent of British and 76 percent of American managers agreed that shareholders should be given first priority. Faced with a hypothetical trade-off between dividend payments and employment level, 89 percent of UK and U.S. managers would maintain dividends even at the expense of employment, whereas 59 percent of German managers would maintain employment even at the expense of dividends.[24]

The explanation for managements' stakeholder preferences is partly to be found in their incentives. International comparisons report that German managers are relatively poorly paid, especially compared with their counterparts in the Anglo-Saxon economies, and stock options were prohibited up to the late 1990s. Without stock options, management does not have a direct interest in promoting the share price, because their salary is not dependent on share performance. Stock option plans are therefore used in outsider systems in order to align managements' interests with investors' interests, and to give highly powered incentives to management to pursue a shareholder-value orientation. Profitability and shareholder value has therefore not been the main concern of German managers. In comparison to British managers, German managers place greater emphasis on productivity improvements and cost reduction, whereas British managers value the meeting of financial goals and mergers and acquisitions much higher.[25] Hence, the prevailing orientation of German managers has been on production and technology. This has been supported by their career paths, which mostly took place within one firm.

Wage Setting, Training, and Technology Transfer

At the meso level of the political economy, German firms and industries have the capacity to govern themselves via associations to a high degree. These associations are legitimized by the state, which delegates much of the economic governance to them or to collective negotiations among them. Owing to strong business associations and unions, wage bargaining is centralized and coordinated and takes place on the industry level between unions and employers' associations. Despite a merely moderately high union density of 25 percent, the members of the employers' associations are bound to these agreements because the results are usually made obligatory for nonmembers by the Federal Ministry for Labor and the Economy. The collective bargaining coverage is 68 percent.[26]

[24] See Allen, Gale (2000), 52–53.
[25] See Jürgens, Rupp, Vitols (2000b), 13.
[26] OECD (2004).

The business associations are not only involved in wage-setting, their functions reach from standard setting to the provision of a "dual" apprenticeship system, consisting of practical training in a company and theoretical training in vocational schools. The vocational training system rests on cooperation between business associations, labor, and the state, and it forms the skill base of the German labor force. The associations negotiate the skill categories and content of training in order to meet the needs of the firms in each sector. Workers are therefore well trained in specialized fields and have a theoretical basis for further skill development within the firm, so that specialized human capital formation is supported and enabled by the apprenticeship system.[27]

The existence of the associations provides a mechanism for conflict resolution between firms and makes cooperation between firms possible, especially in the same industry. It can be seen as a way to overcome the free-rider problem when common interests are affected. One of the main advantages of strong associations for firms lies in the diffusion of new technologies. Business associations promote new technologies by collaborating with public officials in the design of public policy programs. Moreover, another way of diffusing new technologies is standard setting in new technologies, which is eased by the collaboration of competing firms in their industry associations.[28] Thus, also on the level of the political economy, there are multiple coordination mechanisms. The system is based on negotiations between the key actors, most of whom have veto power. Put differently, all key actors are connected via relational or implicit contracts which coordinate their behavior. In its traditional form, German corporate governance has arguably been a consistent system whose institutions and the internal mechanisms of control supported a general stakeholder orientation.

Product Market Strategies, Innovation, and Specialization

The institutional setup has been significant not only for the way companies are run and controlled, but also for the predominant business and innovation strategies on the firm level and consequently for the specialization patterns on the level of the political economy. According to Michael Porter, there are two generic strategies by which firms can build competitive advantage: cost leadership or differentiation.[29] Owing to the institutional framework, the high wage level, and their technical orientation, German firms gravitate toward differentiation strategies: "German

[27] Porter (1990), 369.
[28] See Hall, Soskice (2001), 26–27.
[29] See Porter (1980), chap. 2.

positions are in segments and relatively specialized industries characterized by high levels of productivity, and in which German firms usually
compete with differentiation strategies."[30] Quality and technological sophistication are stressed, so that premium prices can be commanded;
the emphasis is on "mastering and dominating sophisticated market segments and earning satisfactory profits."[31] This specialization has been
called diversified quality production (DQP).[32]

DQP is linked with incremental innovation, which means small scale
innovation to existing technologies with high know-how requirements in
established markets. Examples include cars, engineering, chemicals, or
metal-working. Innovation patterns in German firms build on existing
technologies, and these are amended to a high level of sophistication, a
pattern that could be called "deepening."[33] Incremental innovation is dependent on highly trained employees with specialized skills. They must
be encouraged to invest in firm- and industry-specific skills, which they
will only do if they can be sure that this investment pays; this can be
achieved by the likelihood of long tenure. Congruent with this, in the
mid 1990s, the median tenure of German employees was 10.7 years,
whereas it was only 5.0 years for British and 4.2 years for U.S. employees.
Since employees' knowledge is often tacit and therefore difficult to monitor for management, they are in a strong bargaining position. Incremental innovation patterns are furthermore supported by long-run finance
and long-term relationships with other firms to sustain information flows
and technological transfer.[34]

In sum, the institutional framework in Germany gives incentives to
build certain organizational competencies, and it particularly encourages incremental innovation and DQP. The DQP strategy has been further supported by the technical competencies of German managers. The
majority of German managers hold an engineering and not a business
degree,[35] so that often technical improvement enjoys priority, possibly at
the expense of entrepreneurial capabilities: "*Technik* exerts a pervasive
influence on German firms and on German managerial thinking. . . .
The German company is *Technik* in organizational form. The skilled
worker, the foreman, superintendent, the technical director are all participants in *Technik* . . . *Technik* transcends hierarchy. It may also tran-
scend particular functions in the company."[36]

[30] Porter (1990), 356.
[31] Ibid., 375.
[32] Streeck (1992).
[33] Junne (1989), 250.
[34] See Soskice (1999), 115–19, and Soskice (1997).
[35] See Eberwein, Tholen (1993), 173.
[36] Lawrence (1980), 248.

The strong focus on incremental innovation in turn implies that Germany has comparative disadvantages in industries that demand radical innovation. The performance in volatile market environments is poor: "As strong as Germany is overall in research, it cannot match the U.S. in inventiveness in new industries. . . . Germany is the undisputed leader in improving and upgrading technology in fields in which its industry is established, but there are weaknesses in newer fields such as electronics, biotechnology and new materials."[37]

Radical innovation has substantially different institutional preconditions. It requires a higher degree of freedom for management to react quickly to new market conditions, particularly in volatile and risky high-technology markets, and it needs an open market for corporate control that allows innovative firms to grow quickly. Radical innovation can be equated with "shifting," which essentially means that resources can be easily transferred from one use to another.[38] Most importantly, radical innovation requires open financial markets that provide venture capital and incentives for entrepreneurs who establish new companies. These facilitate the emergence of new sectors and firms. Because of lengthy bargaining processes involving risk-averse employees and banks, complex systems, such as the German one, hinder that sort of strategy. Institutional support for industries such as biotechnology or computers has been poor in Germany, since their needs seem to be "at odds with the prevailing logic within the economy."[39]

Congruent with this distinction between incremental and radical innovation, Germany's patent and export specialization is strongly biased toward medium-high-technology products—characterized by incremental innovation patterns—whereas there are weaknesses in high-technology products, as the table 3.2 indicates.[40] The same picture emerges when looking at trade patterns. Here again, Germany's specialization is clearly in medium-high-tech industries, whereas the Anglo-Saxon economies have comparative advantages in high-tech industries (see table 3.3). In sum, various insiders affect the decision-making process within German firms, while the financial markets play only a limited role. This influence is guaranteed by codetermination as well as by the representation of several stakeholders on the supervisory board. These

---

[37] See Porter (1990), 377.

[38] Junne (1989), 251.

[39] Casper (1999), 5.

[40] According to the OECD classification, high-tech industries, include aircraft and spacecraft; pharmaceuticals; office accounting and computing machinery; radio, television, and communication equipment; medical precision and optical instruments. Medium-tech industries include electrical machinery; motor vehicles, trailers and semiconductors; chemicals; railway equipment and transport equipment; and machinery and equipment.

TABLE 3.2
Patent specialization Germany, Japan, United
Kingdom, United States, 2003

	High-tech	Medium-high-tech
Germany	−28	10
Japan	−12	11
UK	15	−7
USA	19	−2

Source: German Federal Ministry for Education and Research (2006), 31. The relative patent share indicates that the share of patents in these areas is higher/lower than in overall patents.

players form what could be called a "governing coalition" in German enterprises. This coalition has a

largely similar long-term objective. It does not consist in the maximization of shareholder value, but rather in ensuring stability and growth, or stable growth: banks want their loans to be secure; employee and union representatives want job security and advancement opportunities for the staff and the protection of the human capital; families as blockholders want the family name and family involvement to last; top managers of other firms want stable structures in the entire German economy; and ex-top managers will probably want to protect their successors and the firms to which they have dedicated an important part of their life.[41]

This has consequences for firms' strategy, for their specialization, and for the orientation of management.

TABLE 3.3
Contribution to foreign trade balance in high-tech and medium-high-tech-industries, 2002

	High-tech	Medium-high-tech
Germany	−28	56
Japan	−17	147
UK	51	−1
USA	53	−13

Source: German Federal Ministry for Education and Research (2005), 62. The value shows the relative contribution to foreign trade balance in one-tenth of a percent of the total foreign trade volume with manufactured products.

[41] Schmidt (2004), 396.

Reforming Corporate Germany

Even though the German financial and corporate governance system has been highly stable in the postwar era, several important reforms of the legal rules governing the system have taken place in recent years. They focused on financial market regulation and better minority investor protection, with the aim of creating more vibrant markets, and on business law.

Reform of Financial Markets

The liberalization of the financial system began in the mid 1980s, but the most significant measures were undertaken from the early 1990s onward. The main motivations for stock market reform were the completion of the European single market and the discussion about *Standort Deutschland* (Germany as a location for economic activities) caused by Germany's weak standing in terms of incoming foreign direct investment (FDI). Part of the reforms aimed at improving the competitiveness of Germany for foreign investors in the *Finanzplatz Deutschland* campaign (Germany as a financial center). It was intended to attract investment banking and more institutional investor business to Frankfurt in order to build a financial center comparable to London or New York. This in turn required changing Germany's fragmented, small, and high-cost markets into more transparent and liquid markets. It meant that the regulations that led to an "active suppression of corporate securities markets in Germany, taking a variety of forms including discriminatory taxation, regulatory fiat and cumbersome mandated issuance procedures"[42] were subject to reform.

Major players in this liberalization process were the private banks, the finance ministry, and bank regulators, all of which feared that as a consequence of an integrated European financial market, Frankfurt would fall further behind London as a financial center. Significant regulatory liberalization since the mid 1980s aimed to stimulate the development of equity and money markets in Germany, and to establish an "equity culture." The purpose of the reforms was consequently to increase market transparency, to remove restrictions on financial product innovation, and to combat insider trading. The results were innovations in derivatives, the beginning of a commercial paper market, and the emergence of money market funds. These measures were accompanied by tax incentives with the aim of encouraging more investment in equities by German households and to give incentives for firms to go public.

[42] Prowse (1998), 90.

The first steps concerned the introduction of new financial products, especially permission to trade in options and futures contracts, which was followed by the opening of the German Options and Futures Exchange (*Deutsche Terminbörse*) in 1990. Also in 1990, the First Financial Markets Promotion Law was passed to eliminate many of the taxes hindering securities trading, while enabling German investment funds to trade in derivatives. In 1994, the Bundesbank permitted the introduction of money market funds, which helped to create demand for short-term commercial paper.[43]

A milestone in the liberalization process was the Second Law for the Promotion of the German Financial Market (*2. Finanzmarktförderungsgesetz*), passed in 1994. Its most important element was that the federal government assumed responsibility for monitoring the stock exchange; this monitoring function was previously performed by the Länder. Furthermore, a supervisory agency for security trading (Bundesaufsichtsamt für den Wertpapierhandel), modeled along the lines of the U.S. Securities and Exchange Commission, was established with the task of preventing insider trading and to oversee the compliance of the banks and investment businesses with the new "rules of conduct." This new and independent agency performs much of the self-regulation previously exercised by the financial sector itself, and it was intended to establish the credibility of the new capital market regulation in Germany.[44] All in all, this law accommodated the framework of the financial markets to international standards.[45]

Further changes in financial regulations were undertaken by the Third Law for the Promotion of Financial Markets in 1998. It aimed at improving the conditions for venture capital and investment companies. The new regulations allowed the creation of private pension funds. Furthermore, capital gains were made tax-free after one year instead of six. Investment companies must no longer go public within ten years and rules about the minimum number of shareholders have been eased. Additionally, the liability of investment companies and financial advisors for prospectus information and for financial information was reduced from thirty to three years. The Fourth Law for the Promotion of Financial Markets in 2002 made market price manipulation a criminal act and introduced the option to privately sue issuers for making false or misleading statements. Another step toward more liberal markets was the

---

[43]Further reforms included the introduction of an electronic exchange system (IBIS) in 1991 in order to facilitate cheaper and faster trading, as well as the establishment of the Deutsche Boerse AG (German Exchange) in order to overcome regional fragmentation and to link the regional exchanges.

[44]See Deeg (1996), 12.

[45]See Schmidt, Grohs (1999), 18.

formal prohibition of insider trading in the Securities Trading Law (*Wertpapierhandelsgesetz*).

The regulatory change with possibly the most far-reaching consequences took place in the framework of the Tax Reduction Act of 2000. The act abolished taxes on capital gains from selling cross-corporation shareholdings from January 2002 onward. This reform eases the unraveling of cross-share holdings, which until then was made hard by a 50 percent tax rate.

There was not only a liberalization of the main stock exchange, but also the founding of a NASDAQ-style stock exchange for small, high-tech enterprises, called the *Neuer Markt* in 1997. It was modeled on the NASDAQ, and it had greater transparency requirements than the main exchange. Reports must be published quarterly, using international accounting standards. The *Neuer Markt* was initially a huge success. It outperformed the DAX index of Germany's leading enterprises temporarily by more than 400 percent and encouraged IPOs, especially of firms in the telecommunications, software, Internet, multimedia, life sciences, and biotech industries. Whereas in the period from 1987 to 1995, only 121 German corporations went public, the number of listed enterprises on the *Neuer Markt* reached 327 at the end of 2001. After several delistings this figure fell to 264 in 2003.[46] However, due to the downturn of the worldwide stock markets with dramatic drops in share prices and several scandals, the *Neuer Markt* was abolished in 2003. It fell from its all-time-high of 9655 points in March 2000 to 375 points in November 2002 with market capitalization dropping from €234 billion to €29 billion.

Despite the ultimate failure of the *Neuer Markt*, the regulatory structure of the German financial markets has significantly changed and has resulted in the creation of much more liberal markets.

Reform of Business Law

Another major reform was undertaken in the field of corporate law. The Law for Control and Transparency in Business (KonTraG), which took effect in 1998, was the first major company law reform since 1965. The aim of the law, according to one of the officials involved in its preparation, was to meet the requirements of the international financial markets and to react to the institutional competition in the sphere of corporate governance.[47]

Its main ambition was to increase transparency and disclosure. One of

---

[46]See http://manager-magazin.de/geld/artikel/0,2828,218477,00.html, accessed March 2003.
[47]See Seibert (1999), 70, and OECD (1998b).

the most important new regulations was a restriction of banks' proxy voting rights. If a bank holds more than 5 percent of a company's stock, the bank may no longer automatically assume the proxy voting rights of its investment customers. The banks have to make a choice whether to exercise their own voting rights or the proxy votes. Voting cross-share holdings stakes in board elections was also prohibited. Furthermore, banks and businesses must disclose holdings over 5 percent and multiple voting rights were abolished; the principle is one share-one vote.

KonTraG also facilitated share buybacks. The Annual General Meeting is now able to permit the management to reacquire up to 10 percent of the capital stock.

Moreover, the new law allowed capital increases for the financing of stock options for management. Other regulations concerned the final audit and the role of the supervisory boards; the maximum of seats one person can occupy was reduced, and the liability of the board has been increased. Taken as a whole, the KonTraG law introduced more transparency, and it tried to meet investors' expectations in order to attract international investors and to establish an equity culture. Nevertheless, the law strengthened internal control mechanisms. In this sense, it did not contribute to higher outsider or market control of companies.[48]

KonTraG was strategically connected with other reforms in the financial sector such as the Securities Trading Law (*Wertpapierhandelsgesetz*), a new insider-trading legislation, the authorization of nonpar value shares, the law governing small nonlisted stock corporations, the acceptance of international accounting standards, and the Third Law for the Promotion of Financial Markets. Most important of these was the Raising of Equity Relief Act (*Kapitalaufnahmeerleichterungsgesetz*), passed in 1998. It allowed German corporations to issue financial statements on the basis of internationally accepted accounting standards in order to improve the ability of German multinational firms to raise capital on the international markets. Instead of having to prepare two types of financial statements, companies were now free to choose. The international accounting standards (IAS or US-GAAP) require much greater transparency about the financial situation of firms and are therefore more investor-oriented than the creditor-oriented traditional standards. Furthermore the international standards make financial statements across countries comparable. In 2002, the Transparency and Disclosure Act (TransPuG) took effect. The aim of the law was to amend the KonTraG and to further strengthen internal control mechanisms.

These laws were partly based on the recommendations of government

[48]See Schmidt (2004), 408.

commissions on corporate governance. The Baums Commission, appointed in 2000, worked on the modernization of company law; their recommendations were the basis of the TransPuG. It was followed by the Cromme Commission, which started in 2001. It developed code of conduct guidelines for the management and supervision of corporations. The code is not a law, and its adaptation is voluntary for firms. Nevertheless, according to the TransPuG, corporations must declare whether they comply with the code; if they do not comply they have to explain the reasons. The code proposes some regulations that go beyond legal regulation, focusing on a more efficient working of the company bodies and on a higher transparency.

In 2002, a new Takeover Act entered into force. It replaced a largely unsuccessful Takeover Code from 1995, which was based on self-regulation, but.lacked acceptance. The new Takeover Act is not particularly shareholder-friendly. Whereas the Takeover Code was based on the principle that the management of the target firm must take a neutral stance, the Takeover Law explicitly allows defensive measures of management and therefore offers ample protection.[49] It is important to note that regulatory reforms have been limited to the presented areas. Labor laws, for example, have remained largely intact and codetermination has been even enlarged to apply to smaller firms.

Evolution toward the Market?—Aggregate Changes in Corporate Governance

The following sections provide an analysis of the aggregate changes underway in German corporate governance and the question if it is converging by using descriptive statistics on the systemic level. I will start with an investigation of recent developments in German corporate finance and stock markets. Following that, I will analyze changes in corporate ownership patterns, in mergers and acquisitions activity, in accounting standards, in the importance of institutional investors, in managements' attitudes, and in remuneration patterns.

Corporate Finance and Capital Market Development

The predictions of convergence theory are fairly clear cut in the field of corporate finance. The hypothesis is that after the advent of global financial markets and the liberalization of national financial markets,

---

[49] Defensive measures under the act include share repurchases, soliciting competing bits from "white knights," counter offers for the bidders' shares, and issuing shares to a third party. Most important, shareholders can authorize management to implement defensive measures at its own discretion. See Schmid, Wahrenburg (2004), 274.

firms are no longer constrained by the old regulations and will take advantage of this. They will choose more market-oriented financial arrangements, because of their higher efficiency and potentially lower cost of capital, and will diversify their financing.[50] Thus what we should see is a shift toward more market-oriented corporate finance patterns with a higher importance of bond and equity financing, a diminishing role for banks, and a deepening of the financial markets.

There are two ways through which corporate finance can become more market-oriented. The first is the securitization of bank loans (and deposits), which implies a decrease in the intermediation function of banks, that is, disintermediation. The consequence is that credits are granted purely on market criteria, because they are ultimately traded on the capital markets. The second possibility is that bank loans are replaced by bond or securities financing.

Econometric research into the issue of intermediation and securitization from the early 1980s to mid 1990s examined the United Kingdom, France, and Germany. Although strong change was found in France and moderate change in the United Kingdom, the disintermediation and securitization tendencies have not affected Germany: "one cannot, on the basis of the alleged association with disintermediation and securitization as potential causal factors, expect that banks are losing importance in Germany, simply because overall intermediation is not on the decline in this country."[51] Change is only visible in the banks' role as mobilizers of savings, which is increasingly carried out by nonbank financial intermediaries. But there is no decline in the role of banks as lenders, which can be interpreted as growing specialization in the banking business without great repercussions on the function of banks as intermediaries.

International comparisons on the relative importance of bond financing versus credit financing have shown that credit financing has remained the dominant form of finance in Germany, if only these two sources are considered. Table 3.4 shows the relative importance of bank loans as opposed to bond financing. However, if we look at a more disaggregated level and also consider financing sources other than bank loans and bonds, the picture becomes more complicated. Table 3.5 shows the absolute amount of internal finance, the ratio of external versus internal financing, and the relative contribution of various financing sources of external finance. At a first glance, it seems as if corporate finance patterns in Germany have been very volatile over the 1990s. The ratio of internal to external finance oscillated between 32 and 81 percent; bank loans as a source of external finance dropped sharply, whereas other

[50] Decker, Lukauskas (2000), 32.
[51] Schmidt, Hackethal, Tyrell (1999), 52.

TABLE 3.4
Sources of corporate credit, 1996–2001 (bank loans as percentage of overall corporate finance)

	1996	1997	1998	1999	2000	2001
Germany	94.4	95.1	95.6	96.1	96.0	95.5
UK	70.4	70.7	67.9	64.4	63.7	63.0
USA	47.4	47.3	46.4	46.1	45.1	44.6

Source: Siebert (2004), 29. Bank loans to corporations as a percentage of the sum total of bank loans plus short- and long-term securities issued by corporations.

lenders and the financing with shares and other interests gained significantly. Also financing with money market papers or bonds as well as pension accruals have been fairly volatile. Loans are still the most important source of external finance, but firms raise their loans more and more not with German banks, but with other lenders, which are mainly foreign banks.

However, looking at the absolute amount of finance raised internally, it is obvious that it has been continuously increasing—except at the height of the stock market boom, but even then, it stayed at a high absolute level. Hence, internal finance is still the most important source of finance, but firms have been very flexible in adjusting their demand for external finance to market conditions and market swings. Therefore, what is changing is the composition of external finance; sources other than the traditional domestic bank credit have gained importance. Nevertheless, external financing remains long-term in nature; approximately two-thirds of all external funds of German enterprises have maturities of more than one year.[52]

Regarding the deepening of equity markets in Germany, there has indeed been an upswing in market capitalization, driven by the higher valuation of stocks. Market capitalization rose from 24 percent of GDP in 1993 to 68 percent in 2000. However, until 2003, market capitalization went down again to 45 percent. The upswing in stock market capitalization has been a feature common to almost all economies during the stock market boom, whereas the differences between them have almost stayed the same, as table 3.6 illustrates. Interestingly, other coordinated market economies, such as Sweden, the Netherlands, or Switzerland have a much higher market capitalization than Germany and even match the United States or the United Kingdom. Regarding the number of listed firms, there has been a modest increase. Whereas in 1990, there were 776 listed German firms, this figure increased to 905 in 2000 and

[52]Deutsche Bundesbank (2004a), 59.

TABLE 3.5
Financing of German nonfinancial enterprises, 1991–2003

| Year | Internal finance (bn. €) | Internal/ external finance (%) | Bank loans (% of external finance) | | | Other lenders (% of external finance) | Money market papers, bonds etc. (% of external finance) | Shares and other interests (% of external finance) | Pension accruals (% of external finance) |
			Long-term	Short-term	Total				
1991	141	51.1	43	27	70	9	3	13	5
1993	140	59.0	42	−10	32	11	41	12	4
1994	150	60.6	16	0	16	16	44	18	5
1995	182	72.5	48	23	71	4	−4	20	9
1996	186	68.6	42	15	57	15	−5	29	4
1997	180	71.7	47	9	56	22	−4	21	5
1998	189	52.5	30	12	42	21	−2	36	3
1999	155	37.9	26	4	30	35	0	32	3
2000	154	31.9	9	4	13	44	3	38	2
2001	177	50.1	19	1	20	33	6	36	5
2002	210	81.3	10	−50	−40	77	11	34	18

Source: Data from Deutsches Aktieninstitut (2005), author's own calculations. A negative sign indicates that more debts were repaid than taken on.

TABLE 3.6
Market capitalization in percent of GDP, 1993–2003

Year	Germany	USA	UK	Sweden	Switzerland	Japan
1993	24	78	122	58	114	68
1994	24	72	112	66	109	77
1995	24	95	122	75	129	69
1996	28	114	142	96	136	66
1997	39	130	151	111	225	51
1998	51	145	168	116	267	64
1999	68	n.a.	196	148	268	99
2000	68	156	182	137	322	66
2001	58	138	151	108	250	54
2002	35	107	114	74	199	52
2003	45	131	137	108	232	69

Source: Deutsches Aktieninstitut (2005).

then decreased slightly to 867. All in all, there are changes underway especially in corporate finance, but these changes only partly point in the direction convergence theory would expect.

Corporate Ownership

The concentration of corporate ownership is the basis for insider governance. It can be hypothesized that financial liberalization leads to a diversification of corporate ownership, reducing ownership concentration. This means that the relative share of foreigners, institutional investors, and private households should increase, whereas banks' and companies' shares of stock should decrease, which would support the argument that long-standing relationships based on bank-firm or on corporate networks are on the decline. A significant dispersion of ownership would also have the consequence of enabling a market for corporate control to emerge, which cannot develop under a situation of concentrated share holdings. The development of share ownership patterns is shown in table 3.7. There is indeed an increase in institutional investors and a decline in bank ownership. Insurance companies have also increased their shareholdings significantly, as have foreigners, whereas nonfinancial companies and households have reduced their holdings. Nevertheless, nonfinancial companies remain by far the most important shareholders.

Turning to the development of ownership concentration, evidence from the manufacturing sector showed that "almost half of the firms being traded on the stock exchange exhibit increasing shareholder concentration over the last five years (47.2 percent). At the same time, more than a quarter of those firms showed a decreasing concentration of

TABLE 3.7
Distribution of share ownership of nonfinancial German firms, 1991–2003 (as percentage of total)

Year	House-holds	Non-financial firms	Banks	Insurance companies	Investment funds	Government agencies	Foreigners
1991	22	39	13	6	5	3	13
1992	22	39	13	6	6	3	12
1993	20	43	13	7	6	2	10
1994	19	45	12	6	6	2	9
1995	19	46	13	6	6	2	8
1996	18	44	13	6	7	2	9
1997	18	40	13	8	9	2	10
1998	18	40	12	7	10	1	12
1999	17	35	13	8	13	0.7	14
2000	17	36	12	8	14	0.6	13
2001	14	37	12	9	13	0.6	14
2002	13	33	11	13	14	0.8	15
2003	14	33	9	13	14	0.9	17

Source: Deutsche Bundesbank (2004b), 99.

shares (27.8 percent). Concentration does not change in the majority of nonlisted firms."[53] In listed public companies, more firms increased rather than decreased share concentration; however, in the median, the negative effect was stronger than the positive effect. The largest share block in 1998 was almost 58 percent on average for listed stock corporations (*Aktiengesellschaften*, AG), while for nonlisted AGs and Limited Liability Companies (*Gesellschaft mit beschränkter Haftung*, GmbH) it was between 80 and 90 percent.

For listed stock corporations, the largest shareholder was a nonfinancial firm in over 40 percent of the cases, but only in 3.81 percent was it a financial enterprise. In almost 6 percent of the cases foreigners were the largest shareholders, and 37 percent of listed firms could be classified as widely held. Almost 60 percent of listed firms had a shareholder who held more than 50 percent of the shares.[54] Although the ownership structure remains concentrated, it is not necessarily stable. The ownership structure by type of shareholders is constantly changing, although ownership concentration in the aggregate continues to be fairly stable. It appears that shares are traded mainly between nonfinancial firms without offering them on the stock exchange. Also financial firms who reduced their ownership stakes have not necessarily sold them on the mar-

[53]Köke (1999), 13–14.
[54]See ibid., 17.

ket, but to other firms, the 2003 sale of the Allianz stake in Beiersdorf to Tchibo being an example of that.

Furthermore, ownership concentration seems to be associated with control. Since the median of the largest block holding is close to 60 percent, more than four times larger than the second largest block, and as the important thresholds in law are 25, 50, 75, and 95 percent, it can be assumed that control is exercised. But only 15 percent of large shareholders control block holdings in more than one enterprise. Franks and Mayer documented that 85 percent of 171 large corporations have a shareholder who owns more than 25 percent, and 57 percent have a shareholder with a stake of more than 50 percent.[55] These figures, from the early 1990s, are representative for all listed firms for the period 1985 to 1997.[56]

To summarize, ownership concentration, which is mainly due to cross-share holdings between nonfinancial firms, seems to persist, albeit at a lower level. Since the cross-holdings between nonfinancial firms are often motivated by strategic reasons, it seems unlikely that they will become dismantled even after the change in tax law.

Institutional Investors

Institutional investors are the most obvious candidates to press for a capital market orientation on the part of firms and practices favorable for shareholders, because their raison d'être is to maximize returns on their clients' savings. Therefore, their interest lies in a strict shareholder value orientation of the firms they invest in. Institutional investors could press for changes in the German corporate governance system toward an outsider system, which would provide them with higher transparency, better minority investors' rights, and possibly higher returns on their assets. Their role in Germany has been negligible in the past, but this has been changing.

Indeed, as documented in the previous section, investment funds and insurance companies increased their share ownership in Germany considerably, so that in 2003 they together held 27 percent of shares in German nonfinancial firms, up from 11 percent in 1991. This rise in institutional investing is a trend common to almost all industrial countries in the 1990s, as table 3.8 on the growth of institutional investors' financial assets as percent of GDP illustrates. Evidently, the importance of institutional investors in Germany has risen massively over the last decade, even if their absolute assets are still lagging considerably behind other countries. A more detailed breakdown shows that investment companies tre-

---

[55] See Franks, Mayer (1997).
[56] See Boehmer (2000).

TABLE 3.8
Financial assets of institutional investors, 1993–2001 (% of GDP)

	1993	1994	1995	1996	1997	1998	1999	2000	2001	Percentage change 1993–2001
Germany	39	41	45	51	59	66	77	80	81	+108
USA	136	136	152	163	178	192	207	195	191	+41
UK	163	144	164	173	195	204	227	213	191	+17
France	74	72	78	87	97	107	125	133	132	+78

Source: OECD Institutional Investor Database, copyright OECD.

bled their assets, from 12 to 36 percent of GDP, insurance companies increased theirs from 24 to 41 percent of GDP, whereas the assets of pension funds stayed marginal, increasing from 2.5 to 3.3 percent of GDP. Institutional investors in Germany concentrate their share holdings in the largest firms. For instance, in 1997, they held 50 or more percent in Daimler-Benz, MAN, Preussag, Deutsche Babcock, Linde, BASF, and Hoechst.[57]

Nevertheless, there are built-in limits to the importance of institutional investors in Germany, especially for pension funds. The first obstacle is the pension system. In the United States and the United Kingdom, pension fund assets amount to 63 and 66 percent of GDP in 2001, twentyfold the figure of Germany. These differences are mainly due to the different structure of the German pension system, which is of a pay-as-you-go character with no surplus funds to be allocated. The bulk of total pension payments, 70 percent in 1995, is based on the state pension scheme, 14 percent come from civil service pensions, while privately organized pension schemes amount to 16 percent.[58] Hence, the pension system reduces the role of institutional investors.

Institutional investors are strictly regulated in their investment strategies. The limit of equities that German pension funds and life insurance companies are allowed to hold in their portfolio is 30 percent for domestic equities and 6 percent for foreign equities. This is reflected in the investment strategy of pension funds, which invested, in 1994, 72 percent of their assets in domestic bonds and only 9 percent in equities.[59] For investment funds, the regulations are much looser, but even so their equity structure is biased against equities. In 1996, bond funds had a 54 percent share of the total assets of the retail funds, equity funds 15 per-

[57] See Jürgens, Rupp, Vitols (2000a), 58.
[58] See Nürk (1998), 180.
[59] See O'Sullivan (2000), 262.

cent, and money market funds 12 percent. Despite a significant growth in investment funds, from 2 percent to 7.5 percent of private monetary assets, investment fund savings in Germany lag far behind other nations. Investment fund assets per head were €1,780 in Germany, €2,170 in France, and €10,800 in the United States.[60] Although the proportion of shares in the portfolios of institutional investors is growing, from 9 to 19 percent in the period 1990 to 1997, this is still comparatively a very small amount. For the United States, the corresponding figure in 1997 was 45 percent, for the United Kingdom 67 percent.

Second, the close connection of German investment funds with German banks limits the capacity of institutional investors to act as independent and influential agents on their own. The biggest investment funds are owned by the banks; this dependence on banks sets narrow limits for the investment companies; they cannot act against the general strategy of their parent bank, which is evident in their voting behavior in general meetings. Their shares are voted exactly according to the parent banks' proposals and the voting behavior of the parent bank.[61] Hence, investment companies cannot always be assumed to maximize shareholder value, since they are not only the agents of the investors but are also the agents of their parent bank, which provokes conflicts of interests. The same is true for institutional investing on the part of insurance companies.[62]

A fairly inactive role on the part of institutional investors in German corporate governance is documented by empirical studies.[63] Survey research on the involvement of institutional investors reports that for a majority of institutional investors, corporate governance is much less important than share liquidity. Forty-two percent consider control on enterprises too demanding. More than 80 percent have no guidelines for corporate control. Only 9 percent try to influence management's decisions, 20 percent consider such influence to be impossible, a third never exercise any influence, and 41 percent try to exert influence from time to time. This largely passive attitude is also mirrored in voting and proxy voting behavior. Only 10 percent always exercise their voting rights, more than half sometimes delegate their voting rights, almost exclusively to banks, and the rest never exercise their voting rights themselves. Hence, direct control and American-style shareholder activism seems

[60] See Nürk, 186, 187.

[61] See Baums (1995), 31.

[62] Regarding the role of foreign institutional investors, there are strong indications that Germany has particularly attracted long-term-oriented investors. See Goyer 2005.

[63] For the following, see Steiger, Max (2000), 149–97.

TABLE 3.9
Total registered acquisitions, 1990–2004 (number)

Year	Acquisitions
1990	1,548
1991	2,007
1992	1,743
1993	1,514
1994	1,564
1995	1,530
1996	1,434
1997	1,751
1998	1,888
1999	1,182
2000	1,429
2001	1,138
2002	1,317
2003	1,135
2004	1,206

Source: Deutscher Bundestag (2005), 213.

not to be what institutional investors are aiming at, they seem to prefer outsider control through the market.

All in all, the role of institutional investors in Germany is fairly complex. The clear trend is that their assets under management have grown massively, which gives them a more prominent place in German corporate governance. However, the system has limits that prevent the institutional investors from playing a leading role, as in the Anglo-Saxon economies. But it is obvious that institutional investors have evolved into players whose preferences must be incorporated into corporate strategy, especially at the blue chip firms, where they are the most important group of investors.

Merger and Takeover Activity

As stock market activity deepens and the markets become more liquid, there should be a rise in merger and acquisition activity, especially in hostile takeovers. Table 3.9 shows how mergers and acquisitions have developed. There is a no general rise in takeover activity. The steep jump in 1991 is due to German unification and the following rise in takeovers of east German enterprises by their west German counterparts. Regarding only international mergers, here the number of inward cross-border mergers into Germany grew from 166 in 1990 to 453 in 1999, with a peak of 560 in 1997; the yearly total deal value grew from $5.3 billion to $47 billion. Outward cross-border mergers of German firms rose from 140 in 1990 to

645 in 1999, the volume of these deals jumping from $6.8 billion to $87 billion.[64] In terms of volume, the peak was reached in 2000, when the total value was €478 billion, mainly caused by the Mannesmann/Vodafone deal; in 2001 the volume decreased to €163 bn.[65] The bulk of mergers takes place among German firms: in 2001, 50 percent of all mergers occurred among German firms; in 29 percent of the cases German firms were bought by foreign firms, and in 23 percent of the cases German firms acquired other firms abroad.[66]

Concerning hostile takeovers, there were two spectacular cases, which are sometimes interpreted as the advent of a market for corporate control. The first was an unsolicited tender offer from Krupp to Thyssen's shareholders in early 1997; the second was Vodafone Air Touch's cross-border offer for Mannesmann in 1999–2000. The Krupp offer, denounced by Thyssen, was motivated by increasing competition in the steel sector and the aim of rationalizing capacity.[67] But the deviation from the norms of the traditional consensus-orientation in German business through the attempt of a hostile takeover provoked public outcry. Deutsche Bank and Dresdner Bank were criticized for a conflict of interest; they had close ties to both firms and had seats on the supervisory boards, but advised both firms and financed the offer.

The unions were overtly hostile and were supported by Thyssen's management. A successful merger would have removed Thyssen from the strong form of codetermination that applies to the steel industry. Furthermore, the unions feared employment losses. They organized demonstrations, the largest one taking place in front of the Deutsche Bank headquarters in Frankfurt. Political reactions from almost all quarters of the political spectrum concerning the offer were also negative, including central government reactions. Although the government of North Rhine–Westphalia had been trying to push rationalization in the steel industry, it opposed Krupp's offer. The governor of North Rhine-Westphalia brought the top managers of both firms together and persuaded them to search for a mutually acceptable solution, and the unions were also to be consulted.

In the end, the two companies merged their steel operations and Thyssen controlled 60 percent of the merged entity, contrary to Krupp's intentions of getting control over the merged entity. The final solution corresponded to the traditional German model rather than to a market for corporate control. Politics and the unions had a say in the bargaining, and the challenge of the first big attempt of a hostile takeover was

[64]See OECD (2001a), tables 3.5–3.8, 129–32.
[65]See http://www.mergers-and-acquisitions.de/fakten1040.htm, accessed October 2002.
[66]See ibid.
[67]See Ziegler (1999), 19–23.

met by finding a consensus. The chairman of Krupp remarked that German financial markets were not ready for a hostile takeover. Thus, despite the fact that there was an unsolicited bid, it was dealt with according to the normal rules of the game.

A change in the rules of the game was more likely to be brought about by the takeover of Mannesmann. The hostile takeover of Mannesmann by Vodafone Air Touch was interpreted, especially in the business press, as the end of "Rhenish capitalism" and the beginning of a market for corporate control. For the first time in German business history, one of its large enterprises, widely seen as the prime example for a successful turnaround—Mannesmann, actually a steel company, had successfully entered the telecommunications business—fell victim to a hostile takeover. Vodafone, a much smaller enterprise, was only interested in the telecommunications business of Mannesmann, which accounted for about 10 percent of employment. Nevertheless, the bid succeeded, being one of the largest merger and acquisition deals in the world, worth almost €200 billion.

The unions and work councils opposed the bid, but did not mobilize opposition as they had in the case of Krupp/Thyssen. They agreed to the takeover after the fulfillment of several requirements on the part of Vodafone, such as guarantees for the nonsale of the nonmobile telephone business, the maintenance of the planned joint stock offerings for the machine tools and automobile departments, and the maintenance of strategic planning for the steel business. However, there were no formal employment guarantees, although Vodafone promised not to reduce employment and codetermination was not put into question. But many of Vodafone's promises were broken. For example, the machine tools/automotive division did not become independent, the name Mannesmann disappeared, the Düsseldorf headquarters lost importance, and the integrated telecommunications strategy was dismissed. The fear of job losses was not very pronounced because of the booming telecommunications business, and the spin-off of the industrial divisions had already been planned. Furthermore, the telecommunications divisions had a lower unionization rate than the other divisions.[68]

The banks and politicians did not try to prevent the takeover resolutely. Mannesmann had no *Hausbank* although one management board member of Deutsche Bank was on the supervisory board. The character of an international bid made actions on the part of the banks or the government difficult. The German government could hardly afford to actively prevent the takeover because it would have meant conflict with the British government over a level playing field in Europe, es-

[68] See Höpner, Jackson (2001), 44.

pecially after the takeover of some British enterprises by German ones shortly before, such as BMW/Rover. Furthermore, the banks themselves had no incentive to hinder the transaction, since doing so would have meant damaging their international reputation in the investment banking business; moreover, German banks had acquired British banks shortly before. Management also did not employ antitakeover tactics such as poison pills, white knights, or court actions.

However, the case must be put into perspective. The bid was made possible by Mannesmann's quite uncommon ownership structure. Sixty percent of its shares were held by foreign investors, 40 percent by Anglo-Saxon investors alone. There were no large shareholders, and shares were completely dispersed,[69] which stands in contrast to the wide presence of concentrated ownership in German firms. Whether the unions, work councils, and politicians would approve of a similar takeover of another German company is doubtful, considering the breach of promises on Vodafone's side.

The sentiment in the business press after the takeover has been nicely captured by the *Financial Times*, which wrote: "Germany's hitherto unbreakable corporate world has finally been broken and many are going to be licking their lips."[70] However, expectations concerning a wave of follow-up hostile takeovers did not materialize. No major hostile takeover since the Mannesmann/Vodafone deal took place, which indicates that it was not the beginning of an active market for corporate control. Barriers to this market, such as concentrated ownership structures and codetermination, remain in place. Also, the elimination of the large tax burden on the sale of corporate shares from 2002 onward, which was expected to unravel cross- and bank shareholdings, has not had any significant effects as yet. According to a survey among managers of DAX firms, only 7 percent of the respondents thought that the new tax regulation eases the selling of shareholdings, and 59 percent did not plan to change their policy toward their equity interests.[71]

In the longer term, banks might withdraw further from direct share ownership, but the bulk of cross shareholdings is found between industrial companies. Since these shares are held for strategic reasons, there is no obvious motivation for industrial companies to unravel their cross shareholdings. On the contrary, industrial companies can be expected

[69] The biggest shareholder of Mannesmann was Hong Kong firm Hutchison Whampoa with a 10.2 percent share, the next biggest shareowner—an U.S. institutional investor—held 2.8 percent.

[70] See *Finanical Times*, "Triumph for Vodafone as Mannesmann Gives in # 113bn," 4.2.2000.

[71] See *Reuters*, "Studie—Steuerbefreiung beeinflusst Beteiligungsverkäufe kaum," 6.6.2002.

to continue exercising control.[72] Hence, ownership concentration is unlikely to dissolve even after the change in tax law.

Accounting Standards

Traditional German accounting standards are lender-oriented and accounting according to German GAAP (*Handelsgesetzbuch*, HGB) gives management considerable discretion in reporting financial results and building up hidden reserves, which can be used to smooth out revenue streams over several years. Accounting according to the HGB does not therefore provide an account of the real financial situations of enterprises. Assuming that outside investors prefer financial statements that are comparable across countries and provide as much information as possible, traditional German accounting should be under pressure. Since 1998, listed companies have been allowed to use IAS or US-GAAP instead of the HGB rules.[73]

Initially, there was a rush toward the application of international accounting standards. Whereas in 1995, ninety-four of the hundred largest listed German companies were using German GAAP, by 2002 only thirty-nine did so. Twenty of them now used US-GAAP and forty-one used the international accounting standards (IAS).[74] The higher transparency seems to be key for these decisions. In a sample of sixty-six firms that are listed in the DAX 100, 76 percent of the respondents thought that accounting according to the HGB is a big or decisive obstacle for the international dispersion of German shares.[75] Furthermore, 69 percent were convinced that accounting according to HGB has a lower information content compared with US-GAAP. Four years earlier, only 40 percent answered in the affirmative. Also of interest is the appraisal of which of the two accounting principles should have priority—the "true–and–fair–view" or the "caution principle." One third of the participants preferred to give an equal weight to both principles, only 10 percent preferred the caution principle, and 54 percent gave priority to the investor-friendly true-and-fair principle. Here again, a shift took place toward the investor-friendly principle, compared to the survey taken four years earlier.

In sum, there is a clear tendency for listed firms to adopt international accounting standards, whereby IAS is preferred to US-GAAP, probably because the requirements of IAS are not as strict as those of US-GAAP.

[72]See Deutsche Bank Research (2002), 14.

[73]It should be noted that the introduction of international accounting rules is not the same as the U.S.-style disclosure. SEC rules require a much higher disclosure than US-GAAP. In this sense, accounting is only part of a whole "disclosure regime." See Wüstemann (2001).

[74]See Leuz, Wüstemann (2004), 477.

[75]For this and the following results, see Förschle, Glaum (1998), 25–43. Data are from 1997.

Management's Attitude toward Shareholder Value

Survey research about the attitudes of German managers toward share-holder value strategies provides a fairly complex picture. In a study from the late 1990s that included the largest companies, 78 percent of the re-spondents agreed with the thesis that German enterprises did not suffi-ciently consider shareholders' interests in the past; however, when asked whether this also applied to their own company, 74 percent disagreed.[76] Ninety-three percent agreed that shareholders' interests have been more strongly considered in the last few years, but for the respondents' own firm the figure was again much lower. A normative question—whether in the case of trade-offs between several stakeholders' interests, sharehold-ers should have priority—was answered in the affirmative by 66 percent of respondents.

Of interest is the manager's definition of shareholder value: 36 per-cent understand it as the equal consideration of shareholders' interests among other interests; the interpretation that it is the prioritization of shareholders' interests appeals to 58 percent; and only 6 percent agree with a more extreme understanding of shareholder value, namely, that it should be interpreted as the exclusive consideration of shareholders' in-terests. A majority is indifferent or disagrees with the thesis that the insti-tutions of German corporate governance, such as the special role of banks, inflexible labor markets, the strong role of unions, and codeter-mination, hinder the implementation of shareholder value concepts. Asked for their opinion about hypothetical future regulations and devel-opments, there was indifference toward a decreasing share ownership by banks, disagreement with an abolition of codetermination on the com-pany level, and disagreement with a strengthening of the CEO's role.

One of the main requirements of the financial markets, the strategy of concentrating on the core business, is enthusiastically shared by man-agers on a theoretical level: 90 percent support the core competencies strategy and most respondents expect this tendency to increase in the fu-ture. However, as for the most radical step—the separation into several independent listed firms—88 percent do not plan to do this, whereas 53 percent of the firms have implemented minimum rates of return.

Of special importance for corporate governance are attitudes toward the capital market. A vast majority of 89 percent thinks that in the long–term, equity markets price shares correctly, with short-term fluctuations that do not mirror the real value. Fifty-six percent are convinced that all management decisions influence the share price, while the rest thinks that share price is only influenced by strategic decisions. Considering these attitudes, the next result is probably the most surprising: despite

[76]This and the following section build on ibid.

this trust in capital markets, only 5 percent consider the probable reactions of the equities markets in every decision they take, 53 percent do so only in the case of strategic decisions, and 42 percent take strategic decisions on principle without regarding the probable reaction of the market. Only 14 percent used shareholder value approaches for the evaluation of strategic investments. Another survey focused on the implementation of shareholder–value-related reference figures; these are used as a complement to traditional accounting figures, while traditional instruments of management dominate.[77] In sum, the survey suggests that German managers agree with a moderate version of shareholder value on a normative level, but that there is not unanimous support for all of its aspects.

Management Remuneration Patterns

The use of stock options is quite atypical for insider systems. From a principal agent perspective, this is not surprising. Since managers are controlled by insiders, there is less scope for managerial discretion, and since share price maximization is not managements' first priority, it would not make sense to link salary to share price development. Generally, managerial compensation tends to be lower in insider systems, and empirically the higher share ownership concentration is in the company, the lower the executive compensation.[78] Hence, whereas performance-based pay in general is not incompatible with insider systems, stock options are. Among the first enterprises to introduce stock-option incentive schemes in 1996 was Daimler-Chrysler as well as Deutsche Bank.

Most large firms introduced stock option schemes following the KonTraG law in 1998, which made the issuance of stock options easier. By 2003, 80 percent of the DAX 30 enterprises had implemented stock option schemes.[79] Nevertheless, stock options are only a supplement to traditional pay components. In 2001, fixed salary accounted for 47 percent and variable pay 36 percent of total CEO pay in Germany; the corresponding figures for U.S. CEOs were 28 and 61 percent, respectively. Most interesting are the components of variable pay. German CEOs received 47 percent of their basic compensation as a bonus and 30 percent as long-term incentives, normally stock options. For American CEOs, the corresponding figures were 56 and 161 percent, respectively.[80] In other words, American compensation is heavily biased toward stock options, whereas in Germany stock options are additional incentives, but less relevant than the basic salary or bonuses. In terms of total compensation,

[77] See Achleitner, Bassen (2002), 624, 633.
[78] Maher, Andersson (1999), 41.
[79] See Bursee, Schawilye (2003).
[80] See Towers Perrin (2002), 24–26.

German CEOs received \$455,000 in 2001, their American counterparts \$1,933,000.[81] All in all, stock option plans themselves have been used intensively, but their importance and extent remains significantly behind Anglo-Saxon standards.

This chapter has discussed the main elements of German corporate governance, the evolution of the system, and regulatory changes. Concerning the aggregate changes in German corporate governance, the evidence is mixed. There is a puzzling combination of change and continuity. We see some indicators pointing toward a greater shareholder orientation, for example in the introduction of international accounting standards or the use of stock options; in other areas, change is more modest, as is the case for the development of equity markets, corporate finance, ownership structures, and management's attitudes. Other elements show no signs of change or the implications of the changes going on are very hard to interpret, such as the growing importance of institutional investors.

Therefore, on the level of the whole corporate governance system, it is not possible to decide whether a transformation of German corporate governance toward a shareholder model is underway. The changes going on are significant if the traditional portrayal of the German model is taken as a baseline, but they seem moderate in international comparison. However, a noteworthy result of the aggregate analysis is that the various dimensions of corporate governance have not changed in a synchronized way. While the aggregate analysis has shown broad trends in German corporate governance, these findings have to be complemented by a more microlevel analysis. Adjustment of firms as well as the link between product market strategy and corporate structures have to be explored on the firm level, because only in the adjustment patterns of particularly globalization-exposed firms are the full effects of globalization likely to be visible. Thus studying firms allows a more subtle understanding of the consequences of globalization and the ways firms accommodate these pressures. Hence, the following chapters will present three detailed case studies in order to see how German "flagship firms" have adapted to the new environment.

[81] See ibid., 20.

Chapter 4

Siemens

Siemens is Germany's biggest electrical concern and Europe's largest private employer. It displays several features that are closely associated with the German model of corporate governance, such as long-term strategies, peaceful labor relations, diversified quality production, comparatively low profits, and a sales growth orientation. Siemens offers an ideal setting for studying the effects of globalization on German firms for four reasons.

First, it is one of the few German companies with dispersed ownership. Over 90 percent of Siemens's stock is dispersed and institutional investors own 45 percent of Siemens's capital stock. Thus, it is exposed to an unusually high degree to capital market pressures compared to most German companies that have a controlling shareholder. Second, Siemens has a very broad business portfolio, which financial markets tend to punish with the conglomerate discount. Furthermore, due to its broad portfolio, it has lagged behind its competitors in terms of profits, which makes it a prime candidate for portfolio restructuring. Third, it became exposed to competitive pressures over the 1990s to a much higher degree than before. It lost its most profitable and protected markets due to privatization of its main customers. Fourth, Siemens decided to list on the New York Stock Exchange, which is seen by convergence theorists as a main mechanism for convergence toward the Anglo-American model of corporate governance.[1]

[1] See Coffee (1999).

Since its foundation in 1847, Siemens pursued a strategy of producing state-of-the-art technology. Owing to its technology orientation, the company has been identified with a "fetish for technical perfection and the in-house awe in which its engineers are held."[2] The focus has been on whole systems. Electronics is the common theme in the business portfolio, which ranges from power plants to light bulbs, and from washing machines to public networks and automotive electronics. Siemens consists of 6 business areas, 12 groups, 74 divisions and 143 business fields. However, Siemens sees itself not as a conglomerate with unrelated lines of businesses, but as an electronics concern with a broad product portfolio. The strategic focus has been directed toward sales growth rather than profit maximization. The reason for the modest profits has been the broad portfolio. Siemens is serving very different markets, which are developing in different cycles. This minimizes the risk for the company as a whole, but lowers overall profitability.

Already in the course of the 1980s, Siemens had to confront far-reaching changes in market structure. Siemens had primarily been a company that produced large systems, such as communications systems, power plants, or railways. Half of the business consisted of these systems, which only public or semipublic institutions could buy. This customer structure had the side effect that customers were not very cost-conscious and Siemens could develop state-of-the-art products for high prices. It was the principal supplier for the German postal service, railways, military, energy suppliers, and several other institutions. These relationships lasted for decades and sheltered Siemens to a certain degree from market volatility. Almost 60 percent of Siemens's customers in the late 1980s were public or semipublic institutions. Siemens itself has often been portrayed as a semipublic institution.

But that comfortable situation changed. First, the privatization wave had the consequence that most of Siemens's largest customers were privatized and therefore became much more price-sensitive, with formerly constant prices falling drastically. Second, the common European market introduced competition for public orders, which also contributed to the fall in prices. The public share of Siemens's orders went down to 20 percent over the 1990s. After the completion of the infrastructure projects following German reunification, of which Siemens got the lion's share, the company had to face tougher competition. This was true especially in the field of telecommunications, where the privatized Deutsche Telekom no longer automatically ordered its equipment at Siemens, and Siemens lost its role as quasi-monopoly supplier.[3] Hence, Siemens had to

[2] *The Economist*, "Kaske as Siegfried," 21.1.1989.
[3] This was especially damaging for the business segment "public networks," which was the most profitable segment with a share of over 50 percent of total profits in the operating business.

enter new markets, approach new target groups, and in general, become
more market-oriented.

Ownership Structure and Financing Policy

Siemens is one of the few German companies with dispersed ownership.
The single biggest investor is the Siemens family, which holds 6 percent
of the equity share and 1.65 percent of the preferred stock. Since 1929,
the family's preferred stock had sixfold voting rights, but only in the case
of strategic decisions; thus at the general meeting, the family's share the-
oretically represented 14 percent. These multiple voting rights were introduced to guarantee the independence of the company, but they were
never exercised; 94 percent of Siemens's stock is dispersed.

The structure of this dispersed ownership, however, has changed significantly since the 1980s. Institutional investors became the most important shareholder group. In 1982, domestic and foreign investment
funds owned 11 percent of Siemens's shares, banks and insurance companies had 15 percent of the common stock; a further 5 percent was
owned by other companies. Foreigners held 30 percent of the capital
stock.[4] In 1996, institutional investors held 45 percent. Among the institutional investors, investment funds held 30 percent in 1996. Banks had
a 15 percent share. In 2000, the share of institutional investors remained
constant at 45 percent. Employees are also, through employee share-
schemes, important shareholders. They own 75 percent of the dispersed
shares held by private investors; their share of capital stock is not exactly
quantifiable, but it lies somewhere between 9 and 17 percent.[5]

Siemens's financing policy has been characterized by strong continuity. The main goal was not to maximize profits but secure the long-term
survival of the company and financial security. Thus, Siemens has pursued a very cautious financial policy within the limits of self-financing
and—in its beginnings—the financial resources of the Siemens family.
Self-financing in connection with very low dividends had the consequence of accumulation of large reserves. Investments were financed
from cash flow. In 1995, reserves amounted to 47 percent of the balance
sheet total. Liquidity has always been extraordinarily high. It normally
amounted to more than €10 billion. Siemens's interest income continuously contributed some 50 percent to total profits, sometimes accounting for two-thirds of profits.

---

[4] See Siemens AG (1984).
[5] See *Financial Times Deutschland*, "Bescherung für Mitarbeiter und Aktionäre von
Siemens," 20.10.2000.

These reserves, to which unknown hidden reserves need to be added, have guaranteed continuity in Siemens's business policy. Even major acquisitions could be financed from its own cash flow and liquidity. Cash reserves have also enabled Siemens to survive the huge losses without any major consequences in semiconductors, computers, and in some of its foreign businesses. Despite attempts to take this liquidity off the balance sheet, in 1999 interest payments still accounted for €925 million,[6] and after assessing liquidity with market values, interest payments nearly doubled to €1.8 billion in 2000.

Thanks to its reserves, Siemens has been dependent neither on the capital markets nor the banks for financing; it sought to secure its independence from both. Siemens avoided close relationships with banks,[7] because it has not needed credit to a large extent. It has also handled most of its financial business itself. It was the first German industrial company to establish its own capital investment fund. It very rarely tapped into capital markets as well. Its last capital increase was in 1972. Otherwise, it has tapped the financial markets only to exercise its option rights and to acquire shares for its employee share scheme. Expansion was financed by its cash mountain. Therefore, Siemens has a reputation as a "bank with sidelines in electronics." But this huge liquidity does not mean that Siemens is completely sheltered from the capital markets. Indeed, it would make an attractive target for a hostile takeover. A possible acquirer would win this cash mountain as a side effect of a takeover. In sum, the cautious financial policy guaranteed long-term strategies, a certain subordination of profitability to strategy, technological leadership, and above all, the survival of the firm.

Industrial Relations

One of the characteristics of the company in its early years was its paternalistic leadership style. In the founding days, the main goal was to run Siemens as a family firm. For most of the company's history, a family member was chairman of the supervisory board, and the family is still the largest single shareholder. This paternalistic attitude also affected industrial relations. From the beginning, the firm's social policy was very progressive. For example, a pension trust was established, as was health in-

[6] See *Börsen-Zeitung*, "Konzern-Ebit steigt um 82 Prozent," 3.12.1999.

[7] Siemens's *Hausbank* traditionally was the Deutsche Bank, but Siemens was even in its beginnings not dependent on bank credits because of its large retained earnings, which came from the telegraph equipment business. For a historical analysis of the relationship between banks and the German electronics industry, see Chandler (1990), 473.

surance. Paid holidays were introduced; there was limited codetermination, profit sharing with employees, a Christmas bonus, and comparatively short working hours. In return, the management expected a very high degree of loyalty and understood the social policy as an instrument to motivate the workers. This tradition was continued in the post–World War II decades with a focus on providing old-age provisions. A new ingredient for social policy was to issue shares that employees could buy at a lower price. This form of profit participation started in 1969. Over the years, it made the employees one of the most important groups of shareholders, giving them additional channels of influence.

There is a close cooperation and consensus orientation between management and employees; however, these characteristics are more rooted in the specific corporate culture than in a particularly strong influence of the unions, in Siemens's case the IG Metall. According to Rainer Zugehör, compared to other German conglomerates Siemens has a weak form of codetermination in terms of labor influence in the supervisory board, owing to the specific role of the supervisory board at that firm.[8] Although Siemens usually has had a very active chairman of the supervisory board—either a family member or in recent times a retired member of the management board—the supervisory board as a whole has only limited competencies. It is not involved in operational matters and no business decisions have to be approved by it. The main right and function of the supervisory board at Siemens is to be informed by the management board about business policy.[9] Unlike other German firms, Siemens also has no subcommittee of the supervisory board that is concerned with strategic investment planning and in which the work councils normally participate. Moreover, a representative of the executive employees of Siemens also holds one seat in the supervisory board for the employees' side, but supports the interests of capital. The personnel director of Siemens is neither nominated by the employee representatives in the supervisory board nor is he a member of a union.[10] Other indicators for the weakness of the unions, according to Zugehör, are that the deputy chairman of the supervisory board, a position occupied by a works councils member, is a Siemens employee and not an external member from the IG Metall union and that the three external IG Metall members are only lower-ranked functionaries.

While the formal institutionalization of the unions in Siemens's supervisory board may be lower than in other German firms, the influence of IG Metall should not be underestimated. First, the three external

[8]See Zugehör (2003).
[9]See *Süddeutsche Zeitung*, "Es sind keine spektakulären Übernahmen mehr nötig," interview with the then chairman of the supervisory board, Hermann Franz, 14.2.1998.
[10]See Zugehör (2003).

union members are high-ranking union functionaries. One of the external union members belongs to the management board of IG Metall; the second is the leader of the Siemens team at IG Metall, which exclusively deals with developments at Siemens; and the third is chairman of IG Metall's codetermination department. Second, out of the ten employee representatives in Siemens's supervisory board—three external union members, and seven work council representatives—nine are members of the IG Metall. The tenth is the representative of the executive employees. Hence, close ties exist between the work council and the IG Metall.

The less-than-average competencies of the supervisory board and the resulting limited formal influence channels of the union are offset by a corporate culture that emphasizes cooperation between management and employees.[11] The consideration of employees' interests is also supported by the management's perspective that it has to consider stakeholder interests and to mediate between them. Employee concerns and employment security are seen as legitimate. Hence, operational layoffs have been seen as a last resort for management.[12] Moreover, because of Siemens's focus on public and semipublic clients, a confrontational approach toward the unions would probably lower its prospects of winning contracts.

Siemens has an extensive system of committees on which management and workers' representatives regularly meet and reconcile their positions to new developments, and where the work councils are informed about new management initiatives. Besides these committees, informal relationships between key players help to prevent serious conflicts. Moreover, even if the union influence in the supervisory board is not particularly strong, the work councils nevertheless possess veto power. For example, after the Siemens management attempted to reduce sick pay—made possible by a 1996 legal change—the divisional works councils announced that they would no longer allow employees to work overtime. Consequently, Siemens's management changed its mind and returned to their previous policy of 100 percent sick pay. Another example for the influence of the work councils is that they struck an agreement (*Betriebsvereinbarung*) with management that committed management to consult the works councils concerning major decisions related to costs. This was the bargain the work councils agreed to in exchange for accepting restructuring programs.[13] Generally, the work councils have many options for issue-linking and for blocking strategic decisions.

[11] The strong role of the work councils prompted the CEO of General Electric once to remark that Siemens looks more like a national employment agency than a firm.

[12] See *Die Welt*, "Ein Bill Gates würde bei uns im Neid ertrinken," 10.2.1997. Interview with CEO von Pierer.

[13] See *Manager Magazin*, "Noch einmal mit Gefühl," No. 12, 1994.

Recession Restructuring

The recession of the early 1990s, the changing economic environment, the saturated home market, and financial integration made restructuring efforts at Siemens and in most other German firms unavoidable. The first significant reaction was the introduction of the TOP program in the early 1990s. The TOP program, an acronym for "time optimized process," was introduced when a new CEO, Heinrich von Pierer, took office in 1992. The goal of the program was to reach a return on sales of 5 percent, a big jump from the 2 percent 1993 return-on-sales figure. The specific goals were to increase productivity, growth, and innovation. It was based on extensive international benchmarking, which showed that Siemens was producing less efficiently than its competitors, largely due to over-engineering.[14]

TOP was an expensive program and required yearly expenditures of between €0.5–1.8 billion, but achieved impressive improvements in productivity. Siemens attained yearly productivity increases of 8.5 percent, which resulted in cost savings of €10.2 billion in the period 1993–96. This compares to productivity gains of 2 to 3 percent in the late 1980s. However, these increases could not be translated into higher profits. Most of the improved productivity was eaten up by falling prices due to increased competition; for example in 1995, productivity increases saved Siemens €3.6 billion, but €3.4 billion was lost by falling prices.[15] Hence, the TOP program allowed Siemens to hold its position but it did not boost profits.

Despite the focus on growth, TOP led to a considerable number of dismissals. Between 1992 and 1996, forty thousand people lost their jobs. Nevertheless, the program has been fully supported by the work councils.[16] The work councils accepted the necessity of cutting jobs and agreed to a socially cushioned program of layoffs. The dismissals were carried out by early retirement, transfers within the company, part-time work, and severance payments; operational layoffs were avoided. Factories were not closed down and spectacular sales of business units did not materialize. This approach brought high personnel costs, as expenses for restructuring-related personnel measures were roughly as high as the profits made in 1994. Thus, the TOP program was not an American-style restructuring, characterized by asset stripping and mass layoffs. It has been a more socially acceptable, soft restructuring, which was planned in consensus with the work councils and fully supported by them. It did

---

[14]See Naschold (1997), 10.

[15]See *Börsen-Zeitung*, "Rückenwind für Siemens," 16.7.1996.

[16]See *Manager Magazin*, "Noch einmal mit Gefühl," No. 12, 1994. Interview with the chairman of Siemens's works councils, Alfons Graf.

not go hand in hand with a "close it, fix it, or sell it" attitude. There was a difference in kind between TOP and restructuring at Siemens's main competitors. General Electric and ABB introduced similar programs much earlier, GE in 1982 and ABB in 1988. Both followed the strategy of a corporate transformation of all businesses, whereas Siemens introduced a modular transformation. Compared to GE or ABB, Siemens's restructuring followed a complex, multidimensional development concept, with aims that were less radical, less consequent, less orientating, and less motivational than at GE or ABB.[17] TOP was focused on internal productivity gains and avoided portfolio restructuring. Siemens's average return on equity between 1990 and 1999 was 9.2 percent, which was far behind its main competitors: in 1998, for example, ABB had 21 percent and GE had 23 percent.[18]

Hence, even after the TOP program, Siemens was far behind its competitors in terms of profits. At the end of 1998, Siemens came under severe pressure. Share price and profits were falling sharply; profits in 1998 were down to the all-time low of €470 million. Overall, profits had fallen by two-thirds from 1996 to 1998. As a reaction, the CEO presented a ten-point program that was supposed to get Siemens back on track. Some of the ten points were intended to amend the capital structure in order to reach the desired financial figures; others were cost cutting or motivational measures. The main points included a focus on increasing the share price and setting clear goals for management as well as the option to float divisions and the decision to list on the New York Stock Exchange (NYSE). The following sections investigate these restructuring measures as well as others that were taken independently from the ten-point program, namely the introduction of stock options and of a new system of financial performance measures, in the areas of financial, organizational, and portfolio restructuring.

Financial Restructuring

Financial restructuring involves changes in the debt equity mix, greater payments to shareholders or stock buybacks, changes in firms' governance structure, and its relationships to shareholders and the capital market. We have already seen that the core features of financial policy at Siemens—its general financing policy and its debt equity mix—show high continuity. In the following sections, we will therefore look at the other elements of financial restructuring, starting with dividend policies.

[17] See Naschold (1997), 20.
[18] See Bloomberg database and *Manager Magazin,* "Die letzte Reserve," No. 11, 1998.

Dividend policies display large differences across corporate governance systems. Companies' decisions to pay high or low dividends are dependent on the type of corporate governance system the firm is operating in and especially from the level of minority shareholder protection: the higher their influence, the higher the dividends. In this way, the growing importance of institutional investors at Siemens should be mirrored in higher dividends.

Historically, Siemens has always paid comparatively low dividends in order to increase its retained earnings and secure the survival of the firm, and so as to maintain its independence from the banks and the capital markets. Early in its history, it relied on the principle that one-third of profits should be given to the shareholders and two-thirds should be retained. In the postwar era, as well, Siemens pursued a dividend policy that made its shares appear as bonds. From 1960 to 1971 the dividend was kept constant at 16 percent, with only one exception. After 1971, the dividend each year was DM8, irrespective of profit changes.[19] Since then, the stated goal has been to introduce flexibility and profit-dependence in the dividend policy. However, flexibility seems to have been rather limited, as table 4.1 shows. Considering that there were large profit swings in the late 1990s—for example between 1996 and 1998 profits fluctuated between €470 million and €1.5 billion while dividends remained constant—the flexible dividend policy seems not to have been forcefully pursued. After 1998, dividends seem to be on the rise; however the ratio of dividends to profits varies in a range between 30 and 42 percent since the early 1990s with no upward tendency. In 2004, for example, it was 33 percent.[20] Thus, it seems that the institutional investors have not been able to convert their rising share of Siemens's capital into a dividend policy that suits their interests. Research and development expenses also did not react to changing profit situations: they fluctuated only marginally around 7.6 percent of turnover.[21]

While there is strong continuity in dividend policy, the most significant change took place in investor relations. In the 1990s, Siemens disclosed much more information to the capital markets than it used to do, and it abolished several traditions that might deter investors. Certainly the most important of the latter was the abolition of the multiple voting rights of the family shares. Whereas in the early 1990s, attempts by shareholder activists to abolish these preferential shares failed, in the late 1990s, the shares with multiple voting rights were—against the will of the

---

[19] The exchange rate €/DM is 1.95583.

[20] Author's own calculations based on Siemens, *Annual Report*, various years. An exception are the dividend payments in 1998 when Siemens paid 130 percent of its profits as dividends, which was due to the above-mentioned crisis in that year.

[21] See Siemens, *Annual Report*, 2000 and 2001.

TABLE 4.1
Siemens' dividends per share, 1991–2004 (€)

1991	0.66
1992	0.66
1993	0.66
1994	0.66
1995	0.66
1996	0.77
1997	0.77
1998	0.77
1999	1.0
2000	1.0
2001	1.0
2002	1.0
2003	1.10
2004	1.25

Source: Siemens annual reports, various years.

Siemens family—exchanged for named shares. The main reason for this decision was the coming of KonTraG, which forbids multiple rights. Furthermore, it must be seen in the light of the preparation for listing on the NYSE. Other capital-market-related moves were the conversion of the DM50 shares into DM5 shares, which made them more appealing to investors, and the move to named shares in 1999 in order to communicate more directly with its shareholders. These decisions can be interpreted as an attempt to minimize transaction costs in acquiring Siemens shares and to adjust Siemens's habits to the standards of the international capital markets.

New standards have also been introduced to increase transparency. The most decisive move was that Siemens published divisional results. This move was controversial within the management board.[22] It made Siemens more transparent than any other industrial company in Germany, as well as its international competitors.[23] This increased transparency gives analysts a better understanding of Siemens's individual divisions, but on the other hand, it makes cross-subsidization between divisions much more difficult. Furthermore, it puts more pressure on poorly performing businesses and constrains the freedom of management to pursue long-term projects. Moreover, Siemens took to organizing three analyst meetings per year, which at least in the mid 1990s, was uncommon for German blue chip firms. Furthermore, the CEO traveled to the six most important stock exchanges in order to explain Siemens's

[22] See *Börsen-Zeitung*, "Siemens noch mit einer Menge Hausaufgaben," 14.12.1995.
[23] See ibid., "Positives Klima für Siemens-Aktie," 8.11.1995.

strategy. It is important to note that all these changes in investor relations took place before Siemens decided to list itself on the NYSE. The
main decisions were made in the mid 1990s. The head of Siemens's investor relations department explained the shift this way:

> The financial landscape has internationalized through the globalization
> of financial markets; by this increase in transparency and the intensifica-
> tion of equity research, big companies have to adjust to a continuous di-
> alogue with shareholders and financial analysts. . . . companies have to
> formulate value creating strategies and communicate these to the finan-
> cial markets. If this does not work, even big companies are in danger
> of falling behind in the global competition for equity and external capi-
> tal. . . . investors have a natural interest in being informed exhaus-
> tively. . . . and we have an interest that our strategies are understood and
> valued by investors.[24]

Thus, it is quite obvious that financial integration had a causal effect on
one part of Siemens's financial policy—information policy—which has
become much more transparent in order to fulfill the informational
needs of investors.

Siemens also decided to get listed on the NYSE, which was seen as the
jewel in the crown of the ten-point program and a symbol for its more
investor-friendly approach. This is a step with far-reaching consequences
for corporate governance because—as convergence theorists argue—by
doing so, foreign firms become subject to U.S. legal standards and will
adopt American business practices. Therefore, for U.S.–listed firms
"movement toward the American style appears almost inevitable."[25] Several steps were necessary in order to get a listing, the most important
being the introduction of accounting according to U.S.-GAAP.[26] In terms
of transparency, Siemens had introduced most of the transparency requirements before the listing and independently from it: for example, the
publication of divisional results.

Apart from being a symbolic step in the framework of the ten point
program, two factors were decisive for the listing. First, the United States

[24]Rothblum (1996) (Translation AB). However, Rothblum, Siemens's head of Investor
Relations, stresses that Siemens would never maximize short-term profits and that the relations to other stakeholders, such as employees, clients, suppliers, and the whole society, are
crucial for the firm's performance.

[25]Davis, Useem (2002), 252.

[26]Accounting according to US-GAAP had the side effect that Siemens could separate
out its pension requirements, which contribute to its enormous liquidity, but which
it did not like to disclose. Pension funds were transferred to a newly founded pension
trust.

had become Siemens's most important single market after Germany, and Siemens had become the biggest foreign employer in the United States. Nevertheless, the company was not very well known inside the United States. Thus, the listing aimed to increase its name recognition, especially at a time when Siemens was eager to enter the American mobile phone market. In this sense, the step followed the logic of the listing in London in the early 1990s, when a significantly increased sales volume led to a listing in that country in order to support an expansionist product market strategy. Furthermore, Siemens could only introduce stock option schemes for its American employees if it was listed on an American stock exchange.[27]

The second and probably most important reason for seeking a U.S. listing had to do with the starkly growing importance of stocks as an acquisition currency. Most mergers and acquisitions in the late 1990s were financed by share swaps. Since Siemens pursued an expansionist strategy in the United States, the possibility of acquisitions with its own shares needed to be secured. This was of special significance for Siemens's information and communications business group, which had been strongly pursuing acquisitions in the United States, especially in the Internet sector. The importance of acquisitions has always been stressed as the prime reason for a listing. In the Siemens CEO's words: "Since we are largely financed from our internal cash flow, listing in the world's biggest capital market wasn't absolutely necessary. The situation has changed now that stock has become an increasingly important acquisition currency in company takeovers and mergers. We also want to have this option available for dealings in the United States."[28] Other indicators support the view that the goal to obtain an acquisition currency was the prime motive for the listing. No capital was raised by the listing: the share was made tradable by American Depository Rights. Furthermore, it was not intended to broaden ownership among American shareholders. Thus, Siemens's listing on the NYSE was not a move to signal shareholder value commitment, but a precondition for acquisitions.

The most significant change that the U.S. listing brought about was Siemens's conversion to U.S.-GAAP. American shareholders cannot exercise more voice because their ownership base remained by and large the same. In 2001, at the time of the NYSE listing, American investors held 12 percent of Siemens's shares; in 2003 their share even

[27] See *Financial Times Deutschland*, "Siemens hängt Start an New Yorker Börse an die kleine Glocke," 9.3.2001.
[28] Speech at the Annual General Meeting, 18.2.1999.

decreased to 10 percent.[29] Also the trading in Siemens's shares at the NYSE has been minor; it was 3 percent of the trading volume at the Frankfurt stock exchange in 2004.[30] Thus listing on the NYSE was more a symbolic step seeking to win investors' confidence in the framework of the ten-point program than an actual shift toward increased American ownership. There is no direct causality linking a listing on NYSE with the outcome that convergence theorists expect, namely a transformation of a firm's corporate governance system toward the preferences of investors.

Hence, in the area of financial restructuring, we find continuity in Siemens's financing policy and in its dividend policies, whereas there are significant and far-reaching changes in its information policy and its transparency. The listing in the United States has not had major repercussions on Siemens's business policy. The next sections deal with the area of organizational restructuring.

Organizational Restructuring

The Economic-Value-Added Concept

The main financial goal of Siemens in the early 1990s was a return on equity of 15 percent, but this target was missed. In order to come closer to the profit goals, a new management and controlling instrument was introduced in 1998, the economic-value-added (EVA) concept. EVA, developed by the management consultancy Stern Stewart, measures the success of each business group and of the whole company by incorporating the cost of internal and external capital. In this perspective, businesses are only profitable if they earn at least their cost of capital. The expectations of the financial markets are thus incorporated into corporate decision making, because, in theory, the cost of capital can be equalized with the profit requirements of all investors, shareholders, and creditors. The economic value added emerges when more than the costs of capital are earned, which is then benchmarked against competitors. Siemens was the first major company in Germany to introduce the concept. It was seen as a continuation of the TOP program and was intended to take TOP one step further.[31] The result of this concept's use is that there are clear financial goals for business group managers, defined in terms of

---

[29] See *Manager-Magazin*, "Italienische Hochzeiten," No. 1, 2004.

[30] See *Financial Times Deutschland*, "Firmen stützen Delisting-Vorstoß," 22.10.2004.

[31] See *Handelsblatt*, "Die Kapitalkosten wurden nicht verdient," 2.12.1997. The goals of the program are equivalent to a return on equity of 15 percent, the former financial goal.

profitability, which should then translate into higher share prices. EVA, an internal controlling instrument, was introduced in order to remedy the unsatisfactory profit results of the TOP program.[32]

The introduction of EVA was a break with Siemens's old strategies in that it made the performance of the business groups more transparent and it tries to lead the firm by financial goals. It can be seen as the most far-reaching and systematic attempt to achieve the long-standing goal of a return on equity of 15 percent. However, the most important feature of the concept is how it is used. The logic of EVA decrees that business groups that underperform their capital costs should be fixed, closed, or sold, in very much the same way as GE handles its business. Siemens seems not to be willing to follow the concept in this crucial regard, which would mean determined and fast disinvestments. When EVA was introduced, more than half of the business groups earned less than their capital costs. In 2001, the biggest loss makers were Information and Communications, Automotive, and logistics systems, but their profit goals were postponed, and the CEO has declared that no division as a whole will be sold, but only minor parts at most.[33] Siemens sees its broad portfolio as an asset, which makes it less vulnerable against downswings in certain markets, because the cash cows and the loss-makers change, and so the single divisions support each other over time. The prime example is medical equipment, which had for a long time been run at a loss, but achieved a turnaround in the 1990s; it is now one of the most successful divisions. The fix-it option enjoys primacy; despite EVA, Siemens is committed to its divisions and markets.

Furthermore, much depends on the definition of capital costs. On the whole, Siemens is operating with a figure of 9 percent, but the definition differs for each business group. This is significantly lower than what Siemens's competitors try to achieve with a similar system: for Ericsson, the figure is 16 percent, for GE 13 percent, Phillips 12 percent, and GEC 10 percent.[34] Hence, Siemens has adjusted the concept to its own needs and its own environment, which ultimately means a soft version of the original concept. The work councils welcomed the introduction of EVA on the grounds that EVA provides higher transparency about the goals to be met and because it did not set uniform profit goals for the company as a whole, which had always been resisted by the work councils, but differentiated between the divisions.

[32]See CFO Baumann in *Börsen-Zeitung*, "Das neue 'Win'-Dach auf dem Siemens-Haus," 2.12.1997.
[33]See *Financial Times Deutschland*, "Siemens verschiebt Renditeziele auf 2004," 7.12.2001, and *Financial Times Deutschland*, "Bei Siemens rücken Sanierer an die Spitze," 15.11.2001.
[34]See *Börsen-Zeitung*, "Das neue 'Win'-Dach auf dem Siemens-Haus," 2.12.1997.

Introducing Stock Options

In addition to EVA, Siemens introduced a share option scheme. The design of stock options is of crucial importance for a corporate governance system, since stock options can alter the managers' incentives, and are the prime vehicle for a capital market orientation. Stock options are seen as the most important explanatory factor for the transformation of the American corporate governance system from a managerial to a capital-market-oriented system: "Thanks to lucrative stock option plans, managers could share in the market returns from restructured companies. Shareholder value became an ally rather than an enemy."[35] Thus, if management's compensation is closely tied to the share price, it can be expected that their primary focus will be on increasing that price. The crucial point is not the existence of incentive schemes per se, but rather whether managerial incentives are directly tied to share price.

Siemens's incentive scheme was introduced in 1999 and affected five hundred top managers, later it was extended to fifteen hundred managers. The stock option plan is part of a broader incentive scheme. For the two hundred top managers, 40 percent of income is fixed, the rest is variable; for the next tier of three hundred managers, the ratio is 60:40. Thirty percent of the variable part is an annual bonus and is based on yearly results: the remaining 70 percent is a long-term bonus and is based on three-year results, taking EVA and accounting figures as a baseline. The long-term bonus has the aim of preventing short-term incentives.[36] The stock options themselves are only a supplement to these incentives. In a best-case scenario, they can add up to 25 percent of the annual income of top management.[37] The whole incentive scheme shows a deliberate long-term orientation. The yearly bonus is not fully paid: two-thirds of it is retained and paid only when the three-year goals are reached.

Compared to U.S. standards the program does not provide high-powered incentives to tie strategic decisions to share price. Between 1980 and 1994, equity-based compensation in the United States increased from less than 20 percent of total CEO compensation to almost 50.[38] It is obvious that Siemens's stock option plan is quite different. The incentive scheme emphasizes long-term performance, and in 1999 the market value of granted stock options for the management board was only 10 percent of their total salary. In 2004, stock options amounted to

---

[35] See Holmström, Kaplan (2001), 3.
[36] See *Börsen-Zeitung*, "Stock Options für 500 Manager," 4.12.1998.
[37] See *Süddeutsche Zeitung*, "Ein Bonbon für die Top-Manager," 15.2.1999.
[38] Holmström, Kaplan (2001), 16.

only 19 percent of total management board compensation.[39] Thus, the design of the stock option program has also been adjusted to Siemens's environment and provides comparatively low incentives to embrace the promotion of the share price as the main goal for management.

Management Recruitment

There are large differences in the market for managers in stakeholder and shareholder systems. In shareholder systems, managers acquire mostly a general business education, preferably in finance, and change jobs frequently; the job market for managers is very active. In stakeholder systems, managers tend to spend their professional life with one firm, acquire firm-specific knowledge, are often technically trained; top management has long job tenure.

At Siemens, the CEO has normally been an engineer. In the 158-year-old history of the company, there have only been two CEOs without a technical or engineering background. Job tenure is also very long. After the inclusion of Siemens's subsidiaries in 1968, there was a three-year transition period with shared responsibility in the management board. The two following CEOs both had a ten-year tenure, and from 1991 to 2005 Heinrich von Pierer has been CEO. He was the second CEO without a technical background, holding a doctorate in law and a master in economics. No CEO was ever fired. All of them have spent their whole professional life within Siemens and climbed up the hierarchical ladder.

There are no signs that management recruitment policy will change in the foreseeable future. Generally, Siemens has developed a sophisticated system for recruiting its top management internally. In order to identify high potentials, every manager has to speak with his subordinates about their development and achievements, which will be reported to the next highest level. Based on these discussions, the most promising candidates are selected, about five hundred people for the 150 key positions, and are trained in different positions within the company.[40]

Management candidates enjoy a theoretical education: they have to work in different positions in different divisions, and since the early 1990s they have had to spend at least three years in a leading position in a foreign Siemens branch.[41] This program lasts ten to fifteen years, and the most successful candidates are promoted to key positions. It is very rare that outsiders come into leading positions. The principle is to pro-

---

[39] See *Frankfurter Allgemeine Zeitung*, "Pierer ist einer der Spitzenverdiener," 29.11.2004.
[40] Interview with former Siemens senior manager.
[41] See *Süddeutsche Zeitung*, "Wie Siemens seinen Manager-Nachwuchs heranzieht," 4.7.1991.

mote Siemens's own talents into top positions, which is legitimized with Siemens's organizational and technological complexity. This complexity, resulting from the many businesses in which Siemens is active, requires in-depth knowledge of these structures by managers. Hence, managers are trained within one firm, develop firm-specific knowledge, and build up strong relations with employees.

Thus there are no changes underway in the realm of human resource management and management recruitment, whereas the introduction of EVA and the stock option scheme indicate the import of instruments from shareholder systems of corporate governance. However, both instruments are differently designed compared to the standards in shareholder systems and do not provide incentives to promote share price as the exclusive goal of management. A similar pattern is visible in the realm of portfolio restructuring.

Portfolio Restructuring

The most spectacular strategic decision of the ten-point program was that the semiconductor division should be spun off. Until then, only marginal businesses had been sold.[42] Spinning off the semiconductor division was on a new scale; it meant giving up sixty thousand jobs and €8.7 billion in sales. It was not only the semiconductor division that was spun off, but also related businesses, such as passive components, electron tubes, and transistors. However, the strategic decision primarily had to be taken for semiconductors. The other areas were spun off because these divisions would have been too small without semiconductors.

Siemens had invested huge sums in becoming competitive in the semiconductor industry from the early 1980s. Semiconductors were seen as a technology that is crucial for all areas of Siemens's businesses. Thus in-house production was given primacy in order to reduce dependence on external supply with the danger of supplier shortages. Siemens was willing to bear huge losses in a very cyclical business, characterized by fluctuating demand and inelastic supply. It has been estimated that Siemens lost at least €5 billion on semiconductors in the 1990s.[43] Yearly investments fluctuated between €1 and 1.5 billion and research and development expenses were about €500 million each year. Only between 1994 and 1996 did the division make profits and contribute €405 and

[42]The disinvestments from 1994 to 1998 had a value of €3.3 billion. See Warburg (1998), 5.
[43]See *Computerwoche*, "Wegen Halbleitermalaise fliegt Siemens in Turbulenzen," 31.7.1998.

308 million to Siemens's balance.[44] The semiconductor division's losses of more than €500 million, triggered by falling semiconductor prices following the economic crisis in Asia, were the main reason for Siemens's crisis in 1998, which led to the ten-point program.

Faced with the acute crisis in the semiconductor industry, Siemens was no longer willing to bear the cycles in this business and to finance the enormous capital requirements of the division. This capital would have been spent at the expense of the other businesses. Because of the extraordinarily capital-intensive nature of the business, semiconductors had absorbed a lion's share of Siemens's investment resources, thereby jeopardizing the growth of other business groups. Equally important, the very short-term product life cycles in the semiconductor business did not fit Siemens's long-term orientation and its incremental innovation patterns more generally.

The division was renamed Infineon Technologies and in 1999 listed on the New York and Frankfurt stock exchanges. Siemens gave Infineon generous startup capital and appointed the chairmen of the management and supervisory boards, both members of the Siemens management board. However, the spin-off was not complete at first and Siemens demerged Infineon gradually. At the IPO 29 percent of Infineon was floated. In 2001 Siemens decreased its stake to 51 percent and by 2004 this figure was down to 18 percent. The work councils supported the spin-off. Crucial for the decision was the agreement of the divisional work councils whose main concern was Infineon's better future prospects as an independent firm.[45] Furthermore, Infineon adopted the employment conditions of Siemens wholesale, joined the employers' association, and made sure that dismissals would be avoided. Although the spin-off marks a break in Siemens's traditions, it was done in a very traditional way; jobs were not affected, the decision was taken in agreement with the work councils, and Siemens was in control of a majority stake in the first years after the IPO.

From a shareholder value perspective, this was not a far-reaching move. The core of the shareholder value approach is that firms should concentrate on one or only a few businesses with the highest profitability and growth perspectives. The valuation of conglomerates on the stock markets is lower due to the conglomerate discount, which results from their lower transparency. Siemens, with its portfolio that covers many more areas of electronics than all its competitors, is therefore under pressure.[46] Criticism by financial analysts thus centered on its missing

[44]See *Neue Zürcher Zeitung,* "Siemens Führung unter zunehmendem Druck," 5.11.1998.
[45]Interview with former Siemens senior manager.
[46]In 1990, it covered 80 percent of the whole spectrum of electronics, the figures for its competitors were Hitachi: 71 percent, Toshiba: 64 percent, GEC: 52 percent, Philipps: 48

core competencies and the broadness of Siemens's businesses. The suggestion has been to split and divest Siemens completely in order to unlock shareholder value; at a minimum, it should concentrate on one or two core businesses, the then-fashionable telecommunications business among them, and continue restructuring. The *Financial Times* suggested that Siemens be split into a high-tech company comprising telecommunications, semiconductors, computers, and medical equipment; and a low-tech company with power plants, rail systems, capital goods, and lighting.[47] J. P. Morgan urged Siemens to concentrate on a few core businesses and get rid of all underperforming business groups.[48] M. M. Warburg thought that Siemens should sell or float businesses accounting for more than two-thirds of its turnover.[49]

However, Siemens has remained firmly committed to its business groups. Even business groups that incurred heavy losses for a long time were kept and an attempt was made to repair them. The same strategy was followed in the semiconductor business, but after the severe crisis in the industry, a spin-off with continuing influence seemed the more promising alternative for a business in which Siemens never really succeeded. Moreover, there are no signs that Siemens intends to further restructure its portfolio on a large scale. According to the CEO, the floating of Infineon and passive components were not intended to be the beginning of a broader restructuring, but rather the end of one.[50]

Generally, Siemens's business policy has not been characterized by downsizing, but very much by expansion. Sales doubled to €84 billion between 1991 and 2002. Siemens's broad portfolio is seen by the management as one of the firm's key assets that enables it to weather economic crises and achieve long-term economic success for the benefit of customers, shareholders, and employees.[51] Diversification means risk reduction for Siemens because it makes it more independent from the busi-

---

percent, General Electric: 28 percent. See *Financial Times*, "Spotlight on Siemens' Changing Act," 24.12.1990.

[47] See *Financial Times*, "Splitting Siemens Up," 6.11.1998.

[48] See *Börsen-Zeitung*, "Siemens fehlt radikale Neuorientierung," 21.1.1998.

[49] See Warburg (1998), 7.

[50] See *Financial Times*, "New Lean Siemens May Still Need Toning Up," 6.11.1998. Siemens has even ruled out selling or floating business groups for which synergies with other divisions are hard to discover, such as the lighting group Osram or the joint venture with Bosch for household appliances. See *Börsen-Zeitung*, "Wir meinen es ernst mit dem Umbau," 17.4.1999. Nevertheless, there was one exception to this rule, namely the sale of the mobile phone division to BenQ in late 2005. However, this sale followed the same logic as the floating of Infineon. Siemens had not succeeded in the fast-moving mobile phone business for years and experienced heavy losses despite many restructuring efforts. So, it finally sold its last consumer business, characterized by very short product cycle and radical innovation patterns, in order to concentrate on infrastructure and systems solutions, in which innovation is of incremental nature.

[51] See Siemens, *Annual Report 2001*, 19.

ness cycles in different industries and helps to contribute to stability.[52] Thus, it is unlikely that Siemens's structure and portfolio will change significantly in the foreseeable future. The spin-off was not the beginning of a general downsizing of the company, but rather an adjustment in business strategy.

Siemens's strategic behavior in the realm of portfolio restructuring with its relative stability differs significantly from those of its main competitors in the engineering business in the course of the 1990s.

ABB, the result of a merger between Swedish Asean and Swiss BBC in 1988, became a role model for companies in the 1990s. After the merger, ABB introduced a matrix organization, through which control over the five thousand autonomous profit centers was shared between business segments and regions. This organizational structure was governed by strict financial control and was seen as a model for globalizing companies. ABB won the Financial Times Award as Europe's most respected company four years in a row in the mid 1990s. ABB pursued a very active portfolio policy. Between 1988 and 1996, ABB bought more than 150 firms.[53] However, the rapid expansion through often-overvalued acquisitions brought ABB to the brink of bankruptcy. Debt exploded to $30 billion in 2001, it sustained considerable losses, and its share price sharply plummeted. In this situation, ABB initiated a far-reaching downsizing. It sold the shares of its rail traffic joint venture as well as its whole power plant and power generation businesses. Combined with several minor sales, the downsizing resulted in an almost complete retreat from the large-scale plant engineering and construction businesses. ABB is now focused on equipment for industry and electricity distribution. During the restructuring, CEOs changed frequently. Between 1996 and 2002, ABB had three different CEOs. All in all, ABB pursued a much more volatile and risky business policy than did Siemens, which resulted in a far-reaching downsizing. Between the early 1990s and 2001, revenues dropped from $34 to $24 billion.

Alstom, the French heavy engineering conglomerate, experienced similar difficulties. Largely due to risky financial transactions—Alstom's off-balance-sheet guarantees for its customers jumped to 60 percent of its revenues in 2001[54]—Alstom was close to financial collapse. Its debts exploded and Alstom's share lost almost 90 percent of its value that year. Similar to ABB, Alstom undertook a far-reaching downsizing plan, supported by the French government. It sold its industrial turbines business to Siemens. It also sold its most profitable unit, transmission and distri-

---

[52]See von Pierer (1996), 4.
[53]See *Manager Magazin*, "Sicherung durchgebrannt," 1.7.2002.
[54]See *Financial Times*, "One of Europe's Biggest Engineering Companies Is in Trouble," 8.12.2001.

bution activities as well as its technology services, leaving only a fragment of its former business portfolio.

The showcase of an active portfolio policy and a shareholder value orientation is GE, Siemens's American competitor in many industrial businesses. Although a widely diversified conglomerate with operations in power and industrial systems, aircraft engines, insurance, consumer credits, media, and many more, GE does not suffer from the conglomerate discount, because of its strict profit orientation. GE follows the principle that each newly acquired firm must be integrated successfully within a hundred days; otherwise it will be fixed, sold, or closed. The same applies to units that are not number one or two in their respective markets or to units whose markets are likely to stagnate; this happened to GE's defense business—at that time constituting one-tenth of the firm's sales—which was completely sold in 1992. Between 1996 and 1999, GE acquired more than a hundred firms each year, with a cumulative value of $51 billion.[55] The active portfolio policy, through which sales doubled in the 1990s to $125 billion, is intended to meet the financial goals of a minimum earnings growth of 10 percent a year and a return on capital of at least 20 percent.

Compared to its competitors, Siemens's portfolio policy has been much more stable and shows a higher commitment to its markets. These differences are partly grounded in the decision-making in German companies and the interests of stakeholders, especially employees, in stable company development. However, it is also a consequence of Siemens's product market policy and the focus on system production. Siemens stresses the synergies between its businesses in producing whole systems for its customers. In this way, it is very reluctant to concentrate on core competencies, because it sees its broad diversification as an asset and the whole company as a strategic holding, as opposed to a financial one, which leverages synergies and engineering capacities.

This systems approach is pursued within the single divisions as well as across divisions. The continuation of the TOP program explicitly put the production of systems and cross-divisional systems solutions at the center of Siemens's strategy and organizational development. Building on the broadness of its portfolio, Siemens aims for competitive advantages in complex, comprehensive, and tailor-made packages of products and services. Thus, an active portfolio policy does not fit this approach, because producing whole systems for its customers requires the presence in many business lines, even if some businesses, taken on their own, are not profitable. This orientation toward systems can be seen as an extension and a deepening of DQP production. It tries to leverage technological

---

[55] See *Financial Times*, "GE's Hidden Flaw," 1.8.2000.

competence, product differentiation, and the adaptation to user needs. Hence, the cautious and fairly stable portfolio policy is a consequence of Siemens's product market policy and is unlikely to change as long as a systems strategy is pursued.

Restructuring Results, Profit Distribution, and Industrial Relations

The restructuring measures managed to significantly increase profits and share price. In 1999, after-tax profits were €1.2 billion, although EVA was a negative €658 million. In 2000, Siemens announced that after-tax profits had increased to €8.9 billion, with all business segments in the black, while EVA was €7.1 billion.[56] Return on equity exploded. In the crisis year of 1998, it was 2.4 percent, it rose to 10.5 percent in 1999 and to 39.6 percent in 2000, but fell down to the usual range of about 10 percent in the two following years.[57] After the announcement of the ten-point program, Siemens's share price started to outperform the DAX index, and it continued to do so for some time. Siemens's market capitalization increased, supported by the high-tech bubble on the stock markets, from €28 billion to €85 billion between 1998 and 2000.[58] However, Siemens remained behind its main competitor, GE, which had a five to six times higher market capitalization. Nevertheless, the restructuring program with its focus on pushing profits and share price achieved its main goals.

The distribution of Siemens's all-time-high profits shows its continuing stakeholder orientation. The company paid a special dividend of €0.66 on top of the regular dividend of €1; yet the ratio of dividends to profits fell from 37 percent the year before to 16 percent. At the same time, Siemens also let the employees participate in the company's success by "Germany's largest and most generous employee-share program to date."[59] The idea was to give an equivalent of the dividends to the employees, in order to satisfy Siemens's two most important groups of stakeholders.[60] Siemens offered shares to its employees at a discount of 50 percent. This scheme involved costs of €600 million for Siemens. Comparing these payments with GE's shareholder orientation, the differences become obvious. Between 1994 and 1998, GE increased dividend payments by 84 percent, and spent $14.6 billion on share buybacks,

---

[56] See Siemens, *Annual report*, 2000 and 2002, five-year overviews.
[57] Bloomberg database.
[58] See Siemens, *Annual report 2000*, 99.
[59] See *Financial Times*, "Siemens to Spend €500m on Employee Shares," 20.10.2000.
[60] See *Financial Times Deutschland*, "Bescherung für Mitarbeiter und Aktionäre von Siemens," 20.10.2000.

which together meant an outflow of 74.4 percent of cash from operations.[61]

Siemens's employee bonus program also led to an increase in employees' shareholdings of 1.2 percent. Before that program, Siemens employees were estimated to hold somewhere between 9 and 17 percent of the firm's equity.[62] Thus, the employees are the most important group of shareholders, which increases their bargaining position. In this regard, the plan also helps Siemens bolster its defenses against potential takeover attempts. However, the scheme also shows that Siemens is not only focused on its shareholders, but is still investing in consensus with its employees.

Generally, restructuring did not negatively affect the cooperative and consensus-oriented character of industrial relations at Siemens. The system of early information sharing, consensus orientation, and co-management with the work councils was not affected by the restructuring efforts. Indeed, the full support of the work councils enabled the restructuring, which was carried out without major resistance and strikes. In exchange for their cooperation, employees were compensated by the avoidance of operational dismissals and a share in the financial success of the restructuring. The work councils were also successful in preventing uniform profit goals. They generally welcomed the higher transparency of the company, because it increased their access to information.[63] Therefore, the change in Siemens's information policy and the introduction of EVA did not lead to resistance on the part of the work councils.

However, restructuring was not the only challenge for Siemens in the 1990s. The second challenge was the globalization of product markets. A firm's internationalization strategy is a direct reaction to this development. Internationalization is important for corporate governance, because it may result in a disembedding from the home country, in which the corporate governance system of the home country would cease to exert influence on the firm's behavior.

Internationalization Strategy

Comparative research on the strategic behavior of multinational corporations (MNCs) has shown that the most distinguishing characteristic of

[61] Lazonick, O'Sullivan (2000b), p. 23.

[62] See *Financial Times Deutschland*, "Bescherung für Mitarbeiter und Aktionäre von Siemens," 20.10.2000.

[63] Interview with former Siemens manager. This confirms Höpner's argument that code-termination is not an obstacle to an increasing capital market orientation, because a higher transparency is in the interest of the work councils and increases their capacities to monitor management. See Höpner (2001), 27.

German MNCs is their deep embeddedness in the German corporate governance system.[64] They tend to rely on their home base as the center for economic activities and to pursue a multidomestic strategy of internationalization in which foreign direct investment is primarily undertaken to be close to customers and to adapt products to local needs. This is seen as a consequence of the high quality strategies of German firms on the product markets, which require local adaptation of products and cooperation with customers.[65] In this approach subsidiaries are appendages of a mainly domestic corporation, while headquarters retain the strategic and financial control. Hence, organizational pressures from internationalization are low and do not threaten the domestic corporate governance arrangements.

Siemens concentrated on the German home market until the mid 1980s, although it was already then a highly internationalized firm. In 1985, it made 53 percent of its sales in Germany, 21 percent in the rest of Europe, and 10 percent in North America. Since then, Siemens has pursued a much more aggressive internationalization strategy with a focus on the United States, which constitutes a third of the world electronics market, and to a lesser degree on Western Europe, especially Great Britain. The motivation was the assumption that Siemens could only stay competitive if it was strongly present in at least two of the three Triad regions—Europe, Asia and North America. Sales in the U.S. market more than doubled in the 1990s to 22 percent of total sales, with the number of employees increasing from 15,100 in 1985 to 76,000 in 2001. Nevertheless, Siemens's presence in the United States has been associated with high losses and the U.S. business was still unprofitable in 2000.[66]

The strategic decision to grow internationally by acquisitions made Siemens the biggest German investor abroad. Because the German market was already saturated, expansion could only take place abroad. Moreover, the growing importance of electronics resulted in an explosion in research and development expenses while at the same time, product life cycles and innovation cycles shortened dramatically. Whereas in the mid 1970s, 39 percent of Siemens's products had been invented within the past five years, the corresponding figure for the mid 1990s was 75 percent.[67] Economies of scale therefore became much more important; thus higher output was imperative to finance investment in research and development.

Consequently, in terms of sales, Siemens's home market has become relatively less important. Over the course of the 1990s, sales in Germany

[64]See Lane (2000a), 208.
[65]See Lane (1998), 477–78.
[66]See *Financial Times Deutschland*, "Siemens baut das US-Geschäft um," 13.3.2001.
[67]See Goth (1999), 97.

decreased from roughly 45 percent to 21 percent of total sales in 2005. Sales in the rest of Europe increased from 30 to 33 percent and sales in the Americas increased from 15 to 25 percent. Business in Asia grew from 6 to 13 percent.[68] In absolute terms, Siemens's sales in Germany remained by and large constant, but the growth came largely from abroad. The sales pattern follows the distribution of electronics markets, whose growth takes place outside Europe. There is a more balanced sales structure emerging, a key strategic goal since the mid 1990s. However, profits have come mainly from German and European business. Hidden behind the relative distribution of sales, there is a pronounced absolute growth. Total sales grew from €32 billion to €84 billion between 1990 and 2002.[69] Thus Siemens reacted to the changing international environment with an expansionist business policy.

In terms of employees, their number in Germany decreased, from 230,000 in 1990 to 165,000 in 2005. By the mid 1990s, Siemens for the first time had more foreign than domestic employees. The employment pattern therefore followed sales development. However, disproportionately large numbers of employees are still employed in Germany: 36 percent of the company's 460,000 employees while 79 percent of sales were made outside Germany. Even more important is the fact that—in the late 1990s—two-thirds of value added originated in Germany.[70] All central management functions are located in Germany; thus all important decisions are made in the home country. Top management is recruited almost exclusively from Germany. Among the eighty most senior managers, only two were non-Germans and foreigners accounted for only 20 percent of senior middle management in the late 1990s.[71] There have been no attempts to internationalize senior management because the recruitment of top management takes place internally and future top managers are selected very early in their careers. However, non-German Siemens managers can reach the top positions in their respective countries, which are all headed by locals. Thus, in terms of socialization of top management, foreign influence remains low.

Other indicators also point in the direction of a continuing embeddedness of Siemens in the German business system. Currently, two-thirds of the research and development employees in central functions are employed in Germany, and of total forty-seven thousand research and development employees, which include thirty thousand software developers, roughly 50 percent work in Germany; in the 1990s 75 percent of all re-

---

[68] Siemens, *Annual Report 2005*, 17.

[69] See ibid., *Annual Report*, various years.

[70] See *Süddeutsche Zeitung*, "Der Riese in der Tretmühle der Globalisierung," 9.10.1997.

[71] See *Der Spiegel*, "Unsere Leute brauchen Teamgeist," Interview with the head of human resource management, Peter Pribilla, No. 20, 1998.

search and development expenses were spent domestically.[72] This is unlikely to change fundamentally, since Germany is seen as the main location for this field. Furthermore, Siemens exports its production model to its foreign subsidiaries. It has introduced the dual education system in twenty countries in cooperation with local colleges. Also the distribution of assets is biased toward Germany; in 2004, 39 percent of its long-term assets worth €10,700 billion were located in Germany, 27 percent in the rest of Europe, and 21 percent the United States.[73]

Overall, Siemens internationalized much more vigorously over the 1990s. However, its style and strategies of internationalization follow its traditional trajectory. The strategic functions remain in Germany, the distribution of assets has a bias toward the home base, top management is not at all internationalized, and research and development as well as value-added activities are heavily concentrated in Germany. Therefore, Siemens follows a multidomestic strategy, which does not threaten domestic corporate governance arrangements. There are also no signs that Siemens is transforming itself into a network corporation without a clear center, with strong influence by subsidiaries, and with no discernible nationality, a model some management theorists have argued for.[74] Thus Siemens's aggressive internationalization, which has been supported by the work councils, has not resulted in a loosening of ties to the home base, and Siemens is still embedded in the German system of corporate governance. However, it would be misleading to characterize Siemens as a slow globalizer, as German firms have been perceived in the comparative political economy literature. It showed a high degree of active globalization during the 1990s; the institutions of corporate governance have not hindered this process nor have they been transformed by internationalization.

Siemens's responses to globalization show a complex mixture of change and continuity. Its adjustment path has been characterized by expansion through internationalization, and by internal restructuring. In terms of its internationalization strategy, Siemens internationalized vigorously over the 1990s, but there is strong continuity in its way of internationalization. Siemens follows a multidomestic strategy with a bias toward the home base in the distribution of activities and assets.

The restructuring measures show varying degrees of continuity. If we recall the main elements of a shareholder value strategy—concentration on core competencies, minimum profit goals for all divisions with the

---

[72]See Siemens (2005) as well as *Handelsblatt*, "Jahresüberschuß soll um mehr als 20% steigen," 23.2.1996.
[73]Siemens, *Annual Report 2002*, and author's own calculations.
[74]See Hedlund, Rolander (1990), 22–26.

consequence of fast divestments, stock option programs for management, and a transparent information policy, the following picture emerges. The biggest change took place in information policy and transparency. In this area, Siemens has become much more investor-friendly and discloses much more information than it used to do. Nevertheless, this greater capital market orientation did not affect other main features of financial policy, namely, financing and dividend policy. In the realm of organizational restructuring, Siemens introduced stock options and profit goals. However, compared to Anglo-Saxon practices, these are designed differently and provide lower-powered incentives for management to prioritize shareholder value.

In terms of corporate strategy, the core concept of the shareholder value approach is the concentration on a few core businesses and the implied consequence of far-reaching portfolio restructuring, also resulting from minimum profit goals. Here, Siemens shows a high degree of resistance to divestments. According to all statements of top management, the spin-off of Infineon was the last major divestment. Divisions that do not meet the profit goals, which also are lower than the corresponding goals of Siemens's competitors, are nevertheless kept. The broad diversification serves the goal of spreading out risks and securing the survival of the company as a whole. More importantly, Siemens's deliberate strategy to offer system solutions discriminates against an active and far-reaching portfolio and downsizing policy. Hence, the broad diversification is used to create and leverage competitive advantages in complex engineering systems.

In terms of consensual decision making, the stakeholder model is alive, and corporate strategy builds on co-management with the work councils. The interests of shareholders and institutional investors have not become the only interests to be considered, even though profits and share prices have become more important aims in Siemens's strategy and have been markedly pursued.

Taking Anglo-Saxon practices as a benchmark, it can be argued that financial and product market globalization have not pushed Siemens down a path leading to a pure shareholder value conception of the firm, even though it is highly exposed to these developments. Siemens imported several, but only several, elements of the shareholder value approach, and the implemented features are not equivalent to Anglo-Saxon standards. The emerging corporate governance system at Siemens combines continuity in corporate strategy, financing policy, and industrial relations with a transparent information policy and certain shareholder value instruments, such as stock options and profit goals. The shareholder value concept has been accommodated to Siemens's environment and governance style, rejecting short-term profit maximization and stressing a long-term orientation.[75]

All in all, wide differences remain relative to Siemens's competitors from shareholder systems of corporate governance. This implies that financial market pressures do not affect all elements of corporate governance, and that partial adaptations, especially in the area of information policy, need not be damaging for other elements of corporate governance, such as industrial relations and corporate strategy. In the case of Siemens, the pressure of financial markets affected above all accurate information about the financial situation of the company, but did not extend to deeper strategic issues.

[75]Rothblum (1996).

Chapter 5

Deutsche Telekom

Deutsche Telekom (DT) is another prime candidate to take steps in the direction of a shareholder value system of corporate governance. The company has faced considerable pressure from the capital markets, because as a former state monopoly it needs to signal its shareholder value commitment to potential investors, who are highly critical of political influence on firms as well as of goals other than profit maximization. In contrast to Siemens with its widely dispersed ownership, DT has a controlling owner, the German government, which allows one to single out the effects of concentrated versus dispersed ownership. In terms of market capitalization, DT has always been among the three most valuable German enterprises; together with Siemens's shares, DT's have been the most traded shares on the German exchange since its initial public offering (IPO).

Until its privatization in 1996 DT was publicly owned and was integrated into one company along with the German postal service and postal bank. Actual privatization took place relatively late. Whereas AT&T's Bell system was dismantled in the early 1980s and British Telecom was privatized in 1984, the road to DT's privatization proved cumbersome.

A political consensus had to be found, because far-reaching reforms concerning the organization of the telecommunications industry required a change of the constitution and therefore a two-thirds majority in the national parliament. On the basis of recommendations of a commission, liberalization took place in several steps. In 1989 *Post Reform 1* separated Deutsche Bundespost into its three constituent units (telecommunications, postal services, banking). *Post Reform 2*, approved in 1994, freed DT from political control, gave it entrepreneurial autonomy, and allowed it to pursue previously forbidden international activities. The regulatory competencies, such as licensing and tariff controls, were transferred from the dissolved Ministry of Post and Telecommunications to a newly created regulatory agency, the Regulatory Office for Telecommunications and Post, in 1998. The IPO took place in 1996, with a 25 percent stake being floated. Subsequent tranches and share swap-financed acquisitions reduced the government's stake to 38 per cent.

Several developments led to DT's privatization. The main reason was that DT desperately needed capital. The IPO seemed necessary because of the large investments DT had undertaken in former East Germany, which amounted to roughly €25 billion in network infrastructure. The cross-subsidization of the postbank and postal service amounted to €6 billion between 1990 and 1995 and payments to the government to €12 billion in the same period.[1] Hence, DT's equity ratio was extremely low, 11 percent in 1995, which compares with ratios of 50–70 percent on the part of its competitors. Its debts were enormous, around €61 billion in the early 1990s, which gave it twenty-fourth place in the league of leading world debtors, one place ahead of Turkey, and with an interest burden of almost €3 billion per year.[2] Given German federal budget constraints, sufficient capital could only be raised by privatization.

Second, in order to take advantage of the new technological opportunities, such as mobile phones, more flexibility was needed, which included faster decision-making and possible international business activities. Third, the European Union had announced that the telecommunication monopolies must be broken up by 1998; hence a solution had to be found to transform DT in order to make it fit for the coming competition. Parallel to DT's privatization, the German telecommunications market was liberalized. Full liberalization was to be realized, in line with European Union directives, by January 1998. There were several steps on the road to full liberalization. In 1995, the German government opened the telecommunications market to alternative networks; in 1993 it opened the corporate networks market; in 1990, deregulation opened the terminal equipment market to competition; and in 1989, all telecommunications services except voice telephony were liberalized. The German government introduced strict regulation, which obliged the regulator to pursue asymmetric regulation, which meant

[1] See Glotz (2001), 60, 232.
[2] See *Financial Times*, "Doubts over Earnings Potential," 19.9.1996.

that the interests of the competitors of DT should be given priority in order to achieve a workable competition in telecommunications.

After liberalization, Germany's telecommunications sector developed into "one of the most competitive telecoms service markets in the world."[3] The new competitors of DT arrived in large numbers. At the end of 1998, around two hundred licenses had been awarded for telephone infrastructure or service enterprises, and an estimated thirteen hundred companies were active in market segments where no license had been necessary.

Among these new competitors were city carriers, such as Colt Telecom or Worldcom/MFS, which built their own networks in the economically most attractive German cities in order to get the lucrative corporate networks business. Additionally, there were competitors such as Mannesmann Arcor, Otelo, and Viag Interkom, which wanted to challenge DT in most of its businesses. All three companies had powerful backing from strong firms, Mannesmann in the case of Arcor and the utilities companies in the case of the latter two, which could finance the enormous investments in the telecommunications business; all three also had international alliance partners. After two years of competition, DT had a market share of 98 percent in local fixed-line telephony, thanks to the "local loop,"[4] 65 percent in long-distance calls, and 62 percent in international calls, thereby losing significant market share in the most profitable business segments.

All in all, privatization and liberalization completely changed the parameters of corporate governance and strategy for DT. Whether this shaped the company toward a higher shareholder value orientation will be explored in this chapter. First, I will discuss industrial relations at DT and then the restructuring efforts.

Industrial Relations

One important feature of corporate governance at DT before privatization was the strong position of the trade union. The postal union, the Deutsche Postgewerkschaft (DPG), was a one-company-union, solely responsible for the employees of the three integrated enterprises under the umbrella of the German postal service. It was one of the most powerful unions in Germany. This institutionalized influence ensured that employees' interests were represented "beyond the norm achieved through

---

[3] Ibid., "Former Monopoly Loses Significant Market Share," 15.11.2000.
[4] The local loop is the wiring between the telephone exchange and the demarcation point at the customer's premises, on which DT has a monopoly, even if it has to make its network partly available to competing operators.

co-determination."[5] Moreover, DPG was one of the players that shaped managerial strategy and policy initiatives, alongside the minister of Post and Telecommunications and the principal equipment suppliers. The crucial decisions were taken in these informal tripartite negotiations.

After the breakup of the national post office into its constituent units, the DPG has nonetheless focused very strongly on DT. This led to a very close cooperation and close institutional ties between the union and the work councils. The unionization rate is high, about 90 percent among management and nonmanagement employees, and the DPG dominates the work councils, holding more than 90 percent of the seats.[6] The union is also influential in that it nominates DT's personnel manager.

The DPG strongly opposed privatization.[7] It feared not only for its own influence and position, but also for employment security, employment conditions, and the obligation to provide universal infrastructure services. Hence, the DPG suggested not privatizing DT, but granting management more autonomy by organizing it as a public sector body. However, even if the union did not reach its main goal of preventing privatization, it managed to reach many of its other goals and shaped the form of privatization. First, DT had to introduce the most extensive form of codetermination. Second, a basic infrastructural obligation was written into the basic law. Third, a lot of personnel issues became part of the collective wage agreement. The Social Democratic Party (SPD) threatened to block the postal reforms, if these requirements were not met by the liberal-conservative government in power at that time.[8]

Privatization itself did not significantly diminish DPG's role. It managed to prevent decentralization of decision making toward the work councils, which would have meant bargaining on a divisional basis. Even when DT began to establish subsidiaries in order to achieve greater flexibility by escaping the civil servant regulations, the DPG was able to introduce the requirement that DT must negotiate not only with DPG in the core firm, but also in all newly established subsidiaries.[9] Employment conditions are therefore uniform throughout the company and control remains centralized. This enables the union to pursue one of its main goals, namely to prevent significant variation in employment practices. Hence, bargaining remains centralized, with the union being involved in all major decisions and being able to dominate the work councils. The

---

[5] See Darbishire (1997), 192.

[6] See ibid., 220.

[7] The most spectacular action in this context was a demonstration of 100,000 DPG members against privatization in June 1994.

[8] See Glotz (2001), 67. The government was a coalition between the Christian Democratic Union (CDU/CSU) and the Free Democratic Party (FDP).

[9] See Katz, Darbishire (2000), 213.

strong role of the union has had ramifications for the adjustment path of DT. Management has to find a consensus with the union, since the costs of potential conflict would be very high, leading to incremental adjustment steps and a high cost base. This setting excludes a pure cost-cutting strategy. Sales growth, which contributes to employment stability, is preferred by the union.[10]

Financial Restructuring

The IPO of DT raised huge expectations. It was seen as a "jump-step in Germany's equity culture."[11] The IPO was the largest in European economic history, worldwide second only to Japanese NTT, and it was intended to raise €7.7 billion. Whether the IPO would be a success was far from certain. DT had low productivity, there was huge uncertainty about market development and future regulations, new competitors had entered the field, and its strategy was considered "too nebulous to convince any skeptical private investor, let alone professionals."[12] Due to its poor client orientation, DT was even portrayed as "the most ridiculed company in Germany."[13] The German financial markets seemed much too small to raise such a huge amount of money: DT's IPO with the estimated €7.7 billion would raise more capital than the previous 220 IPOs in Germany stretching back to 1983 combined, although only a 25 percent stake of DT was to be floated.

For its IPO, DT focused on individual German investors. First, there were political reasons. In order to justify privatization, its supporters created the catchphrase of the "people's share of the 1990s." Second, owing to the sheer size of the IPO, new investors, who previously had not held shares, had to be targeted. Hence, German retail investors were the key to DT's stock issuance. Demand among them had to be generated, which then should lead to further demand on the institutional side. That the issue had to have a strong international component followed also from its size.

Third, and most important for corporate governance, management pursued the wide dispersion of ownership among individual investors, which—combined with the government's controlling stake—would free DT's management from major interference on the part of larger investors. The declared aim of DT was to have as many individual investors as possible because they were considered to be long-term shareholders.

---

[10]Darbishire (1997), 218.
[11] *The Economist,* "To War," 12.12.1998.
[12]*Euromoney,* "Nowhere to Hide," February 1996, 36.
[13] *The Economist,* "Launching Deutsche Telekom," 26.10.1996.

A wide distribution among individual investors was seen in 1992 as a weapon against a possible takeover by the Post and Telecommunications minister. Internal control in the supervisory council has been weak and mainly performed by single members and employee representatives.[14] The actual majority owner, the German federal government, had not been active in the formulation of DT's strategy, and its two representatives on the supervisory board took a very passive stance. The banks had only one seat on the supervisory board, and this was held by a retired CEO of Dresdner Bank.

In order to convince private investors to buy stock, DT applied two strategies: an unprecedented corporate image and advertising campaign[15] and an incentive program, targeting individual investors. Probably most important among these incentives was the quite unusual guarantee to pay substantial dividends in 1996 and 1997. This step was intended to convince risk-averse investors of the security of DT's shares.

Banks and financial markets did not exert much pressure on DT to conform to shareholder value expectations—instead, it was the other way around. Almost a hundred banks were involved in the transaction in one way or the other, an exceptionally high number. Fees alone amounted to roughly €255 million.[16] This had two effects. First, through the placing power of the banks involved a huge number of potential buyers was mobilized, six times as many hopeful buyers as stock for sale. Second, it allowed DT to dictate the rules and to make sure that there would be no interference by analysts. DT was on the "restricted list" of all participating banks. Therefore, any major international bank was represented in the consortium; its analysts were not allowed to publish analyses or make any public statement. The banks were only allowed to make public statements when they had an agreed message to transmit. This meant that DT controlled the flow of information about the company, and every deviation from its rules was sanctioned with the threat of being ejected from the syndicate; this in turn would have meant exclusion from subsequent DT tranches. In this way, "Telekom achieved not only the broadest coverage of the investor market but also won the right to impose discipline on practically the entire international banking community."[17]

The targeted group of individual investors, galvanized by the incentive program and the dividend guarantee, ordered massively. The focus

---

[14]Interview with a former supervisory board member.

[15]The costs for the product and image campaigns were estimated to amount to €500 million in 1996 alone.

[16]See Glotz (2001), 87. DT chose Deutsche Bank, Dresdner Bank, and Goldman Sachs as leaders of the international consortium There were also five regional consortia for Germany. Moreover, consulting banks for the government and DT were appointed.

[17]*Euromoney*, December 1996, 33.

on individual investors was mirrored in the distribution of the shares. Ultimately, German investors were allocated 67 percent of shares, 60 percent of which went to retail investors. Despite a much higher foreign demand, American investors received 14 percent, UK investors 8 percent; 6 percent were allocated to continental Europe, and 5 percent to Asia and the rest of the world. In the allocation of the shares a hierarchy emerged. Domestic individual investors enjoyed priority, then domestic institutional investors, and finally foreign investors. Institutional investors received only 11 percent of their orders, whereas private investors received 32 percent of their orders, and in the second tranche, institutions received again only 12 percent of their demand.

Since individual German investors indeed held their shares much longer than institutional investors, they were also the prime target group for subsequent tranches in 1999 and 2000. With the second tranche, in which a similar number of banks was involved, DT collected €10.7 billion from the investors, through which it met its main financial goal: the equity ratio had increased to 40 percent. Two-thirds of the second tranche were placed with individual investors, and one third went to institutional investors; the same was true for the third tranche. The assumption that individual investors would have a long-term orientation again proved accurate. Fourteen months after the second tranche, more than 60 percent of private investors still held their shares.[18] In summary, DT did everything it could to minimize the influence of financial markets by promoting long-term shareholders.

Surprisingly, the listing on the New York Stock Exchange (NYSE) did not much affect DT's practices. DT sought the listing mainly for pragmatic reasons. Because of the size of the issue, it was assumed that the offer could not be absorbed by primarily German or European investors. Apart from that, listing in the U.S. stock market was intended to signal the growing international ambitions of the company, which is why DT was also listed in Tokyo. DT was the second German firm to be listed on the NYSE after Daimler-Benz. The NYSE was very interested in attracting foreign enterprises in order to increase its market volume. In 1996, only 10 percent of the firms listed at NYSE were of foreign origin, and the new chairman of Securities and Exchange Commission (SEC), Arthur Lewitt, was concerned that NYSE could lose lucrative businesses. This made the SEC more willing to show flexibility and refrain from putting too much pressure on DT.[19] The vice president of the NYSE stated that German

[18] See *Börsen-Zeitung*, "Telekom mit 10 Millionen Treueaktien," 21.9.2000.

[19] See *Süddeutsche Zeitung*, "Die Telekom setzt auch in New York Signale," 19.11.1996. The chairman of NYSE even hailed DT's listing in New York as the most important event for the internationalization of Wall Street.

practices and internal organization are good for German enterprises and that therefore no convergence in corporate governance systems need take place.[20]

Because the SEC relaxed its usual requirements, DT did not have to introduce those features that are associated with shareholder systems, namely quarterly results and divisional breakdowns.[21] In this way DT could avoid providing more transparency than it wished. Thus there was no automatic mechanism connecting the listing at NYSE to full adaptation to the U.S. rules of corporate governance. DT was even awarded the "golden lemon" for poor transparency by a minority shareholders association (*Deutsche Schutzvereinigung für Wertpapierbesitz*) in 1997 exactly on the grounds of the missing quarterly reports and divisional breakdowns.[22] Also in a 2001 survey of corporate governance and transparency, covering the Euro STOXX companies, DT was ranked as intransparent. Out of forty-three companies, DT was ranked thirty-fourth in terms of transparency. Among the ten German firms covered, it was in last place in the transparency list.[23] The point here is simply that listing on the NYSE has no direct and linear relationship with transparency and strategy. The SEC rules per se did not force DT to converge on American disclosure standards and its corporate governance rules. This contradicts Coffee's argument that listings of foreign firms in the United States lead—through the adaptation of American standards and rules of corporate governance—to convergence of strategies and structures.

Regarding ownership structure, in 2004, several years after the IPO, the German government directly or indirectly held 38 percent of DT shares, institutional investors 45 percent, and private investors 17 percent. Thirty-nine percent of the free float was held by German investors, 30 percent by European ones, and 29 percent, due to acquisitions, by American or Canadian investors.[24] DT's shares have mainly been traded within Germany. Concerning its shareholder-value orientation, DT's top management has constantly emphasized over the years that the DT share is a long-term investment and that the strategy is designed to serve long-term investors. The CEO stated that he was not willing to lay off thousands of workers for speculative investors, and that the long-term value of

---

[20] See ibid., "Die Telekom setzt auch in New York Signale," 19.11.1996.

[21] See *Börsen-Zeitung*, "Telekom gibt sich aktionärsfreundlich," 5.10.1996. DT finally introduced quarterly reports and divisional breakdowns in 1998, while divisional breakdowns in the quarterly reports appeared 2001. The main reason for these introduction of the divisional breakdowns was that the new strategy, based on four columns, should also become clearer in the financial statements.

[22] See ibid., "Goldene Zitrone' für dürftige Information," 27.6.1997.

[23] See DWS (2001).

[24] See Deutsche Telekom, *Annual Report 2004*, 24 (German edition).

the company and of the share should be maximized.[25] In this sense, there was not even lip service to a strict version of a shareholder value concept. DT's understanding of shareholder value has been embedded in a stakeholder context, as the CEO explained: "We will not develop a corporate culture, which only concentrates on profits for the shareholders. Shareholder value is an important element in equilibrium: The shareholders, the customers and the employees must be satisfied."[26]

A feature that was intimately linked to the focus on private investors in Germany was DT's dividend policy. Because German investors were known to prefer bonds to equities, it was widely assumed that they compared the DT shares not to other shares, but to German government bonds. This risk aversion of the main target group therefore had to be taken into account. DT guaranteed the dividends for 1996 and 1997. Though not in a legally binding sense, they figured prominently in the IPO prospectus. It promised, at a time when the restructuring process was far from being finished, to pay in 1996 €0.30 dividend per share as well as €0.60 per share for 1997. DT in fact did pay the promised dividends, although this meant a complete distribution of the company's profits. Rather than being a "downsize and distribute" policy, this action is linked to the characteristics of the IPO. The risk for private investors was reduced since they could rely on a guaranteed interest rate, which was also in line with German government bonds. In the following years, dividends remained constant at €0.60, although profits per share were quite volatile, fluctuating between €0.7 and €2.8.[27] Thus, the dividend policy in the years after the IPO was independent of profit development and had the goal of reducing the risk for private investors.

Another measure to reduce risk and to promote share price was that DT managed to manipulate the stock market index. DT received a weighting of nearly 5 percent in the DAX index, substantially more than it would have been assigned on the basis of its subscribed capital; in the MSCI Germany index, DT even got a weighting of almost 10 percent. After the second tranche, when the DAX was reformed and considered more the market capitalization, DT managed to have the government's shares, then 70 percent of its capital and not traded at the stock exchange, added to its market capitalization. The intention was clear: index funds, and most other investment funds to a certain degree, track

---

[25]See *Süddeutsche Zeitung*, "Wir sind kein Unternehmen für Zocker," Interview with Ron Sommer, 18.3.1999.

[26]*Die Woche*, "Hat weh getan," Interview with Ron Sommer, 28.6.1996 [Translation by author].

[27]See Deutsche Telekom, *Annual Report 2000*, U2 (German edition). Due to its huge debts, DT paid no dividend in the years 2002 and 2003 and returned to a dividend of €0.62 in the year 2004.

the index in order to minimize risks. A higher weighting in the index therefore leads to immediate higher demand by institutional investors.

To summarize DT's financial policy and the strategy during the flotations, it first assured the support of all major international banks by inviting them into its consortium in order to multiply placing power and discipline all major players on the financial markets. It targeted private investors, since they were believed to display a long-term orientation. Although all tranches took the form of a global offering, the overwhelming majority of shares was allocated to German investors. Furthermore, by gaining a disproportionate weighting in the major indexes, DT could stabilize the share price by generating demand on the institutional side. Lastly, DT lowered the risk for private investors by committing itself in advance to a competitive dividend.

Therefore, the IPO itself was not the start, whether hoped or feared, of a robust equity culture and a shareholder value orientation of German investors. The design of the IPO "insulated the purchasers from the key elements of equity investment: risk and significant governance rights" and "the explicit and tacit assurances of dividend protection and the ownership and governance structure are far from a robust version of shareholder capitalism."[28]

Organizational Restructuring

One of the key goals of the restructuring process was employment reduction, mainly because DT had a much lower turnover per head than its main competitors. The other challenge was to introduce more market- and client-orientation instead of focusing on technology alone. Overall efficiency had to be improved significantly. But it was not only the privatization process that led to the necessity of dismissals; it was also technological progress. The network digitalization underway in the 1990s made a significant number of blue-collar workers superfluous.

The productivity gap between DT and its main competitors was large. In 1994, each DT employee earned the firm €128,000, whereas the corresponding figure for AT&T was €205,000. Compared to American companies, DT employed 45 percent more people and employee costs were 25 percent more than the average across Europe.[29] There seemed to be no alternative to a reduction of personnel. The goal was to achieve an employee productivity of €205,000 per employee. In 1993, DT announced that it would downgrade its workforce from 230,000 people to 210,000 by

[28]Gordon (2000), 11, 16.
[29]See *Manager Magazin*, "Gestörte Leitung," No. 1, January 1995 and *Financial Times*, "Doubts over Earnings Potential," 19.9.1996.

2002. In the mid 1990s, the aim became to cut the workforce further to 170,000 employees. However, pointing to job reductions in other privatized telecoms, especially in the Anglo-Saxon countries, most experts considered this 25 percent cut insufficient.[30]

However, laying off workers was difficult. Slightly more than the half of DT's employees were civil servants, a legacy from monopoly times when DT was a public administration. These civil servants enjoy certain privileges. Above all, they cannot be dismissed. Furthermore, the structure of their career as well as their pay and working conditions are determined by law, and if they are to be reassigned, the job must have similar status. The blue-collar workers (*Arbeiter*) and white-collar workers (*Angestellte*) also had de facto job security after having spent at least fifteen years on DT's payroll. Thus, an additional 20 percent of the workforce could not be fired.[31] The DT management's freedom to reduce staffing levels was therefore constrained beyond the normal legal limitations. Given these institutional constraints and the need to significantly reduce employment, DT's management entered into negotiations with the unions and the work councils. After initial protests, the DPG agreed to job cuts, but in turn the management conceded that there would not be any compulsory redundancies. The contract that committed the two parties to this policy was struck in 1994. It ended in 1997, but was renewed twice, so that it extended until 2004. Recently, the agreement was again extended until December 2008.

The means by which the downsizing was to be achieved were early retirement and voluntary redundancy programs. The voluntary redundancy program targeted white- and blue-collar workers with a minimum service of two years and offered them eighteen to twenty-two months' salary if they left. The cost of this program was estimated at around €2.5 billion.[32] An alternative job was offered to those employees who were unwilling to leave. The early retirement program addressed the civil servants, who are unlikely to quit their job, because that would mean that they would lose their status and their lifetime employment guarantee. Younger civil servants were offered one-time payments to give them an incentive to change careers.

This agreement reached its goals, although it was quite expensive. DT was indeed able to reduce its work force to 170,000 in 2000, and the turnover-per-employee rose to €170,000. No involuntary redundancies were necessary. Management was also happy with the outcome. The CEO and other top managers had always emphasized that DT should not

---

[30] See *Business Week*, "Europe's Toughest Job," 9.10.1995.
[31] See ibid., "We're Making a 180–Degree Turn," 21.11.1994.
[32] See *Die Welt*, "Telekom: 5 Milliarden DM für Abfindungen," 14.1.1995.

become a "hire and fire" company. As one manager put it: "We won't fire people, so we'll grow."[33] An agreement was also reached concerning the transfer of employees to the newly established subsidiaries, by which employees were guaranteed the same employment and salary conditions as they enjoyed before.

Management has cooperated with the unions and the work councils from the beginning of the restructuring process, and there were no attempts to challenge the institution of codetermination.[34] A precondition for cooperation was that no operational dismissals were undertaken, even if their avoidance would result in a very expensive program. The work councils' representatives did not exert pressure on the management, but their preferences were incorporated into the decision making: the management was aware that otherwise the work councils might block strategic decisions in the supervisory board, because issue-linking has always been an option for the work councils.

In this way the veto power of the employees through codetermination was taken into account by management when evaluating its options, even though it was never actually exercised. Because some options would have been unacceptable for the work councils, management excluded them from the outset. The way of dealing with potential labor-management conflicts has been that the personnel manager, who had been proposed by the union, had built up an extensive system of committees where all issues are discussed with employees and where compromises are sought in the early stages of the decision-making process. Thus employees are tied into the decision-making process from the beginning and can become vocal, which leads to lengthy bargaining but quick implementation without major conflicts; the dismissals by the means mentioned are a prime example for this pattern.

Putting this strategy into perspective, it can be said that it differs in quantitative and qualitative terms from the experience of Anglo-Saxon telecoms. After its privatization, AT&T reduced its employees from 430,000 in 1984 to 299,000 in 1995,[35] whereas the privatized BT shed 90,000 jobs, half of its workforce.[36] Involuntary redundancies were employed in both cases. DT preferred a growth strategy instead of pure cost cutting, and it did so in close cooperation with the union and work councils.

Another feature of industrial relations that was also evident in the case of Siemens is staff shares. DT's management intended to place al-

[33] See *Business Week*, "We're making a 180–degree turn," 21.11.1994.
[34] The following paragraph is based on an interview with a former supervisory council member.
[35] See Gerpott (1998), 140.
[36] See *Business Week*, "Europe's Toughest Job," 9.10.1995.

most 14 percent of the volume of its IPO with employees. Before the IPO, DT's management made its employees an offer to participate in a share program; in total, 150,000 employees chose to participate. It was hailed as the "world's largest employee share ownership program."[37] The program was subsidized at €50 million, and employees could either buy shares with a 40 percent discount or participate in a risk-free trust, which insured them against any losses. All in all, during the restructuring phase, DT's management cooperated closely with the work councils and employees and sought to ensure their backing. The bargaining over staff reduction took place within the realm of German industrial relations institutions, producing a bargained adjustment path. In this sense, no adversarial constellation emerged, despite the heavy job losses.

The long management tenure is harder to verify in the case of DT because identification of systematic forms of management recruitment or tenure is difficult in the short period that DT has been a private company. Almost all high-level managers were recruited from other German companies, simply because DT lacked internal management expertise. Due to the various restructurings of the business units and the development of new ones, the composition of the management board changed frequently. However, it can be said that the first CEO, despite some heavy crises, stayed on board quite a long time compared to other telecommunications companies. He was removed mainly because of political pressures in the election campaign, when the losses of the shareholders became an issue. The successor, the CEO of T-Mobile, was recruited internally and was a close collaborator of his predecessor. Other key departments also show continuity: the departments of finance, personnel affairs, networks and purchasing, technology, and marketing were all led by the same person in 2001 who was in charge in 1996. Thus a sense of stability existed in the management board; a hire-and-fire attitude did not gain ground.

DT also introduced a stock option program in 2000. Before the introduction of the stock option program, a certain amount of the salary was variable, which accounted in 1999 for 39 percent of the total salary of the management board.[38] DT did not publicize the exact design of the stock option plan, but the lock-up period for the options lasted until 2002; after 2002 the options could be exercised until 2005. In the first six months after the introduction of the program, only 1,024 options were granted. Altogether 25 million shares for the first five-year program were agreed by the general shareholder's meeting. Only members of the management board, managers one layer below the management board, and

[37] *Financial Times*, "Deutsche Telekom Plans Staff Shares," 14.12.1995.
[38] See Deutsche Telekom, *IPO prospectus*, 26.5.2000, 145.

top managers of the business units are eligible for stock options, so the beneficiaries are a small group. It was not revealed what percentage of their total salary management could earn by stock options, but the basic design of the program was heavily criticized. It allowed the options to be exercised at a 20 percent increase of the share over 10 years, which is a yearly increase of only 2 percent. In other words, the exercise hurdle is very low and gives no incentive for an outstanding share performance and seems designed more to serve the self-enrichment of management.

The stock option scheme was one of the critical factors that led to the demise of CEO Ron Sommer in 2002. Management's compensation was being increased, mainly by raising the basic salary, which was supposed to rise from €9.2 million to €17.4 million for the management board in total, but also by stock options, and this led to public criticism. Management renounced its stock options for the years 2002 and for 2003. But the plan was also opposed by members of the supervisory board, not by the work councils' representatives, but by representatives of the shareholders. Furthermore, due to political pressures in the 2002 federal election campaign, the Finance Ministry changed course and paved the way for the CEO's demise. The combination of bad share performance, the intended increase in compensation, and the dispersed ownership with 3 million private investors, an important target group in the election campaign, led to the firing of the CEO, whose contract had been renewed not long before. Thus, a reward system that would have tied management's compensation closely to share price performance and would have led to a massive increase in compensation could not be asserted. Finally, in 2004 DT's stock option program was abandoned and replaced by a system in which compensation is based on personal goals, company performance, and share price development. Hence, the incentives for management to focus exclusively on the promotion of share price were rolled back again. The problems with the stock option program as well as its discontinuation indicate that the corporate governance system at DT discriminates against far-reaching steps toward a shareholder value orientation.

Portfolio Restructuring

The process of strategic change began long before the IPO and even before privatization. One of the key challenges was the introduction of greater market and client orientation. DT was widely seen as a purely technology-orientated company, a fact that the CEO and other top managers also publicly stated.

On the other hand, DT had one of the most modern phone networks, a near monopoly over the densest cable TV network in Europe, and was second only by a slim margin in the German mobile phone market. The fixed-line network offered especially large opportunities for growth. DT invested large sums in the ISDN broadband network, needed for interactive services. These investments made Germany the country with by far the largest ISDN network worldwide.[39] However, despite these technological possibilities, DT was very slow to capitalize on its advantages. There were hardly any services available and if services were offered they did not meet customer demand. Mainly for that reason, the traffic in American telephone networks was seven times higher than in DT's network in the early 1990s.[40] Achieving flexibility and customer orientation was therefore the top priority of management and the basis for DT's new strategies.

Substantial change was necessary to move DT "from a bureaucratic, public service, technologically focused company, to being commercially and consumer driven, and with a shift from a universal service requirement (characterized by mass production of simple dial tone) to a significantly differentiated market."[41] Specialization and focus on single market segments instead of the provision of standardized universal services was one of the key requirements in the changed telecommunications market. In order to operationalize its ambition to become a global player, three main strategic goals were identified: the protection of the core business (fixed-line telephony); entry into the markets of the future, which aimed at the provision of new and innovative services and products in growing markets; and the internationalization of business.[42] The latter two were necessary to compensate for expected losses in market share, whereas the upgrading of the telephone network was the precondition for generating new business. An important step for doing that was the digitalization of the network. The initial timeframe for complete digitalization projected that it would be finished by 2006. However, business pressures caused DT to rush its completion to 1997.

These strategic goals necessarily had implications for the organization of DT. The first important step was taken before the decision was made to privatize the firm. In 1993, DT reorganized itself into four client-oriented departments: private customers, corporate customers, systems

---

[39] In 1996 one in three ISDN connections worldwide was in Germany. See *Financial Times*, "Doubts over Earnings Potential," 19.9.1996.

[40] See *Frankfurter Allgemeine Zeitung*, "Die Telekom wird kundenorientiert organisiert," 13.8.1992.

[41] Darbishire (1997), 225.

[42] See then CEO Helmut Ricke in *Frankfurter Allgemeine Zeitung*, "Schlanker, flexibler, schneller," 6.9.1994.

customers, and mobile telephony. Furthermore, DT founded a subsidiary for its mobile phone business. The new subsidiary, fully owned by DT, was intended to enable the company to circumvent the legislative salary rules for its staff, which made it hard to attract specialists in the field, as well as to practice a more aggressive marketing strategy.[43]

This strategy of founding organizationally and legally independent subsidiaries has been pursued ever since. In the course of the 1990s, DeTe mobile (mobile telephony), DeTe system (systems solutions for corporate clients), DeTe media (DT publications), Multimedia Services GmbH, and several others were founded. For all these subsidiaries, the work, employment, and pay conditions were held constant with those of the original DT; however, their creation gave DT more flexibility in terms of payment and working hours, because no civil servants were employed in the subsidiaries.[44] The subsidiaries could pay higher wages, because they were not bound to the civil service regulations, and this opened up better possibilities to attract outside experts, who were needed especially in the areas of marketing and finance, where DT lacked experience.[45] Thus in its subsidiaries, DT could introduce a different incentive structure, which was supposed to lead to higher flexibility. Additionally this change allowed for greater specialization.

These steps toward greater specialization under the DT umbrella finally led to a four-pillar strategy, which stands for the four areas DT considers as its core businesses. These businesses were constituted as operating divisions in 2000:

- T-Mobile; mobile phone activities
- T-Online; Internet service provider
- T-Systems; building and operation of global high-speed networks for large customers
- T-Com; traditional telephone business

This division of the company into operating units clearly followed the strategy to diversify DT's products in order to generate growth, whereby higher autonomy should help the firm as a whole to get closer to the differentiated markets. Decision-making should be accelerated. T-Com has the role of a "cash cow" for the company, whose profits were used to finance investments in growing markets. At the same time, large investments took place in T-Com, especially the further upgrading of the network with broadband technology, called T-DSL. With this technology,

[43] See *Süddeutsche Zeitung*, "Die Telekom will ihre Mobilfunk-Sparte als GmbH privatrechtlich organisieren," 25.1.1993.

[44] If a civil servant wanted to be transferred he could surrender his civil servant status for a certain amount of time.

[45] See Darbishire (1997), 214.

the telephone network can operate with broadband access, enabling high-speed Internet access, e-commerce, and video on demand. The already large number of ISDN connections, almost a third of all telephone connections, can be upgraded to this new technology. Investments here are intended to compensate for future losses in the traditional fixed-line telephony business. But through the wide use of the Internet and the continuing near monopoly of DT in local calls, the profits of T-Com have still remained high.

T-Online is, in terms of total number of clients, the largest Internet provider in Europe, with 5 million subscribers. It is strongly focused on Germany; the presence in other European countries is limited to Austria and France. Its strategy in foreign markets has been to acquire Internet providers and media companies in order to offer local services. T-Online's competitive strength is the "precious link to the mobile phone, which could make T-Online a monster of the coming age, the mobile Internet."[46] Furthermore, T-Online's link to T-Com is intended to be exploited for the cross-marketing of products, and a subsidiary of T-Online and T-Mobile has been established in order to enter the mobile commerce market.[47]

Like T-Online, T-Systems is a business that is considered to be in a growth market. T-Systems provides IT and telecommunications services and solutions. The target group is commercial firms, which are offered the whole spectrum of these services. T-Systems gained importance when DT acquired Debis Systemhaus from Daimler-Chrysler for €5.5 billion and merged it with its systems division. Debis also possessed a worldwide data network, which was very attractive to DT. Through this acquisition, DT jumped to the number-two position in systems solutions in Europe after IBM.

The last pillar is T-Mobile. It has managed to catch up with D2 Mannesmann in the German market, and the internationalization of T-Mobile is far more advanced than that of the other segments. T-Mobile has 35 million customers in Europe,[48] but it is lagging behind the European market leader Vodafone. Italy, France, Spain, and Sweden are not covered by T-Mobile.

The four pillar strategy was started before DT was listed on the NYSE and accelerated in the late 1990s. The adjustment path was clearly not

[46] *Business Week*, "Designs on the Web," 13.3.2000.

[47] See Ron Sommer, Speech at the General Meeting 2000, 8. In late 2004 T-Com and T-Online were merged into a new organizational unit called broadband / fixed line business so that the four-pillar-strategy became a three-pillar-strategy. However, this did not signal a strategic change, but was due to the growing importance of the broadband business and its links to the fixed-line business.

[48] See *Frankfurter Allgemeine Zeitung*, "Die richtige Strategie, aber noch keine spektakulären Erfolge," 26.2.2001.

cost-cutting, but emphasized growth and quality. DT did not want to compete on price. It considered itself similar to the German car industry, especially its more luxurious brands, such as Mercedes, BMW, or Porsche,[49] and it aimed at competing with differentiated products with a concentration on quality, service, innovation, and systems competency. The strategy focused on expansion into new market segments and international business.[50] Both strategies are interconnected. One of the main goals was that every operating unit should become, through acquisitions, one of the leading international firms in its segment, which is easier to achieve with a more autonomous status.

The decision to list the subsidiaries on the stock market must be also seen in this light. T-Online was listed in 2000, whereas T-Mobile's listing was postponed several times due to the market environment and finally abandoned. However, DT decided only to list a small stake of T-Online—10 percent—in order to retain full control. The main ambition is to give the units more financial resources for their internationalization through acquisitions and "creating of a paper currency for the acquisition of operators in Western Europe and the US."[51] According to the then CEO Ron Sommer, the stakes to be floated should be as small as possible and only large enough to create a paper currency.[52] The creation of an acquisition currency for the expansion of the respective business units was the only goal of the flotations, according to DT's CEO; acquisitions were decided by DT, not by the floated companies. There is no splitting-up of DT, and the listed subsidiaries remain under its full control.[53]

The new structure was certainly not imposed on DT by the financial markets, although more transparency, a better structured business portfolio, and clearer strategies for the market segments is clearly appreciated by financial market actors. But it was rather the need to compete in product markets, the need for a sharper focus on market segments, and finally the need to internationalize in the market segments that motivated the changes. A shareholder value strategy would have looked very different. DT remains the most diversified telecommunications company worldwide, as a glance at its competitors illustrates. Vodafone concentrates on the mobile phone business, IBM on systems solutions, and AOL on the Internet.

---

[49]See interview with Ron Sommer in *Süddeutsche Zeitung,* "Wir sind kein Unternehmen für Zocker," 18.3.1999.

[50]See speeches of Ron Sommer at the Annual Meeting 1998 and 2000.

[51]*Financial Times,* "Deutsche Telekom Plans Mobile Phone Arm Listing," 15.1.2000. See also Sommer, *Speech at the General Meeting,* 25.5.2000, p. 14.

[52]See *Börsen-Zeitung,* "Börsenwert der Telekom könnte höher sein," 22.12.1999.

[53]In the end, DT even bought back T-Online's shares in 2004 and reintegrated the company.

DT's strategic focus is on systems. A shareholder value strategy would require unprofitable units to be spun off completely as well as concentration on a clearly defined business area. However, the systems business and T-Online had or have been operating at a loss for quite a long time. Nevertheless, DT retains them. The strategy is explicitly long term. The differences with its competitors became obvious in the crisis of the telecommunications industry after the downturn in stock markets from 2000 onward. All telecom companies were faced with high adjustment pressures. The stocks of DT, British Telecom (BT), and AT&T showed a similar decline, losing between 47 and 52 percent in the first ten months of 2000.[54] BT as well as AT&T resorted to massive layoffs,[55] and both have since split up their companies. AT&T demerged into four companies with the explicit aim of promoting the share price and spun off the mobile telephone unit completely. Each of its units is intended to become a listed company or will be sold. Analysts expect that none of AT&T's former parts will survive in the long run as independent firms.[56]

BT did something similar. After firing the CEO and reorganizing according to its main products—broadband, mobile, fixed-line, and data—it floated its mobile arm as MMO2, selling its complete stake. Furthermore, BT partly divested its international business. The joint venture with AT&T, Concert, was dissolved in 2002. BT cut its international activities and gave up its ambitions to be a global carrier. It now wants to concentrate on its landline business in Britain and in continental Europe, although the company considered selling its landline business shortly before.[57] Thus, the adjustment patterns remain very different in comparison to DT. Sticking to a more long-term and diversified strategy, DT has managed so far to cope better with the crisis than its Anglo-Saxon counterparts, which are disappearing as integrated telecommunications firms and are going back to the times when they were exclusively in the landline telephone business.

DT's strategy has not been to split the company but rather to achieve a clearer focus and specialization on market segments with semiautonomous units under the roof of a holding company. This specialization occurs within the supply of universal telecommunications services, which makes DT a conglomerate compared to other telecom companies. This diversification strategy is justified by the assumed synergies to be derived from the markets of the future, when the markets for

[54] See *Business Week,* "Did BT Miss the Boat?" 23.10.2000.

[55] This was done even though in 1999 BT employed 70,000 fewer people than DT, despite an almost identical revenue. See OECD (2001c), 18.

[56] See OECD (2001c), 15, and *Financial Times Deutschland,* "AT&T verschwindet Stück um Stück," 2.10.

[57] See *Financial Times Deutschland,* "British Telecom behält ihr Festnetz doch," 29.1.2002.

telecommunications, information, media, entertainment, and security converge. If this materializes, DT can offer convergence solutions, incorporating all its divisions. Using its multiple businesses, DT wants to capitalize on its synergies, because it possesses all the relevant and modern networks for the converging technologies.[58]

These synergies are not only important for the markets of the future, they are considered to be a competitive advantage today. The strategy aims especially at being able to serve business clients with all telecommunications products and services, thereby primarily producing systems solutions that incorporate mobile and landline phoning, Internet access, and business solutions. Furthermore, through its many businesses, DT sees huge savings potential in purchasing by cooperation between divisions. The main goal of the divisions is sales growth, which is to be realized by participation in the fastest growing market segments.[59] Thus, the main pillar of DT's strategy is to capitalize on the synergies between the divisions, which are assumed to multiply with technological convergence. In this sense, diversification is the precondition of DT's systems strategy, even if this strategy is antithetical to a shareholder value strategy and a concentration on core competencies.

The following section deals with DT's approach to cope with the internationalization of telecommunications markets by investigating its internationalization strategy.

Internationalization Strategy

Internationalizing business has been a key challenge to DT's strategy. The introduction of competition in its home market produced the inevitable consequence of a loss to DT's market share and revenues. Thus DT decided to enter international markets. As this happened, DT's international competitors made inroads into Germany, especially in the market for business clients. Hence, in order to be able to compete in the business-client market, DT had to build up an international presence. A crucial motivation for internationalization was based on the necessity to be as international as its clients. Hence internationalization of business became one of the top priorities of DT's management. In operational terms, the goal was to realize 20 percent of its sales outside Germany by 2000.

DT pursed internationalization forcefully, but did so in a way characteristic of German multinational corporations. It kept its strategic functions and its center of gravity in Germany and pursued a multidomestic

---

[58]See Sommer, Speech at the 2000 General Meeting 25.5.2000, 3–6.
[59]See Deutsche Telekom, *Annual Report 2001*, 65–66 (German edition).

strategy, which left its corporate governance system unaffected. The prime motivation was the entry into new markets in order to generate new business. Therefore, internationalization was pursued with full agreement of the work councils and DT's controlling owner, the German federal government.

When the constitutional constraint on foreign business was lifted through the *Postreform II*, DT turned first to Eastern Europe, acquiring stakes in Hungary, Poland, the Czech Republic, and Kazakhstan.[60] In Eastern Europe, DT could capitalize on its experience in building up and modernizing networks in the former East Germany. It followed a piecemeal approach to internationalization and created a patchwork of minority holdings. By the time DT went public in 1996, it had acquired (mostly minority) stakes in firms in Indonesia, Malaysia, the Philippines, Thailand, Kazakhstan, Russia, Ukraine, Hungary, Austria, Poland, the Czech Republic, Switzerland, and the Netherlands. Nevertheless, DT was looking for a strong partner in order to join forces on the international markets and to compete in the $500 billion market for international telephone services against Worldpartners (AT&T, Singapore Telecom, KDD of Japan, and Unisource) and Concert (BT, MCI). The rationale behind these alliances was the assumption that in the long run, only a few global carriers would be able to survive, so a global presence was required.

Partly for political reasons, DT found this partner in France Telecom (FT) in 1993, uniting the third and fourth largest carriers worldwide, respectively. An American partner, Sprint, was found shortly afterward and incorporated into the Global One alliance.[61] However, Global One incurred considerable losses, $790 million in 1998 alone.[62] Cooperation with FT proved to be difficult, and it was a constraint on DT's international activities, because FT intended to prevent further DT expansion. On the initiative of FT, there was an agreement that neither company should become involved in a country's mobile market where the other was already engaged. FT defined Western Europe as its zone of influence, whereas DT should concentrate on Eastern Europe.[63] Moreover, FT prevented DT from acquiring Sprint, alone or with FT, and it refused the merger of both firms' foreign mobile activities. These difficulties contributed to a step taken by DT—that was sure to destroy the al-

[60]See *Börsen-Zeitung,* "Globaler Anspruch and lokales Geschäft," 17.9.1996.
[61]DT and FT acquired a 20 percent stake for the sum of $4 billion each. On the U.S. market FT and DT were handicapped by the fact that U.S. regulations did not allow more than a 25 percent stake in American telecommunications companies if the home market of the acquirer was not as open as the U.S. market. That meant that they could not fully acquire a U.S. company. After a lengthy process, Global One was approved by the regulatory agencies in the United States as well as by the EU Commission.
[62]See *Die Woche,* "Glückloser Jäger," 15.10.1999.
[63]See Glotz (2001), 157.

liance—which was the attempt to merge with Telecom Italia, acting as a "white knight" in a hostile takeover battle.

Olivetti made a bit for Telecom Italia (TI), which was already largely privatized at that time with the state only holding 3.35 percent and a golden share. Trying to defend its independence, TI searched for a white knight and a friendly merger, which corresponded with DT plans for international expansion. The management boards agreed on a friendly merger, as did German politicians, but Italian politicians objected. In the end, the deal did not succeed. Fifty-one percent of the shareholders sold to Olivetti, whose offer was actually below that of DT. In the aftermath, the alliance with France Telecom collapsed.

This led to a shift in approach. Instead of a patchwork of minority stakes and a focus on alliances, DT now aimed to acquire full control of all its international activities. The goal was no longer worldwide presence, but to become a pan-European company. Nevertheless, a partner in the U.S. mobile market was still sought, whereas Asia and landline telephony in the United States ceased to be primary targets. Only 7 percent of sales came from abroad in 1998, which was far below the self-set goal of 20 percent by 2000. DT was the least internationalized company among the big telecommunications companies.[64] After the second tranche of its IPO and the listing of T-Online, DT also had the necessary financial power for big purchases: its war chest was estimated at $100 billion.[65]

Following the new strategy, in 1999 DT acquired, at a high premium, a majority stake in One2One, the fourth largest British mobile company, as well as mobile phone operators in Austria and Croatia and Club Internet in France. However, these were small acquisitions compared to the planned merger of MCI and Sprint, involving a sum of $130 billion. Fears were expressed that DT might either fall victim to a hostile takeover, after the government reduced its stake, or be shoved aside by its rivals if it did not build up international presence quickly.[66] Various merger talks failed.

Entering the U.S. market proved difficult, as DT had already experienced. In the first wave of telecom takeovers, DT was not yet privatized, so it could not pay the required sums. Then it was committed to FT and could not make an acquisition on its own; and finally it faced a roadblock thrown up by a group of U.S. senators, who tried to convince the Federal Communications Commission to block U.S. telecom purchases

---

[64] See *Wirtschaftswoche*, "Aufbauen oder verabschieden," 9.2.2000.
[65] See *Business Week*, "Deutsche Telekom sets off alarm bells," 24.7.2000.
[66] See *Wall Street Journal*, "Deutsche Telekom Is on the Prowl Again to Buy Global Heft," 3.3.2000, as well as *Financial Times*, "Deutsche Telekom Left on the Sidelines," 28.1.2000.

by companies that were more than a quarter state-owned. However, DT made its American deal and acquired Voicestream in 2000.

Voicestream was the sixth largest mobile company in the United States, with a market share of 3 percent. DT made an outstandingly high offer for Voicestream of $50 billion. This meant that DT paid $22,000 per subscriber, about three times the price of the previously most expensive deals.[67] After the announcement, DT's share lost 12 percent, and later 20 percent in the following days. The deal was defended by strategic and technological arguments. The technological attraction lay in the fact that Voicestream was the only U.S. company that used the European GSM mobile telephone standard and the company possessed licenses for 88 percent of the U.S. market. DT's focus was on the market potential of Voicestream. Voicestream's acquisition enabled DT to become the only global GSM mobile company that could offer mobile telephony on the same network worldwide.

The takeover was approved by the U.S. authorities, and the final price was half of the initial offer—$30 billion—owing to the stock market downturn and DT's decrease in share price; it was the last of the big deals in telecommunications. DT guaranteed Voicestream wide-ranging autonomy and independence within the limits of DT's general strategy; a decentralized leadership was installed. In 2000, DT nearly met its goal of making a fifth of its sales abroad. Foreign sales jumped from 8 to 17 percent in 2000, to 27 percent in 2001 and to 39 percent in 2004. In quantitative terms, the goals of internationalization were met.

To sum up DT's internationalization strategy, DT had to compensate for expected market losses in the home market, so there were was no alternative to internationalization and entering new markets. This policy of aggressive internationalization was supported by the majority owner, the German federal government, as well as by the work councils. The work councils' representatives on the supervisory board never expressed any resistance against internationalization because they considered this strategy necessary to international competition.[68]

Internationalization has not resulted in a disembedding from DT's homebase and follows a multidomestic strategy, which does not affect the corporate governance system of the parent company itself. The traditional multidomestic strategy of German MNCs is motivated by being close to customers and by the possibility of adapting products to local needs. In telecommunications, this strategy fits the growing tendency to provide systems solutions that require cooperation with customers.[69]

---

[67]See *Business Week*, "Deutsche Telekom Wireless Merger," 7.8.2000.
[68]Interview with former supervisory board member.
[69]See Lane (2000b), 202.

From DT's total assets of €90 billion in 2004, 46 percent were located in Germany, 29 percent in Europe outside of Germany, and 24 percent in North America.[70] Thus, the plurality of assets is still located in Germany, as well as all strategic functions. DT also employs 70 percent of its workforce in Germany. Thus, a wide dispersion of assets is not what DT is pursuing: they are concentrated in Germany and, as a recent development, in the United States.

There is also no tight coordination of the subsidiaries, nor strict control by DT over its subsidiaries. The subsidiaries are tied to the general strategy, but enjoy a considerable degree of autonomy on an operational level and in the way they serve their markets. They have their own management and are not coordinating closely with subsidiaries in other countries.

Major decisions are made by the parent firm without much involvement of the subsidiaries. This stands in contrast to the predictions of management theorists, who claim that in internationalized companies, a transnational organizational form will "intersperse," which essentially means that networks of regional and decentralized units will dominate decision making; this would lead to a diminished role for the headquarters and to multicenteredness within the corporation.[71] The lack of a center could lead to disembeddedness from the country of origin. However, this pattern is absent in the case of DT. The center is embedded in the home base and all strategic decision making is done there. Furthermore, its seeking of majority stakes, labeled a "stand-alone" strategy in contrast to a "partnering strategy,"[72] indicates that DT builds on internal resources and routines and seeks leadership in its international investments. This suggests that the company intends to transfer its own strategies to its subsidiaries without much influence on their part. All in all, regarding the style and the pattern of DT's internationalization, it does not seem that competition in international markets has meant the need for changes in corporate governance. Internationalization has been pursued in a manner that leaves DT's institutions of corporate governance unaffected.

In terms of its self-set goals, the restructuring at DT has been successful. DT reached the goal of a revenue of €40 billion in 2000 exactly; however, profits fluctuated between €0.9 and €2.7 billion. Jobs were reduced from 230,000 in 1994 to 170,000 in 2000. However, the personnel reduction could not lower the personnel costs. These were €9.3 billion in 1997 and €9.7 billion in 2000, the main reason being the high expenses of the re-

---

[70] Author's own calculations based on Deutsche Telekom, *Annual Report 2004*, 194.
[71] Proponents of this view are Bartlett, Goshal (1987a, b) and Hedlund, Rolander (1990).
[72] See Dörrenbacher (1999), 137.

ductions, which relied on voluntary actions by the employees. Thus, costs remained more or less constant, despite the loss of 60,000 employees. After 2000, revenue continued to grow from €40 billion to €58 billion in 2004.

DT chose a pronounced expansion strategy as an adjustment policy to liberalization and the loss of market share in its core business. The expansion focused on international activities as well as on fast-growing domestic markets, especially mobile telephony and online services. It was an aggressive strategy, concentrating on market share in the targeted segments.[73] DT managed to increase revenues by one-third between 1994 and 2000 and by a further 45 percent between 2000 and 2004. In sum, DT's strategy, despite financial market pressure and a listing on the NYSE, is a far cry from a shareholder value strategy.

DT underwent several organizational restructurings that all related to the transformation of an administration into a market-oriented company. The major part of the financial restructuring was the IPO, which was intended to reduce the enormous debts and give DT the opportunity to compete in the changing telecommunications landscape. However, before and during the IPO, the financial markets did not put pressure on DT, it was the other way around. DT could discipline all the important actors by giving them functions in the consortium of the IPO. Of course, that would not shield DT from financial market pressure afterward, but because of the company's heavy focus on long-term-oriented private investors and with help from the government's controlling stake, it tried to minimize its dependency. The listing in New York did not have far-reaching effects on corporate governance; some of the rules of the SEC were negotiable. Therefore, the pressure was not pronounced: not even quarterly reports and divisional breakdowns were compulsory for DT.

Portfolio restructuring, which should follow from capital market pressure, is completely absent in the DT case. The company did not concentrate on core businesses, which would imply an active portfolio policy, a concentration on the most profitable business lines in a firm's portfolio, and the spinning off of businesses that do not meet certain performance goals. Although DT is the most diversified company in the telecommunications industry, downsizing was not even considered. The spinning off of T-Online was only intended to create a paper currency. That is why only very small stakes were floated. The operating units remain under full control of DT. Hence the listing served the goal of a higher flexibility of the division, in order to enable the overall growth

---

[73] Despite market share losses, the fixed line business still accounts for the bulk of profits. In 1999, €2.3 billion of the €2.9 billion profits before taxes came from network communications, which is fixed-line telephony. See DT, *Annual Report 1999*, 18.

strategy by giving it the possibility for acquisitions with its own shares. It is in no way intended to be the beginning of an active portfolio policy with a quick entry and exit from markets.

The strategy of diversification contrasts sharply with the strategy that British Telecom and AT&T have pursued. Both split into separate companies during the crisis in the telecommunications business. DT is committed to its divisions and develops them in a long-term perspective, irrespective of the current profit situation. This follows from its strategic focus on being able to provide all telecommunications services and sell them as comprehensive system solutions.

Most other features of a shareholder value strategy are also not to be found in the case of DT. A prominent ingredient of such a strategy are profit goals, for the company as a whole and for the operating units, normally via a measure such as return-on-equity (ROE) or the economic-value-added (EVA) approach, which accounts for the cost of capital. DT employs neither of these tools for the internal allocation of resources or for deciding which parts should be sold. Indeed, there were never any profit goals, neither for the company as a whole nor for the units. Success has been mainly measured as market share. That profit is not the prime driver in decision-making can be seen when revenue and profits are compared. Between 1994 and 1999, revenue increased by €3 billion whereas profits decreased by €500 million. Earnings before interest, taxes, and amortization (EBITA), a financial indicator of profitability, in this period fell by almost €3 billion.[74] Thus, the internal control does not rely on capital-market-related tools; the main financial goal is revenue growth. This adds to the general approach, in which strategy—namely to provide integrated systems solutions—enjoys priority over immediate profit goals.

[74]See ibid., *Annual report*, various years.

Chapter 6

Bosch

Bosch is a highly internationalized, but nonlisted company. Hence it is not exposed to capital market influence, but only to product market pressures. It is one of Germany's most internationalized companies. In the internationalization index of the one hundred largest German companies for 1996, Bosch holds tenth place, before Siemens, Daimler-Benz, or Mannesmann, and only just behind BMW and BASF.[1] Bosch is a private limited-liability company, and 92 percent of the capital stock of the Robert Bosch GmbH is held by the Robert Bosch Foundation, to which the dividends are paid. Due to this rare ownership structure compared to other multinational companies, research on Bosch allows one to disentangle the effects of financial and product market globalization and find an answer to the question of whether increased international competition in isolation leads to a transformation of traditional German corporate governance arrangements and associated strategies.

Founded in 1886 as "workshops for precision engineering and electrical engineering" in Stuttgart, Bosch is active in the business areas of automotive equipment, power tools and equipment, thermo-technology, household appliances, communications, automation, and packaging machines. The most important sector is the car supply business; Bosch is the largest independent car supplier worldwide. In particular, the company

---

[1] See Hassel, Höpner, Kurdelbusch, Rehder, and Zugehör 2000, 35.

focuses on the areas of vehicle economy, performance, and safety. Bosch became famous for pioneering the antilock braking system (ABS), the electronic stability program (ESP), and for its technological dominance in the market for high-pressure electronic diesel injection pumps. Bosch is the second largest electronics company in Germany and has 239,000 employees, of which 54 percent work outside Germany. The company manufactures at 193 locations, 150 of them located outside Germany, and it is represented in almost 50 countries by subsidiaries and associated companies.

Bosch's corporate culture is shaped by several characteristics that were introduced by the founder and have been preserved ever since. Central to the corporate philosophy is an uncompromising quality orientation.[2] Hence, Bosch has always been a highly production-oriented company. This quality orientation is supported by a high degree of innovation. Bosch has the highest number of patents in its industry worldwide and holds second place in terms of patents in German industry. Thus Bosch is a very important part of the German car industry. As the former BMW and now Volkswagen CEO Bernd Pischetsrieder states, "Without Bosch the German car industry would not have achieved its leading international position."[3]

Bosch has always struggled for its independence, especially from the capital markets. This principle also goes back to the firm's beginnings. The ownership structure of Bosch—established in 1938—was intended to preserve Bosch's independence. This structure and the goal of staying independent have two strategic implications. First, diversification has always been of high priority in order to avoid dependence on the car supply business,[4] and second, investments had to be financed out of reserves or the cash flow. Thus the three principles of Bosch's business policy have been independence, quality, and a solid financial policy. Hence, the firm may be characterized as "proud, canny and secretive, Bosch has a long history of innovation, aggressive marketing and high quality. . . . Bosch . . . seemed to have hit upon a magic formula welding the vitality of the money-spinning *Mittelstand* . . . with a size giving truly international clout."[5]

[2] As Robert Bosch put it in 1918: "It has always been an unbearable thought to me that someone could inspect one of my products and find it inferior. I have, therefore, always tried to ensure that only such work goes out as is superior in all respects."

[3] *Manager Magazin*, "Der Klub der Honoratioren," 1.4.2001 (translation by author).

[4] See Herdt (1986), 14.

[5] *The Economist*, "Braking," 25.4.1992.

Ownership Structure, Financing Policy, and Financial Restructuring

The Robert Bosch Foundation owns 92 percent of the company; the rest is owned by the Bosch family. The foundation receives the dividends and distributes them for charitable projects. It runs three medical care and research institutions, and supports projects in many areas, such as public health, science, social sciences, and culture. In 2001, for example, it spent €40 million. Although the Bosch Foundation owns the company, the voting rights are exercised by the industrial trust, which is the most important decision-making body. The two most important Bosch managers—the chairmen of the management and supervisory boards—as well as external managers are represented on the board of the industrial trust. The supervisory board itself has only limited influence.

The dividends paid are extremely low, compared to listed companies. Between 1992 and 2004, they fluctuated between €31 and €63 million, whereas sales increased in that period from €17 billion to 40 billion. Dividend payments as share of profits fluctuated between 4 and 13 percent of profits between 1995 and 2004. It has been estimated that as a listed company, Bosch would have to pay at least five times higher dividends to meet the requirements of the financial markets.[6]

Thus status of a private company means for Bosch that it does not have "to bother about outside shareholders and can plough almost all of its profits back into the business."[7] As a nonlisted company, its possibilities to raise money are constrained by the fact that it cannot utilize the equities markets. However, several options remain. In principle, Bosch could issue bonds, take loans from banks, or rely on self-financing. The third option has been given preference for almost all of the firm's history. The overarching aim of securing the independence of the company was operationalized as being able to finance expansion and innovation internally as well as to hold enough money for difficult times.[8]

Indeed, Bosch's finance relies only to a very limited extent on bank credits, which gives the company independence from banks' interference. Financial liabilities made up only 5 percent of total assets in 1999.[9] Bosch approaches the bond markets very rarely, eight times in the last fifty years.[10] There were two capital increases in the 1990s in order to achieve the necessary financial reserves for expansion and to strengthen

---

[6]See *Börsen-Zeitung*, "Das Phänomen Bosch," 17.7.1991 and Bosch, *Annual Report 2004*, 93.

[7] *The Economist*, "Braking," 25.4.1992.

[8]See *Handelsblatt*, "Bosch setzt ein Signal," 27.2.1991.

[9]See *Frankfurter Allgemeine Zeitung*, "Bosch ist mit der Ertragslage nicht zufrieden," 12.5.2000.

[10]See *Handelsblatt*, "Robert Bosch geht auf Roadshow," 4.7.2001.

the firm's financial position. Bosch's equity capital as a percentage of sales has remained very stable over the decades: in the 1990s it was always a little more than 30 percent. Furthermore, its reliance on internal financing also enables Bosch to hold enough liquidity to secure its independence, even in market downswings. Thus, the general course of Bosch's financial policy has been to have sound finance, which means that debts should be kept as low as possible.

Despite the limits of self-financing, Bosch was able to pursue a highly expansionist strategy over the 1980s and 1990s; for instance, reserves were almost €5 billion in 1996. The massive investments of the last two decades were financed from depreciation and amortization of fixed assets as well as from cash flow; these two sources were sufficient to cover investments.

From the principles of Bosch's business policy it also follows that purely financial goals are not of prime importance. As the CEO declared in 2001, Bosch wants to earn sufficient money to finance its expansion.[11] In order to reach that goal, a return on sales of 7 or 8 percent is pursued. However, that goal was never reached during the 1990s. Return on sales was 2 percent in the beginning of the 1990s, increased to 4 percent by the mid 1990s and has stagnated since, with the exception of 1997 when 5 percent was reached. Considering that sales went up from €18 billion in 1995 to €32 billion in 2000, it can be safely assumed that there is a strong focus on sales development at Bosch, yet not on profitability. Also the second financial goal, namely a cash flow of 13 to 14 percent of sales, which is seen as a precondition for its future growth plans, could not be reached. Bosch's cash flow as percent of sales fluctuated between 9 and 12 percent between 1991 and 2004, but has not crossed the 12 percent threshold. Nevertheless, the cash flow was high enough to finance a strongly expansionist business policy.

In summary, Bosch's approach to financial policy is embedded in the company's larger business strategy, and its prime goal is to secure the independence of the firm and to be able to finance growth from appreciation and cash flow. Bosch's complete reliance on internal finance is made possible by the very low dividends paid to the Bosch Foundation. There are no purely financial goals that shape the strategy; it is the other way around. Performance indicators such as return on sales and cash flow are subordinated to the larger strategy. The financial policy and financial goals are part of the production orientation of Bosch's business policy. There have been no efforts to restructure the company in the financial realm.

[11] See *Die Zeit*, "Kulturrevolution auf schwäbische Art," 30.8.2001.

Industrial Relations

Bosch's special company structure sets limits to institutionalized influence of the unions. The Robert Bosch foundation is the majority owner, but the industrial trust has the voting rights of these shares. Therefore, the industrial trust is the main controlling body. It is traditionally chaired by the current or former CEO. The other seven members include a Bosch family member, a former member of the management board, a banker, an industrialist, and the former president of a German enterprise association. The chairman and the deputy chairman are general partners; the other members are limited partners. Bosch has a code-termined supervisory board, but the supervisory board does not have much say. Control, or noncontrol, and the general ownership functions are carried out by the industrial trust. The supervisory board is not even a company body.[12] Moreover, the personnel director is neither a member of the unions nor officially proposed by them.

Nevertheless, industrial relations have been peaceful and cooperative: they follow a trajectory of the company that emphasizes social peace, social benefits, and mutual trust between management and employees. There is a long tradition of social and job security at Bosch. The social commitment of the company dates back to the intentions of the founder. The company implemented several, at that time revolutionary, social improvements for the workforce, such as the introduction of the eight-hour working day in 1906; a free Saturday afternoon in 1910; paid breaks; continuation of payments to sick workers; and the five-day week with compensatory wage payments in 1952. Furthermore, since 1934, Bosch has paid a work and success bonus to its employees and provides extensive social benefits. Employees receive wages above the industry average, voluntary pension benefits, work and performance bonuses, interest-free loans, and preventive cures. These voluntary payments add up to 160 percent of a monthly salary on average and amounted to more than €500 million in 1992. Employees have traditionally enjoyed a nearly lifetime employment tenure.

Thus the relationship with the unions and industrial relations in general have been very peaceful and cooperative, and employees strongly identify with the company. A former CEO remarked about Bosch's corporate culture that everybody there is proud of its products and social benefits.[13] This social trajectory results in a corporate culture that is paternalistic in several respects but gives employees, if not the unions, great influence on management and a strong position. This workplace

[12]See *Manager Magazin,* "Hüter des Grals," 1.4.2001.
[13]See *Der Spiegel,* "Im Stile eines Allmächtigen," 3.5.1993.

harmony is the result not only of the product market strategy, which is dependent on highly skilled employees, but also of the social traditions, which confer a high degree of legitimacy to the employee concerns. Worker influence is obvious as well in the area of organizational restructuring and especially in the way Bosch reduced employment, which will be investigated next.

Organizational Restructuring

The need for restructuring became urgent for Bosch in the early 1990s. After a decade of expansion that took place mainly in Germany, Bosch was heavily affected by the worldwide recession of the late 1980s and by the prolonged recession in Germany. The recession particularly affected the car industry; in Germany, at that time the company's most important market by a wide margin, car and commercial vehicle production fell by 23 and 28 percent respectively in 1993.[14] Between 1992 and 1993, Bosch's sales dropped. Profits plummeted as well. Net income fell until 1995. In 1993 and 1994, Bosch experienced operating losses for the first time since World War II and had the first fall in sales since the 1970s.

Reducing Staff Levels

During this crisis, tensions between management and employees emerged. As a reaction to the recession, employment reduction began in 1991 with 8,300 jobs being cut, 6,000 of these in Germany.[15] Job reduction continued in the following years: in 1992, 12,000 employees lost their jobs, and in 1993 the figure was 13,000. In 1994, job reduction continued at a more modest pace, and before it came to a halt 4,000 more employees were made redundant in 1995. During these years, a considerable number of employees also had to work short hours. The majority of these jobs were cut domestically, the reason being that Bosch wanted to build up a stronger international presence in order to become more independent from the German business cycle and to enter new markets.

This massive employment reduction was carried out without compulsory redundancies. The measures used were severance pay, natural fluctuation, and early retirement, for which the entry age was lowered. The job cuts especially affected middle management and administration as well as blue-collar workers in low-tech activities. Management positions were cut by 20 percent in order to achieve faster decision-making and

[14]See *Financial Times*, "A mark of respect for German supplier," 12.7.1994.
[15]See *Börsen-Zeitung*, "Bosch ist 1991 nur im Inland gewachsen," 31.1.1992.

flatten hierarchies with the aim of a leaner company.[16] These measures were part of a cost-cutting program, acknowledging that Bosch's production costs were almost 30 percent higher than those of its competitors.[17] The measures that aimed at cost-cutting as well as simultaneous productivity improvements were negotiated with the work councils. However, although the work councils agreed to the job reductions, another part of the cost-cutting program—namely the cutting of some voluntary bonuses—led to massive protests.

These voluntary bonuses included the work and performance allowance, the contributions for shift workers, the company contribution for lunch and other allowances that were Bosch-specific payments and that added to the standard wage. The management entered into negotiations with the work councils in early 1993 about the reduction of these payments, but no agreement could be reached. Thus the management terminated all respective agreements unilaterally; the savings amounted to €128 million.[18]

However, this unilateral decision provoked a massive reaction on the part of the employees. The work councils saw it as a breach of the social traditions of the company as well as the end of the cooperation policy on part of the management. In response, the councils mobilized the workforce. Demonstrations were organized that involved tens of thousands of employees. For the Bosch management, protests or demonstrations by its employees were completely unknown and largely inconceivable, due to the hitherto very peaceful management-labor relationship. In the end, the management reached agreement with the work councils and softened the cost-cutting measures; the company set voluntary payments at €383 million and agreed to pay the work and performance bonus in 1994.[19] Hence, the conflict ended in favor of the employees, even if they had to bear some reductions. A longer conflict could have been damaging for the management, because apart from the direct costs, management needed the cooperation of the employees to complement the cost-cutting measures through productivity improvement in production.

Inspired by its Japanese competitors, Bosch introduced a production approach that included group work in production as well as greater responsibilities and commitment on the part of the employees. Labeled CIP (continuous improvement process), it began in 1991 and was sup-

---

[16]See *Die Welt*, "Bosch setzt auf Exportmärkte," 1.7.1994.

[17]See *Frankfurter Allgemeine Zeitung*, "Bosch schreibt beim Betriebsergebnis jetzt einen Verlust," 3.3.1993. However, the job reduction resulted in additional expenses of €195 million in 1992.

[18]See ibid., "Bosch kürzt die freiwilligen Leistungen," 20.3.1993.

[19]See ibid., "Bei Bosch Einigung über Kostensenkungen," 1.10.1993; ibid., "Sonderzahlung für Bosch-Beschäftigte," 28.10.1994.

posed to encourage the employees to realize their own potential for cutting costs and enhancing productivity at their workplace and to introduce more flexibility, customer-orientation, and faster reaction to changing market situations. Employees had to develop a stronger identification with their functions, accept greater responsibilities, and be willing to take part in group work. This and other programs were aimed at increasing internal flexibility in order to facilitate just-in-time production.

However, the success of the CIP program obviously depended on the employees, who needed to be motivated. The work councils were involved in the program and its projects from the beginning. But cooperation with employees could not be achieved in an adversarial situation. Because of the reduction in their allowances, workers did not readily commit themselves to these new programs.[20] Hence, social peace and the labor-management cooperation needed to be restored. Because of management's partial retreat, this was achieved after the conflict was resolved.

Because of the necessity of reaching consensus with the work councils and conforming to the social traditions of the company, the cost-cutting programs could only be carried out within narrow limits. Bosch's production model and the efforts to introduce lean production in the early 1990s were dependent on cooperation from the employees, which made management seek a compromise after the initial adversarial policy. This outcome speaks for the need for consensus seeking in the German corporate governance system. In the following years, restructuring took place with the full cooperation of the work councils, even when it proceeded at a much more modest pace. In exchange for job security, the work councils bargained to achieve productivity pacts for several plants in Germany, which included flexible working time models and longer machine run times.[21]

Management Tenure and Recruitment

Another area in which Bosch exemplifies the German model of corporate governance is management and employee tenure. Regarding the tenure of its CEOs, Bosch even takes this institution to the extremes. The present CEO is only the sixth in the 120–year history of the company. All of the CEOs were recruited internally and most of them had spent their whole professional lives with Bosch. The long tenure of the CEOs and their internal recruitment, together with the influential posi-

[20] See *Die Zeit,* "Der Nimbus geht verloren," 9.4.1993.
[21] See *Frankfurter Allgemeine Zeitung,* "Bosch Standort Leonberg bleibt doch erhalten," 27.3.1996.

tion of the predecessor as chairman of the supervisory board and the Industrial Trust, create a very high degree of continuity and stability in Bosch's strategy. This is strengthened through the influence of the industrial trust and the Bosch Foundation, which are obliged to act in accordance with the principles of the founder. Thus the basic traditional goals—independence, quality, and a solid financial policy—are still valid.

Management pay and incentives were reformed in 1999. For the 250 senior managers of the Bosch group worldwide, the variable part of pay has been increased. As a nonlisted company Bosch could not introduce stock options. However, the fixed salary was lowered from 75 percent to 45–55 percent of total compensation. The criteria for the variable part consist of the general business results, the performance of the respective business area, and personal goals.[22]

The composition of the supervisory board indicates Bosch's technology orientation. Traditionally, Allianz and Deutsche Bank are the financial institutions represented. Besides these, two scientists have a seat on the board, and the remaining two or three seats are held by representatives of other companies. This technology orientation also manifests itself in recruitment policy. Bosch recruits about a thousand graduates a year, of whom 80 percent have a science or engineering background.[23] This recruitment policy mirrors itself in the composition of senior management; two-thirds of the senior managers are either scientists or engineers. Vacant management positions are filled internally in 90 percent of cases.[24] Candidates from other firms are very rarely considered. The employment relation at Bosch is very long-term; for managers it is a slow climbing up the career ladder, with several positions in different departments and abroad. But the principle of long-term tenure also applies to shop-floor workers. Bosch offers secure employment and tries to bind its employees to the company.

Thus the features of stylized German corporate governance in the area of internal labor markets, career paths, and long-term tenure apply fully to Bosch. The institution of long-term tenure is applied from the CEO to the workers; senior management is recruited internally with a strong emphasis on technical education, and there are strong efforts to bind employees to the firm, including investment in education. Thus firm specific investments on the parts of managers and workers are likely to be undertaken, which is a necessary precondition for the general quality and production orientation of the company.

[22] See *Handelsblatt*, "Bosch sucht Telekompartner," 7.5.1999.

[23] See *Frankfurter Allgemeine Zeitung*, "Der schnelle Aufstieg an der Schnittstelle von Markt und Technik," 14.3.1992.

[24] See *Karriere* (Supplement of Wirtschaftswoche and Handelsblatt), "Die Personalentwickler der Bosch GmbH erwachen aus ihrem Dornröschen Schlaf," 12.1.1990.

Portfolio Restructuring and Product Market Policy

Because it requires much higher flexibility, intensified global competition has the potential to disrupt the long-term strategies of German companies. Greater flexibility can, in strategic terms, be equated with an active portfolio policy. This would indicate a sharp break with Bosch's corporate strategy, which has traditionally been aimed toward the stable development of the company and diversification in order to secure independence.

Divesting and Diversifying Again

Divestments are actually not part of Bosch's generic strategy. The strategic goal has been diversification in order to minimize risk and become more independent of the business cycle in the car industry. A major part of the diversification strategy was Bosch's decision to develop its communications business, which had been substantially strengthened by acquisitions in the 1980s.[25] In the following decade, Bosch's communications business enjoyed, similar to Siemens, a status as "royal supplier" for the German postal service; thus long-term relationships with its main customer and a near monopoly characterized this business. This changed when the communications market was liberalized and competition increased.

In the early 1990s, the communications business, consisting of public networks, private networks, and mobile communications, contributed almost 25 percent to total sales; foreign sales were 28 percent.[26] The strategic goal was to take advantage of the liberalizing international markets by increasing foreign share to 50 percent and to defend the home market.[27] Neither goal was met, sales went down, and the company incurred operating losses. International acquisitions did not succeed and by the mid 1990s growing competition, falling prices, and a reduction in the number of orders from Deutsche Telekom had put the communications business under growing pressure. As a reaction, the business was reorganized, employment was reduced by more than five thousand jobs, and two of the nine German plants were closed.

Despite the acquisition of the Danish company Dancall—a leading research centre for Global System for Mobile Communications (GSM) technology—in 1997, Bosch still could not compete with the major play-

[25]Bosch acquired parts of AEG's communications engineering business and the telecommunications company Telenorma, one of the then three biggest German telecommunications companies.
[26]See *Börsen-Zeitung*, "Bosch Telecom verstärkt die Forschung," 23.3.1990.
[27]See *Frankfurter Allgemeine Zeitung*, "Bosch Telecom will das Auslandsgeschäft ausbauen," 27.3.1990.

ers. Its market share in mobile phones in Europe was just 3 percent in 1998. It grew much more slowly than the market and had been losing money since 1992.[28] Although Bosch had always declared itself committed to its long-term plan in communications, divestment started in 1999 when Bosch sold more than 80 percent of its communications business.[29]

The main reasons for divesting the business were that Bosch did not have the necessary size to carry out economies of scale, it lacked international presence, and its research and development costs were too high. The company was not able to find a niche in the telecommunications sector and was not a leader in marketing or technology in a single area. In order to catch up, Bosch would have had to undertake massive investments that it was not willing to make.[30] First and foremost, this was because such expenditures might have threatened the existence of the firm altogether, and also because the main business was still automotive technology. Investing heavily in the risky communications business did not fit the general strategy, in which telecommunications were intended to minimize the risks incurred by the main business, automotive technology. Related to this, and equally important for the exit from telecommunications, was industry development. The telecommunications business developed over the 1990s in an industry characterized by short product cycles and radical innovation. It therefore did not fit Bosch's engineering orientation and its focus on incremental innovation.

However, the exit from telecommunications is an exception to the general business strategy. Other than telecommunications, Bosch divested only marginal activities, such as medical electronics or hearing aids. Generally, it prefers to stick to its business sectors and to develop them in the long term, even if they lose money in the short term. Car multimedia is a case in point. Although this business incurred losses or only marginal profits in the 1990s, there is no intention to divest. One reason is that car radios and the corresponding equipment are closer to Bosch's main business, and these products are a showcase for its competence in car electronics. Furthermore, Blaupunkt is at the center of Bosch's strategy to build integrated car multimedia and onboard navigation systems. In these systems, Bosch dominates the market, which shows low demand so far as a result of high prices and limited software, but de-

---

[28] See *Börsen-Zeitung*, "Bosch will auch bei Handys Spitzenposition," 21 October 1998.

[29] The public networks business was sold to British company Marconi, the private networks business was acquired by U.S. financial investors Kohlberg Kravis Roberts & Co. (KKR). The mobile phone division was split and sold to Siemens and the American firm Flextronics.

[30] See CEO Hermann Scholl quoted in *Börsen-Zeitung*, "Bosch und Siemens sind sich einig," 21.3.2000.

mand is expected to rise.[31] Generally, business lines such as Blaupunkt are kept when they fit into the general strategy.

After selling the telecommunications business, which was the second largest business sector, the diversification strategy was in danger. Bosch was more dependent than ever on automotive technology. During the 1990s, this sector was strengthened through several medium-sized acquisitions in Germany and major acquisitions abroad. Bosch tried to strengthen its other business divisions in order to keep a diversified business. There were considerable investments in the power tool division, which made Bosch the biggest power tool producer worldwide in terms of sales.[32] Furthermore, the French thermo-technology company Leblanc was acquired in 1996. Nevertheless, because of rapid growth, the overall share of automotive equipment increased even further. After the telecommunications business was finally sold, Bosch searched more determinedly for acquisitions for its other sectors. Thanks to the hostile takeover of Mannesmann by Vodafone in 2000, Bosch could strengthen the industrial technology division, since Vodafone intended to sell all businesses except telecommunications, which were united in the subsidiary Atecs.

Siemens and Bosch made a joint offer. Siemens got the automotive division, which Bosch was not allowed to control due to competition law, and Bosch the automation technology division, Rexroth. The remaining three divisions were to be controlled jointly, similar to a Siemens-Bosch joint venture in household appliances. The acquisition of Rexroth was Bosch's biggest acquisition ever. It compensated for the loss of about €1.8 billion in sales from telecommunications. Rexroth had a business volume of €1.3 billion. The automation technology division of Bosch until then had sold products for €820 million.[33] Thus, in exchange for the telecommunications business, Bosch built up a similarly strong pillar, automation technology, which fits better into its engineering orientation and its focus on incremental innovation.

All in all, despite the selling of the telecommunications business, Bosch continues its diversification policy by building up other sectors. The spinning off of telecommunications shows that such measures are not necessarily related to capital market pressures but can be caused by the structure of the industry, that is, product market pressures. The next section deals with Bosch's product market and research and development policies in order to find out how it reacted to the severe crisis in the 1990s.

[31] See *Financial Times*, "Bosch Benefits from Mercedes' Mishap," 5.2.1998.
[32] See *Süddeutsche Zeitung*, "Bescheiden und pflichtbewußt," 17.6.2000.
[33] See *Handelsblatt*, "Bosch hat ein Auge auf Rexroths Automatisierungstechnik geworfen," 18.4.2000.

Product Market Strategy

As Bosch entered the 1990s, the competitive situation in its main market, the automotive technology sector, began to change dramatically. New competitors entered the market, and Japanese car supply companies, the cost leaders, built plants in Europe in the wake of the common European market; Siemens, the ITT subsidiary Teves, and Mannesmann all entered the high-tech segments of the market. The competition in Europe was especially dangerous for the company because in the beginning of the 1990s the overwhelming part of its sales, more than 80 percent,[34] was made in Europe. The consequence was that profit margins fell considerably, and the car industry tried to pass on its own cost pressures to its suppliers. This was a new situation for Bosch. It was used to having long-term relationships with its biggest clients; it followed their development cycles and enjoyed a near monopoly in its most important products, above all the antiskid system (ABS)[35] and fuel injection systems. Bosch's dominance in these markets stemmed from a sophisticated patent and licensed manufacturing policy. Furthermore, in both areas Bosch was the only firm that was able to master the complete systems: in ABS it had a world market share of 80 percent and in fuel-injection systems 75 percent.[36] Thus, Bosch's strength traditionally has been the production of high-end products in connection with a strong market position.

The new competitive landscape threatened Bosch in its core and most important business and should—according to convergence theorists—lead to an imitation of the competitors' cost structures and corresponding strategies. However, to enter a pure cost competition would have been an unrealistic option for Bosch. It has had higher research and development and labor costs than its competitors, while drastic measures in order to compete on costs could not be undertaken due to the institutional environment as well as the tradition of the company. Bosch cut costs in only the most obvious voluntary allowances and even this measure largely failed. By the end of the 1990s, its products were on average still about 10 percent more expensive than comparable products of its competitors.[37] Nevertheless, in the 1990s sales almost doubled and the share of the vehicle component sector rose significantly.

Bosch essentially pursued a strategy that was built on moving upmarket by concentrating on systems and on the creation of new products.

[34] See ibid., "Wettbewerbsdruck verwandelt auch die Struktur der Automobilzulieferer," 6.7.1990.
[35] The most important difference between ABS and conventional brakes is that ABS is based on electronics, whereas normal brakes work mechanically.
[36] See *Manager Magazin*, "Fin de siecle," No. 8, 1991, as well as *Wirtschaftswoche*, "Wachsen oder weichen," 6.7.1990. By the late 1990s Bosch still had a share of 40 percent in the ABS world market.
[37] See *Manager Magazin*, "Ancien Regime," No. 3, 1997.

The first measure undertaken to secure its markets was to enter long-term contracts with the car producers. Due to cost reasons, car producers in the early 1990s were increasingly interested in "single sourcing," which means that they relied on one supplier to deliver whole equipment systems. The supplier firm has to undertake several specific investments in advance, such as the building of plants close to the customer, but in exchange receives all orders for a certain product or system. These contracts normally have a time frame of between five and ten years, corresponding to the life cycle of a certain car type. The prices decrease incrementally over the period of the contract, which forces the supply firm to increase productivity continuously. Bosch concentrated on making such deals, because they enable the suppliers to have longer-term perspectives and market shares can be secured or increased. The contractually fixed falling prices, however, force the supplying companies to achieve falling costs in production too. This contributed to the shifting of low-tech production to lower-cost countries as well as to the development of Bosch's production network; these contracts required Bosch's further internationalization, since closeness to customers became even more important.

Because Bosch could not compete on costs, it intensified its efforts to retain technological leadership in the upmarket segments. The goal was to stay ahead of competition through the development of technologically sophisticated new products that create new markets, similar to the earlier successes of ABS and fuel injection systems.[38] Bosch achieved this by means of massive investments and further development of exactly these products. On the basis of ABS, Bosch developed the electronic stability program (ESP), which is an extension of automated braking systems and stabilizes the car automatically. In its beginnings, ESP was limited to luxury cars but has trickled down to the mass and small car markets.[39] The second innovation was based on Bosch's leadership in fuel injection machines, namely common-rail diesel fuel injection, which is the precondition for improved vehicle economy and performance. In this area, Bosch became the undisputed market leader due to heavy investments.[40] In these two segments, Bosch managed to dominate the markets.

These successes with ESP and diesel injection systems came at a price, namely that, due to the necessary high investments, they were profitable

---

[38] See *Handelsblatt*, "Kraftfahrzeug-Ausrüstung trägt das Wachstum," 14.9.1995; *Handelsblatt*, "Elektronikkonzern wieder im Aufwind," 27.1.1995.

[39] This was helped by Mercedes-Benz's infamous "elk test." As a reaction and as a signal to care about safety concerns, it introduced ESP into the small car segment, which set a benchmark for competitors, which followed this example. See *Financial Times*, "Bosch Benefits from Mercedes' Mishap," 5.2.1998.

[40] Bosch invested about €2.5 billion between 1995 and 2000 in diesel technologies.

only in the long-run and yielded small profits in the short-run. However, since these products are technologically very sophisticated, the profits per car are higher, and again, Bosch enjoys a near monopoly for a certain period of time with profits coming over the long-run.[41] Furthermore, these markets that require innovative and sophisticated products grow much faster than the world car market in general. Bosch managed to grow twice as much as the relevant market in the mid 1990s.[42] Thus Bosch can uncouple itself to a significant degree from the business cycle in the car industry, which is not expected to grow continuously in the foreseeable future.[43] In the presence of growing competition and cost pressures, Bosch chose a strategy that leveraged its traditional competitive advantages, namely high investments and a high research and development intensity for upmarket items, innovated its products incrementally, and achieved market leadership in new products for which a premium has to be paid.

Closely connected to this, and another way to bypass cost competition, has been that Bosch made package offers. The high-tech products of Bosch, on which the car producers are dependent, can only be purchased in a package with its low-tech items, such as windshield wipers. In this way, the higher prices of the low-level goods are offset by their connection with the more sophisticated products. This strategy obviously depends on technological leadership in the high-tech products as well as on reasonable prices for the commodities. In a way, by making conditional offers, Bosch forces its clients to subsidize its production of low-tech goods.

Another crucial feature of the upmarket strategy in the 1990s was Bosch's focus on systems solutions. Bosch's products have been combined and sold as whole systems. This tendency covers all of Bosch's business sectors, with a corresponding move to diversification within sectors in order to be able to offer all relevant items. In the automotive business, the national and international acquisitions mainly had this systems strategy as a goal. Acquisitions made the braking division the largest within the car equipment sector and aimed at the creation of systems solutions for brakes and the possibility of offering all types of brakes for all types of vehicles.[44] The ABS and brakes divisions as well as other divisions of automotive equipment were reorganized so as to be able to offer systems solutions in their respective business fields, such as body electronics, car multimedia (centered around Blaupunkt), and chassis systems.

---

[41] See *Handelsblatt*, "Die Zukunft des Dieselmotors ist Bosch viele Milliarden wert," 2.2.2001.

[42] See ibid., "Mammut-Akquisitionen im Ausland gut verdaut," 16.5.1997.

[43] See *Börsen-Zeitung*, "Der stille Bosch," 29.6.2000.

[44] See ibid., "Bosch bremst mit Knorr," 15.10.1998; *Handelsblatt*, "Bremsen-Joint-Venture besiegelt," 15.10.1998.

Reorganization with the explicit aim of offering integrated systems solutions and the expansion of the range of products also took place in
other business areas. Several business lines were merged to create the
new sector automation technology. The reasoning was that customers'
requirements are becoming more and more differentiated. Anticipating
that customers are likely to ask for tailored systems, Bosch has increased
the number of variants of one product.[45] The same concept was pursued
in packaging technology. The most important clients in this industry are
pharmaceutical companies. They have usually outsourced their packaging activities to the manufacturing firms, so here again tailor-made solutions were required by the clients. Thus Bosch pursued a systems strategy
relying on its traditional engineering strengths. It diversified within the
power-tool sector, making itself into one of the biggest players on the
world markets and aiming to provide a complete range of products.

This orientation toward the production of systems has been made
possible by the introduction of electronic engineering in items that were
previously characterized by mechanical engineering; in the words of
Bosch's CEO: "We don't make simple products. All are complicated
items which can be made on automated production lines and where we
can add value by combining electronic and mechanical engineering."[46]
Due to technological complexity, modules and systems are expected to
become paramount: "We have a growing trend towards modules."[47]
Hence, Bosch's innovation lead results from its combination of electronic and mechanical engineering, which was applied to its most successful products, such as ABS, ESP, and petrol and diesel fuel injection.
The importance of electronics for the company can also be seen in its
semiconductor production. Because semiconductors lie at the heart of
all sorts of electronic items Bosch produces and it did not want to be dependent in this key area on other producers, a new plant was built in the
mid 1990s. Moreover, this in-house production and development enables the company to build its semiconductors exactly according to its
needs and to keep the know-how of new developments, especially in systems.[48] This strategy is also apparent in most of its activities; high-tech
products are not outsourced, but rather all manufactured in-house to
preserve the company's competitive edge.

The focus on systems also reinforced Bosch's concentration on market shares. Since systems need a certain market share to be produced
profitably, market share has to be secured, even at the expense of profitability in the short-term because of high initial investments. Thus, during the recession in the early and mid 1990s, Bosch lowered prices in

[45] See *Frankfurter Allgemeine Zeitung,* "Bosch Automation hat 1996 stagniert," 16.4.1997.
[46] *Financial Times,* "Bosch Enjoys the Benefits of a Varied Portfolio," 6.7.2000.
[47] Ibid., "Gently with the Brakes . . ." 23.2.1998.
[48] See *Handelsblatt,* "Kraftfahrzeug-Ausrüstung trägt das Wachstum," 14.9.1995.

order to keep its market share.[49] The strategy emphasized not profit maximization but quality maximization, with a corresponding long-term view toward profits.

Research and development and investment policy are an essential ingredient for the focus on high-quality products and systems solutions and Bosch's highly productionist orientation. The declared goal is technological leadership.[50] Thus research and development expenses are high: they fluctuated between 6.4 percent and 7 percent as a portion of sales in the 1990s. This high research and development intensity is mirrored in Bosch's number of patents. It is among the top ten companies worldwide in registering new patents.

Research and development, as well as investment activity, is largely independent of profits in the case of Bosch. In order to fulfill its claim to technological leadership, Bosch's research and development and investments are not influenced by changing profit situations. During the recession in the early 1990s, both remained more or less stable, and research and development expenses even increased. Even "in the face of falling turnover, therefore, Bosch has maintained its research and development momentum."[51] Research and development is seen as a precondition for the quality of the products and for business success. Moreover, the constant share of research and development expenses as a percentage of sales hides considerable increases in absolute terms even in the years of recession.

Internationalization Strategy

From its very beginnings, Bosch has been a highly international company. At the end of the nineteenth century, it opened its first branch in Great Britain; in 1914, the first plant in the United States was established, and at that time Bosch was exporting 88 percent of its production to twenty-five countries, among them Japan.

At the beginning of the 1980s, foreign sales amounted to 55 percent of total sales and decreased to 51 percent in 1990. Despite the falling contribution from international markets, Bosch's sales rose significantly during the 1980s, from €7 to €16 billion; domestic sales grew, including exports, from €5 to 13 billion.[52] Hence, Bosch entered the 1990s as an already internationalized company, but grew primarily in the domestic market while keeping international business by and large constant.

[49]See ibid., "Boxberg-Teststrecke kostet 100 Mill. DM," 2.2.1996; *Börsen-Zeitung,* "Bosch sieht Planung für 1995 stark gefährdet," 30.6.1995; *Frankfurter Allgemeine Zeitung,* "Bosch will im Inland noch einmal 4000 Stellen streichen," 27.1.1995.
[50]See *Handelsblatt,* "Halbleiterwerk läuft rund um die Uhr," 11.10.1995.
[51]*Financial Times,* "A Mark of Respect for German Supplier," 12.7.1994.
[52]Figures are all taken from Bosch, *Annual Report 1991,* 64.

TABLE 6.1
Bosch's sales and foreign sales, 1991–2004

Year	Total sales (mil. €)	Foreign sales (mil. €)	Foreign share in %
1991	17,179	8,246	48
1992	17,604	8,274	47
1993	16,601	8,134	49
1994	17,628	9,519	54
1995	18,327	10,263	56
1996	21,038	12,833	61
1997	23,955	15,570	65
1998	25,735	16,727	65
1999	27,906	18,418	66
2000	31,556	22,720	72
2001	34,029	24,501	72
2002	34,977	25,183	72
2003	36,357	25,813	71
2004	40,007	28,805	72

Source: Bosch annual report, various years.

Bosch strongly accelerated its internationalization during the 1990s and became one of the most internationalized German companies.

However, the company internationalized in a way that closely followed its traditional multidomestic style of internationalization. Bosch used international expansion not as means to escape its home base but rather to enter foreign markets and leverage its traditional strengths there. Internationalization complemented its product market strategy with the focus on the production of systems. Bosch kept all of its strategic functions in Germany, which remains the undisputed center of the company. Internationalization—supported by the work councils—has not resulted in pressures to transform Bosch's corporate governance model; on the contrary, it reinforced it. Table 6.1 shows the development of Bosch's international expansion during the 1990s.

There are several reasons for Bosch's focus on the international markets in the 1990s, which resulted in a foreign share of total sales of 72 percent in 2004. First, domestic expansion of the 1980s necessarily reached a saturation point. Second, intensified competition in the car supply market lowered the premium for Bosch's products in the home market. Hence, it had to enter new markets. Third, as a car supplier, Bosch has to be close to its clients. Therefore, "globalization among vehicle manufacturers means successful suppliers have to follow."[53] It has to be present near the plants of its clients; therefore presence is required

[53] *Financial Times*, "Gently with the Brakes . . ." 23.2.1998 as well as *Financial Times*, "Bosch Enjoys the Benefits of a Varied Portfolio," 6.7.2000.

at least in Europe, North and South America, and Asia. Fourth, Bosch tried to diversify its operations geographically to avoid dependence on national business cycles, which might threaten the company's independence.[54]

From the early 1990s onward, Bosch entered many joint ventures and has acquired many companies for all of its divisions. The main target countries have been the United States, Japan, and South Korea, as well as several Western European countries. Minor investments were undertaken in Russia, Thailand, China, and the Czech Republic. In countries where market access is difficult, it entered the markets via joint ventures but attempted to gain full control later.[55] Internal growth is the preferred strategy, but where it seemed infeasible, Bosch resorted to external growth.

Internationalization had an impact on Bosch's distribution of sales. Whereas in 1990, 83 percent of its sales were made in Europe, in 2004 this figure had decreased to 68 percent. The Americas and Asia increased their share in Bosch's sales from 11 to 18 percent and from 6 to 14 percent, respectively.[56] Hence, Europe has lost importance, but still accounts for two-thirds of sales. The major acquisitions took place in the United States and Japan: U.S. firms Emerson Electric and Bendix, until then the largest acquisitions, and Zexel of Japan were bought. Contrary to Siemens and Deutsche Telekom, Bosch targets all Triad markets and not only the United States.[57]

Bendix, the braking division of the American conglomerate Allied Signal, was by far the largest foreign acquisition, with a value of €1.1 billion. The dimension of the deal shows that it clearly deviates from the principle of internal growth. However, Bendix fitted nicely into Bosch's strategy to produce whole systems. Until the acquisition, Bosch produced braking systems only for passenger cars and for heavy commercial vehicles. Bendix was specialized in braking systems for all categories of commercial vehicles, for which Bosch produced the complementary electronic equipment.[58] With this deal, Bosch was able to produce braking systems for all categories of vehicles and could deliver whole braking systems, including ABS and the electronic equipment the car industry demands. Moreover, the bargaining position with the car industry was strengthened, since only a few firms are able to offer these systems. With

[54] See *Börsen-Zeitung*, "Bosch sieht in USA starkes Wachstumspotential," 5.11.1996.
[55] See *Frankfurter Allgemeine Zeitung*, "Bosch verstärkt im Ausland," 23.9.1996.
[56] See Bosch, *Annual Report*, various years.
[57] This happened in the cases of Emerson Electric, Diesel Technologies, Zexel, Vermont American, and several Korean firms.
[58] See *Frankfurter Allgemeine Zeitung*, "Bosch: Komplettanbieter von Bremsanlagen," 2.3.1996.

the acquisition, Bosch became the fourth largest brake producer world-wide[59] and earned €1.5 billion in sales.

The step-by-step acquisition of Zexel strengthened Bosch's network of stakes in Japanese car supply companies. It was the first majority stake that a foreign company bought in an important Japanese car supply firm. Bosch increased its stake from an initial 14 percent to 50.04 percent. By the time of the deal, Zexel had sales of €1.5 billion. Zexel could offer a complete range of car components, which allowed Bosch to offer whole systems to its Japanese customers. The deal also enabled Bosch to gain further access to the supply networks of Japanese car producers, because the second largest stakeholder in Zexel is Nissan. Bosch had already bought minority stakes in two of Nissan's affiliates, which are key Nissan parts suppliers. Behind this joint venture is the same strategic consideration as in the case of the Bendix, namely to produce systems solutions. But Bosch not only entered the Nissan network; it also holds a 5.4 percent stake in one of its most important international competitors, Denso Corporation, which belongs to the Toyota conglomerate. Thus, Bosch's activities in Japan can be regarded as the attempt to gain market access; however, the company has also succeeded in having "nimbly positioned itself in the vast supply networks that radiate out from automaking giants Nissan Motor Co. and Toyota Motor corp."[60]

A major foreign investment was a plant for lightweight alternators in Cardiff, opened in 1991, worth €150 million. It was not the high German wage level that led to the investments in Wales. Due to the low share of personnel expenses, which results from the high degree of automation, the cost advantage over German plants was only 5 percent.[61] Much more important than personnel expenses was the proximity to car producers. In the years before, Nissan, Honda, and Toyota had established plants in Wales. Since a new generation of alternators was to be produced, their success depended on their introduction into new car models, which were produced in Wales.[62] In terms of work organization and education, Bosch transferred the German production model completely in order to achieve its quality standards. The dual system was copied, in close cooperation with technical universities in Wales. Vocational training consists of on-the-job-training as well as theoretical education at the universities. Bosch invested heavily in the education of its employees, because, as the

---

[59] After ITT and Kelsey-Hayes of the United States and Lucas of Great Britain.

[60] *The Nikkei Weekly*, "Bosch Seeking Niche in Car-Supply Network," 19.10.1992.

[61] See *Handelsblatt*, "Die 'dritte industrielle Revolution' vollzieht sich im Bosch-Werk in Cardiff," 19.11.1991.

[62] Bosch's then CEO stressed that the prime motivations were access to a new market, access to new technologies, risk minimization through geographic diversification, as well as economies of scale through an international division of labor. See *Die Welt*, "Bosch überquert den Ärmelkanal," 27.9.1991.

director of the plant explains, "There is no equivalent to the way in which we understand vocational training. . . . We had to set up training programs to match our needs and were very fortunate in having the greatest co-operation of the local authorities."[63]

These initiatives in vocational training are not restricted to the plant in Wales; Bosch introduces them in all of its plants. Bosch copies the dual system, collaborates with local technical colleges, and invests heavily in its employees.[64]

Internationalization and Embeddedness

An important indicator of how Bosch controls its international operations is research and development policy. Generally, the research and product development work is carried out overwhelmingly in Germany; 80 percent of Bosch's research and development is undertaken there.[65] The company very closely follows the product life cycle; development takes place in the home location where the new products are also produced in the first part of their life cycle; production costs can be neglected at this stage, economies of scale and learning effects play the most important role. If the product is mature, then it is also produced in the foreign plants and adjusted to the needs of the respective markets.[66] The new products are locally adapted by application centers in the most important regions. Bosch has established application centers in several European countries, North America, South America, India, and Australia. The biggest application center was opened in 1992 in Yokohama, Japan, in order to deepen cooperation with local car producers. Hence these centers not only serve the purpose of adapting and distributing the technology to foreign markets, they also enable Bosch to participate in the development of new cars, to gain access to technology, and to develop its own technology accordingly. Another example is Bosch's decision to build a test site for brakes in Detroit in order to provide engineering support for American car producers in the development of new vehicles.

Investment policy follows this pattern. The production of high-tech goods is located overwhelmingly in Germany or, to a lesser degree, at plants close to the main customers in the Triad; low-tech products, such as loudspeakers or head lights, with a high share of wage costs, are pro-

---

[63]*Financial Times*, "It Was Love at First Sight," 21.10.1992.

[64]See *Handelsblatt*, "Erfolg ist nur mit Mitarbeitern möglich, die mitdenken und verantwortlich handeln," 21.10.1993.

[65]See *Frankfurter Allgemeine Zeitung*, "Bosch wirbt im Ausland um Führungskräfte," 6.10.2000.

[66]See interview with CEO Scholl in *Handelsblatt*, "Neue Produkte sichern die Zukunft der Inlandswerke," 14.6.1994.

duced in low-wage countries, for example Malaysia.[67] In the case of investments that are considered to be essential for Bosch's future, Germany remains the preferred location, the new semiconductor plant, a €110 million investment, being an example of that approach.

The foreign production of Bosch is integrated into an international production network in order to lower costs and to take advantage of international production and cost differences.[68] The foreign plants cover their regions, but they also produce certain single components that are needed for various products; these components are manufactured in only one plant and delivered to the others. The final assembly, however, takes place in the respective markets, which allows adjustment to local needs. Market access considerations are crucial. The first motivation of foreign investments is the location of the client and only then do cost considerations enter into consideration. U.S. production was sold almost entirely (87 percent) to U.S. clients.[69] Thus, foreign production is primarily intended to serve the local markets. Bosch set up a production network even before its customers in the car industry followed similar strategies.[70]

The expansive international strategy has been pursued in cooperation with the work councils. The main reason for the support of the work councils has been that production was not withdrawn from Germany, but that additional work has been generated abroad.[71] Nevertheless, international expansion did affect the development of the workforce; the ratio of domestic to foreign workforce has significantly changed over the 1990s, as table 6.2 shows. It can be seen that during the recession in the early 1990s, the domestic workforce was shrinking, whereas the number of foreign employees more or less stayed the same. From the mid 1990s onward, employment in the home location was kept constant but increased significantly abroad. In 1998, the number of employees abroad equaled the number of German employees for the first time. From 2000 onward Bosch employed slightly more employees abroad than in Germany, while employment has been increasing in Germany as well as abroad. However, considering that the share of foreign sales was 72 percent in 2000, the distribution of employees lags far behind. Regarding the internationalization of management, senior management still consists overwhelmingly of German citizens. In 2000, 84 percent of

---

[67] See Interview with CEO Bierich in *Wirtschaftswoche*, "Wettlauf von Hase und Igel," 25.6.1993, as well as *Handelsblatt*, "Erste Zeichen einer Umkehr im Ergebnis," 27.5.1992.

[68] See *Wirtschaftswoche*, "Wettlauf von Hase und Igel," 25.6.1993.

[69] See *Börsen-Zeitung*, "Bosch sieht in USA starkes Wachstumspotential," 5.11.1996.

[70] See *Manager Magazin*, "Ancien Regime," No. 3, 1997.

[71] See *Die Zeit*, "Kulturrevolution auf schwäbische Art," 30.8.2001.

TABLE 6.2
Domestic and foreign employees at
Bosch, 1991–2004 (thousands)

Year	Domestic employees	Foreign employees
1991	117	64
1992	113	64
1993	104	61
1994	95	61
1995	92	66
1996	91	81
1997	91	89
1998	94	94
1999	97	97
2000	91	106
2001	99	119
2002	103	123
2003	105	124
2004	110	129

Source: Bosch annual report, various years.

senior managers were German; among the heads of department world-wide, the share of German managers was 68 percent.[72] An even stronger indicator of the continuing embeddedness of Bosch in its home base is the concentration of value-added activities and research and development in relation to the share of sales. In 2000, 28 percent of sales were made in Germany, but 80 percent of the research and development activities took place there; 55 percent of value added was realized in Germany.[73]

In summary, Bosch strongly internationalized its business in the course of the 1990s, although it had always been a highly international company. The main reason was that domestic markets were saturated and that the company had to follow its clients, who internationalized as well. Since such a marked international expansion has not been possible by internal growth alone, Bosch resorted to external growth. However, internal growth remains the preferred path. Bosch has still centered its main functions in Germany, employment is disproportionately located in Germany, research and development almost exclusively takes place in Germany, and it transfers its production model to its foreign sub-

[72] See *Frankfurter Allgemeine Zeitung*, "Bosch wirbt im Ausland um Führungskräfte," 6.10.2000.
[73] See Ibid.

sidiaries. The last point demonstrates that Bosch pursues the transplant model, where the foreign affiliates are modeled on the parent company, in order to achieve the same quality results as in the home location by transforming the labor force. Also considering the approach to develop and introduce new products first in Germany and then bring them to foreign markets with application centers tailoring them to local needs, it can be said that Bosch's internationalization strategy is a clear-cut case of a multidomestic strategy, which is traditionally associated with German enterprises and a consequence of the high-quality production model.[74] Foreign direct investment in this strategy is undertaken to be close to the customer and the products are tailored to the customers' needs without much influence of the affiliates on the parent company.

Compared to Siemens and DT, Bosch pursues a higher coordination between its subsidiaries through the production network. However, no network structure in the company emerged. The parent company controls the operational matters of the subsidiaries quite strictly, but leaves them autonomy in local adaptation. Strategic decisions are taken exclusively in the home location, which indicates an ethnocentric management style. Therefore, it can be said that Bosch continues its traditional style of internationalization that does not challenge its traditional model of corporate governance but rather complements its domestic strategy. The international strategy transfers Bosch's corporate governance model; it does not threaten it.

This chapter opened with the question as to which strategy Bosch pursued in the 1990s in the wake of a severe recession, a dramatic drop in sales and earnings, as well as increasing competition, nationally and internationally, in its main business of car equipment. Bosch's strategy has been straightforward. In the early 1990s, Bosch reacted to the crisis by cost cutting in order to lower its labor costs and to catch up with its competitors. However, despite these measures, Bosch could not compete based on cost for three reasons: the firm's traditions, prior modest cost-cutting measures had provoked massive reactions on part of the employees, and threats to the firm's quality principles.

Bosch thus first reduced its workforce significantly, though without compulsory redundancies. The prime measures were early retirement, natural fluctuation, and severance payments. The production of simple items was transferred abroad, sold, or brought into joint ventures. This job reduction, as well as the transfer of activities, was undertaken in co-operation with the work councils; decision-making remained coopera-

[74]See Lane (2000b), 201–3.

tive. The only unilateral decision by management led to protests and then management concessions. Since then, industrial relations have continued to be peaceful.

In terms of management tenure, Bosch is an example of extremely high continuity. There have been only six CEO's in its 120–year history and top management is recruited internally, with a strong emphasis on individuals with a science or engineering background. A unique feature of Bosch's structure is that management controls itself via the Industrial Trust. There is no outside control by banks or financial markets. Financial policy is subordinated to the goal of maintaining the independence of the company. Bosch has very low debts, no house bank, and finances its investments and expansion exclusively from cash flow. Although there are some financial goals for business activities, they concern cash flow and profits as a percentage of sales. The prime goal is to be able to finance investments internally—profit maximization is not of prime concern. There are absolutely no signs that Bosch intends to be listed.[75] On the contrary, some observers see its nonlisting as its biggest asset. "While this status does not mean, of course, that there is no pressure to secure satisfactory financial returns, the company undoubtedly enjoys the luxury of not having to satisfy an outside group of hungry investors on a quarterly or half-yearly basis, as is the case with the principal American or British component groups. This has provided the necessary conditions to focus on long-term targets—notably in research and development—an especially valuable characteristic during the recent downturn."[76]

After its attempts to cut costs, Bosch's strategy switched to massive expansion and a concentration on upscale products. Bosch expanded internationally, especially through acquisitions and joint ventures in the United States and Asia. Foreign sales increased from 48 to 72 percent of total sales over the 1990s and remained constant at this level. Total sales jumped from €18 billion to €40 billion between 1995 and 2004, after having stagnated in the first half of the 1990s. The automotive equipment division was particularly strengthened. Bosch acquired Bendix of the United States and Zexel of Japan in the brake sector in order to be able to offer whole brake systems for all kinds of vehicles.

The internationalization and the establishment of a production network were caused by the internationalization of Bosch's customers, from which followed the necessity to be close to its customers. Moreover, the expansion possibilities in Germany had already been saturated by the end of the 1980s. In 1990, more than 80 percent of sales were made in Europe. In 2004, it was 68 percent. This trend is likely to continue, be-

---

[75]See *Die Zeit*, "Kulturrevolution auf schwäbische Art," 30.8.2001.
[76]*Financial Times*, "A Mark of Respect for German Supplier," 12.7.1994.

cause on average, Bosch items worth €510 are built in European production cars. The corresponding figure for the United States is €150 and in Japan the figure is even lower.[77] Growth potential is therefore evident in the United States and Asia, where Bosch makes 18 and 14 percent of its sales, respectively. Furthermore, Bosch wants to diversify even further geographically in order to minimize risks.[78] The general goal is to achieve growth of 8 to 10 percent p.a. in order to be able to maintain cash flow and profit levels as well as research and development intensity.[79] However, despite its internationalization policy, the overwhelming majority of Bosch's research and development is undertaken in Germany, and this also applies to the production of high-tech and high-value-added items.

Bosch's long-standing goal of diversification in order to minimize risk has been in danger after the selling of the telecommunications sector, which was its only major divestment in the 1990s. The reasons for the exit lie in the development of the industry, which evolved into a business characterized by radical innovation. This did not fit Bosch's focus on incremental innovation and its engineering orientation. Thus Bosch compensated the loss of the telecommunications business by strengthening its industrial technology division, a business that fits its innovation patterns and strategic orientation much better.

In terms of product market strategy, Bosch has focused on the development of upscale items and systems, for which the market pays a premium in all businesses. Bosch had used technical innovations to dominate the markets, such as the markets for ABS or petrol injection systems, and it built on these strengths by massive research and development expenses and other investments in order to achieve innovation in these areas. It innovated its products incrementally by building on existing products, and the outcome was products such as ESP and diesel fuel injection systems; these products secure Bosch's technological leadership, provide the company with a quasi-monopoly for a certain period of time, and shelter it from cost competition as long as it is the only firm that manages to produce whole systems in these sectors.

The mastering of whole systems also gives Bosch a competitive advantage in its other sectors. The basic strategy of the 1990s has been a concentration on systems. Corresponding to this strategy are very high research and development expenses and investments. Thus new products may not pay over the short run but secure Bosch's position as technological and market leader. These investments, especially in research and de-

---

[77] See *Handelsblatt,* "Bosch sieht gute Chancen in Asien und in USA," 4.2.2000.

[78] See *Financial Times Deutschland,* "Bosch will Anteil des Autozuliefergeschäfts zurückschrauben," 19.6.2000.

[79] See *Frankfurter Allgemeine Zeitung,* "Bosch ist mit seiner Rendite unzufrieden," 17.5.2001.

velopment, are undertaken regardless of the market or earnings situation.

All in all, as a response to the recession crisis, Bosch concentrated on its traditional strengths: long-term strategy, high research and development expenses and investments, incremental innovation, and diversified quality production, which are also associated with the German corporate governance system in general. There are no signs of change in financial policy, in management tenure, or in cooperation with the work councils. The general strategy has been to develop high-quality products, especially systems, and to target the high-end segments of markets, either by creating new markets or by offering technologically superior products. This strategy has allowed Bosch to grow significantly faster than the market. Thus, by relying on and reinforcing its traditional strategy, Bosch could compete very successfully on world markets, and it is market leader in most of its businesses. There are no signs that the growing competition in world markets affects its corporate governance system or undermines its general strategy. On the contrary, it seems that competition, nationally and internationally, reinforces Bosch's traditional strategy in all areas.

Chapter 7

Lessons of German Corporate Governance

This last chapter summarizes and compares the findings across the three cases. The main question to be examined is how the firms investigated have adapted their strategies to capital and product market pressures. I will then briefly investigate developments in other German firms in the chemical/pharmaceutical and automobile industries during the 1990s in order to broaden the argument. Equipped with these findings, I will then try to answer to what extent the German corporate governance system has transformed itself and will draw out the theoretical implications of the study.

Financial Restructuring

If convergence theory is correct, what we should see in the realm of financial policy is a higher dependency on the capital markets and a finance conception of the firm, subordinating strategic goals to financial results. Furthermore, the pressure of financial markets is supposed to lead to an increased transparency of firms. Whereas the higher dependency on the stock markets is not supported by the empirical evidence, the listed firms have indeed become much more transparent.

In the case of Siemens, institutional investors considerably increased their ownership to today's 45 percent. Nevertheless, there is continuity in the core features of corporate finance. Owing to its high reserves, Siemens is independent from the financial markets in terms of financing investments, which are financed from cash flow or reserves. Dividends remained constant over the 1990s. They rose significantly after the record year 2000, but simultaneously this success was shared with the employees, who benefited from a generous employee-share program. The biggest change in Siemens's financial policy is to be found in transparency and information policy. The company discloses much more information than it used to, including business segment information. Transparency was increased before Siemens's listing on the NYSE; the listing itself did not have a significant impact. No capital has been raised on the NYSE, and the share of American investors stayed the same.

DT has been much more dependent on the financial markets in terms of financing. Its financial policy has been shaped by its enormous debts. Its IPO was a success, and the distribution of the shares showed a strong bias toward German private investors, because they were considered to be long-term investors. To this end, stable and high dividends were announced in order to shelter private investors from risk. Several other measures were undertaken to make the IPO a success, ranging from a bank consortium, in which every major bank was included, to a disproportional weighting in the stock market index. DT listed on the NYSE because the size of its stock offering was simply too big for Germany alone, and it wished to indicate its international ambitions on the product markets. The SEC's rules proved quite elastic: not even quarterly results and divisional breakdowns had to be introduced.

Bosch's financial policy is characterized by strong continuity and has been embedded in the production-orientated strategy. The aim is to secure the independence and long-term survival of the firm. Bosch finances its investments from retained earnings and cash flow and very rarely taps the bond market. This is made possible by the very low dividends Bosch pays to its owner, the Bosch Foundation. Financial goals do not enjoy priority. There are also no strict profit targets that units or the firm as a whole must reach. More important for Bosch is the development of cash flow to finance expansion. In none of the case studies do we find the feature that is mostly associated with German corporate governance: the strong influence of banks. Financing patterns rely on self-financing as much as possible.

Organizational Restructuring and Industrial Relations

Union influence differs across the three firms. Its institutionalization is highest at DT, where the union preserved its exceptionally strong position during and after privatization. It is weaker at Siemens, where the supervisory board is not involved in strategic decision making, and it is weakest at Bosch, where the supervisory board has virtually no power or responsibilities. Despite this variation, industrial relations and adjustment in the realm of employment policy at all three firms show strong similarities.

All three companies reduced domestic employment to a significant extent over the 1990s. DT shed sixty thousand jobs, Bosch and Siemens about thirty thousand each. These reductions, however, did not lead to compulsory redundancies and hire-and-fire policies but were accomplished through such means as severance pay, natural fluctuation, and early retirement. All measures were taken in close cooperation with the work councils. Interestingly, the nonlisted Bosch is the only company in the sample in which management attempted to introduce unilateral decision-making in a crisis situation and in which major strikes took place.

Codetermination as an institution has not been under pressure. On the contrary, the restructuring efforts examined here have to a large degree been dependent on the cooperation of the employees and work councils. This sort of co-management, with its emphasis on bargaining, produces a consensual adjustment path that includes dismissals, but only as a last option. Hence, codetermination seems to be alive and uncontested in all three companies, regardless of their ownership structure and capital market exposure.

Management recruitment and tenure also largely follow traditional patterns. Bosch is an extreme example of the recruitment of managers with a scientific or engineering background as well as the very long tenure of the CEO. Also in the case of Siemens, the CEO and the overwhelming majority of the management board are internally recruited, and there are no signs that this policy will change. DT differs from this picture. Owing to the special situation of privatization, its CEO was externally recruited. The tenure of the first DT CEO was quite long, compared to DT's international competitors. His successor was internally recruited. There are no signs that this feature of the German corporate governance system—the internal recruitment of management and the long tenure—is fundamentally changing: what we see points more in the direction of continuity.

The most prominent instruments of shareholder value are stock options and divisional profit goals. Siemens introduced both. However, the stock option scheme does not provide very high-powered incentives. Only top management is affected and most of the incentives are based on accounting figures with a long-term bias. These incentives are complemented by stock options, which can, in the best case, add up to 25 percent of annual income. This share of equity-based compensation is as high as in U.S. firms in 1980, before the transformation of the American corporate governance system toward shareholder value principles. Regarding profit goals, these are lower at Siemens than at its competitors, and crucially the company refuses to follow the concept that units that do not meet the profits goals should be closed or sold. Despite the EVA concept, Siemens is committed to its product lines and is biased toward fixing. No splitting of the company is intended.

DT also introduced a stock option program in 2000. The number of granted stock options was very small in the first year of the program, as was the number of potential beneficiaries. However, the program encountered problems. Its design led to accusations of self-enrichment of management by the public and, because the exercise hurdle was remarkably low, was opposed by the supervisory board. The program was one of the major factors that led to the demise of the CEO in 2002. Management renounced its stock options afterward, and the program was finally abolished in favor of more balanced incentives. Hence, far-reaching steps toward a shareholder value orientation at DT were not possible to sustain against the pressure of various stakeholders.

Bosch obviously cannot introduce stock options. However, the company changed the structure of management compensation. The fixed salary was lowered from 75 percent to 45–55 percent. The criteria for the variable parts consist of the general business results, performance of the respective business area, and personal goals

Portfolio Restructuring and Product Market Strategy

The rapid restructuring of a firm's portfolio and its entry into new markets is a crucial feature of Anglo-Saxon corporate governance. Financial markets favor the spinning off of business lines in mature markets with average profit perspectives and a focus on fast-growing markets. However, German firms traditionally stick to their markets, and this commitment is seen as a precondition for DQP strategies, incremental innovation patterns, long-term investments, and a market share-orientation with stable, but not spectacular, profits. From a convergence perspective, the growing role of financial markets should lead to increased portfolio restructuring in response to financial market expectations, which may then also threaten DQP strategies. It should be kept in mind that all three firms are the most diversified in their respective industries in a worldwide comparison, and the two listed firms should therefore be the prime candidates for portfolio restructurings.

Siemens spun off its semiconductor and passive components divisions and listed them in the late 1990s, when it was faced with a critical situation in terms of share price and profits at an all–time low. This divesture was the first time Siemens spun off major loss-making divisions. However, the semiconductor business had experienced difficulties since the 1980s and was the main cause of Siemens's general problems. It was extremely capital-intensive, absorbed the lion's share of Siemens's investment resources—which threatened other divisions—and the innovation patterns in the industry did not fit Siemens's incremental innovation orientation.[1] The Asian crisis in 1997 accelerated the long-standing problems of competing in a highly cyclical business. The spin-off was undertaken in full agreement with the work councils. Further demergers are not planned, despite the demands of financial market actors to split Siemens completely in order to concentrate on core businesses and increase profitability. Siemens remains committed to its markets, even if several divisions do not meet their profit goals. The spin-off was therefore not the beginning of a broader restructuring; it was rather the end of one. Nor has Siemens followed a policy of downsizing. Expansion remains the dominant strategy: via domestic and international acquisitions, sales grew by almost €40 billion between 1996 and 2002. Siemens's strategy shows strong differences in comparison to its competitors. Both GE and ABB pursued a highly active portfolio policy over the 1990s and have had a much lower commitment to their markets, congruent with a stricter profit orientation.

The nonlisted Bosch took a similar step as Siemens. Its telecommunications department had been chronically unprofitable, and eventually Bosch sold all parts of the division. Here, too, the investment requirements, which were thought to damage the prospects of the other businesses, were the main reason for moving out of telecommunications. This took place without any influence from the financial markets. Simply, the costs of gaining a competitive edge were considered to be too high. However, Bosch still gives priority to strategic considerations as opposed to financial results, if divisions fit into the general strategy. The loss of communications has been compensated with major acquisitions in other areas in order to reach a higher degree of diversification. Expansion has also been the dominant strategy in the case of Bosch. Sales almost doubled between 1991 and 2000. A further common feature of Siemens and Bosch is that both have constantly

---

[1] The sale of the mobile phone division in late 2005 followed the same logic; Siemens was not able to gain a competitive edge in this fast-moving business with its short product cycles and radical innovation patterns.

kept their research and development expenses at a very high level, irrespective of profit swings, worsening market situations, or in the case
of Siemens, a falling share price. Thus, although Siemens is heavily exposed to the capital markets and Bosch is a nonlisted firm, in terms of
portfolio restructuring and general strategy, both have behaved almost
identically. It is important to note that the spun-off divisions were in
both cases active in fast-moving businesses that require patterns of radical innovation and fit poorly with the incremental innovation patterns
German corporate governance—and these two firms in particular—is
associated with.

DT had a very different starting position. However, it too shows a
strongly expansionist strategy. It first reorganized itself in order to give
the different businesses more flexibility. We see no major demergers in
the case of DT, despite its debt mountain and its position as the most diversified telecommunications company worldwide. Its strategy has been
focused on expansion into new market segments and international markets. The listing of units is an integral part of this strategy. Only small
stakes were listed with the goal of creating an acquisition currency for international expansion of the units. The parent firm retains full control.
DT's focus on expansion contrasts sharply with its competitors' strategies. The crisis in the industry led to a division of both BT and AT&T;
AT&T demerged into four companies, BT divested its mobile business
and parts of its international business. Nothing similar took place at DT.
DT has tried to cover much wider areas than its competitors, and its adjustment path excluded downsizing. It remains committed to its diversified and expansionist strategy. Sales grew by two-thirds between 1995
and 2001.

In sum, all three enterprises have withstood the pressure to demerge
significantly; they pursued a strongly expansionist strategy and have diversified within technologically related areas, a pattern Porter sees as a
characteristic of German enterprises.[2]

In terms of product market specialization, the DQP specialization has
increased rather than decreased. Until the 1990s, Bosch's competitive
advantage lay in its technological leadership, especially in the mastering
of whole systems. Confronted with new competitors, cost pressures, and
falling margins, Bosch did not enter into cost competition; it moved
even further to the higher end of the market. Bosch concentrated even
more strongly on the production of systems and the creation of technologically leading new products by means of massive investments. The
company managed to regain a near-monopoly status in upmarket products with higher profits over the long term, but with lower short-term

---

[2]See Porter (1990), 374.

profits due to the high investments involved. The second pillar of its product market strategy was the bundling of its products into whole systems. Systems bring with them a focus on market share, because they need a certain market share to be profitable over the long run at the expense of short-run profits. In this way, the adjustment to tougher competition resulted in a reinforcement of Bosch's upscale strategy with a concentration on technological leadership.

DT also enjoyed technological leadership in its business. Its telephone network was one of the most modern worldwide at the time of its privatization. It continued to invest massively in its network, especially in digitalization and broadband, which are both necessary for multimedia and interactive services. The problem was to commercialize DT's technological advantages. DT did so by a clearer focus on market segments through four operating units, responsible for the traditional telephone business, mobile business, Internet, and systems solutions for business. The profits from the fixed line segment have been used to finance growth in the growing markets. DT sees its competitive advantage in quality, service, innovation, and systems competency. Its main strategy has been to integrate its activities in order to offer systems solutions, thereby capitalizing on the convergence of information and communications technologies.

Siemens also tried to leverage its engineering strengths and its broad portfolio by concentrating on systems solutions. The focus of its product market policy has been to integrate the products and services of its numerous divisions, mostly involved in large-scale infrastructure projects, and offer comprehensive, tailor-made solutions to its customers. In this sense, Siemens further pursued its traditional engineering orientation and tried to create a competitive advantage out of its wide-ranging portfolio. This strategy has discriminated against downsizing, because the broadness of its portfolio is a precondition for the systems strategy. In sum, all three firms have deepened their existing product market strategies and developed them into systems strategies.

Internationalization Strategy

One of the most remarkable features of the corporate strategy of the firms under investigation has been their aggressive internationalization during the 1990s. All three companies have strongly expanded internationally; this strategic choice could be termed "adjustment by expansion." The companies share two important characteristics in their internationalization. First, international expansion was fully supported by the work councils in each of the cases. The work councils agreed to this strategy because the firms sought not to escape the high-cost German home base but access new markets. Second, the three firms sought full control over their subsidiaries, whose influence on the general strategy has been very limited. No networklike structures or a multicenteredness exist in any of the three firms. There were no attempts to consolidate international operations into a single worldwide entity without a commitment to the home country. Despite international expansion, Germany remains the undisputed center of gravity for all three firms, where the strategically important functions are located.

Siemens reacted to increased competition in the German electronics market and its loss of status of privileged supplier for all sorts of public institutions by expanding massively. The share of the German market in its distribution of sales dropped from about 50 to 30 percent over the 1990s and further to 21 percent in 2005; in absolute terms, sales in Germany remained by and large constant, but growth came from abroad. Siemens's employment structure follows that pattern only loosely. In the mid 1990s, Siemens for the first time employed more people abroad than in Germany. However, the company has disproportionately more employees in Germany.

Bosch's international sales remained constant over the 1980s at roughly 50 percent, but increased to 72 percent in 2004. The main reasons for internationalization have been saturated markets in Germany, the internationalization of the car industry in general, and the minimization of risks by geographical expansion in order to avoid dependence on national business cycles. Also, Bosch now employs slightly more people abroad than in Germany. Despite these massive internationalization moves, both companies are far from footloose. They remain anchored in the German business system. Research and development activities are kept in Germany. In the case of Siemens, 75 percent of research and development expenses are spent domestically; Bosch carries out 80 percent of research and development activities in Germany. The bulk of other value-added activities also remains in the home location. The style of internationalization also favors Germany. All strategically important management functions are located there, top management is recruited there, and acquisitions have only a limited degree of autonomy, while the production model is transferred to the subsidiaries.

DT also reacted to the adjustment pressures with international expansion. Formerly a purely national enterprise, it increased its foreign sales from zero to 27 percent in 2000 and to 39 percent in 2004. The main reason was to compensate for losses in the domestic market after deregulation and to follow its business clients. Similar to Siemens and, to a lesser degree, to Bosch, its main target has been the American market.

Also in the case of DT, we find that assets and strategic and financial functions are mainly located in Germany.

Overall, the marked international expansion does not threaten the corporate governance model; it seems to reinforce it. The style of internationalization is consistent with the stakeholder model of corporate governance. Their internationalization can be seen as an effective strategy to cope with increased competition. It is not a move away from the home base: internationalization complements the domestic corporate strategy.

An Assessment

The adjustment path of all three companies over the 1990s was characterized by expansion through internationalization, and by internal restructuring. There is a combination of continuity in some institutions, whereas there is substantial change in others. The degree of change does indeed vary with capital market exposure—with the degree of change being highest in the case of Siemens—but even high capital market exposure does not result in a transformation of corporate governance and in patterns prevalent in shareholder systems.

Looking at the degree of change, the results are most clear-cut in the case of Bosch. Its exposure to product market competition did not significantly affect its corporate governance arrangements. Change is visible in three indicators. Bosch internationalized determinedly, but within the limits of its traditional internationalization style. Management-labor cooperation temporarily weakened, and confrontation did occur once. Finally, Bosch undertook a major divestment but compensated for this by big acquisitions in other business areas.

DT's shareholder value orientation remains limited despite its listing on the NYSE and the need to signal its investor-orientation after privatization. The biggest change took place concerning its extent of internationalization, but it pursued a style of internationalization congruent with stakeholder governance. Its financing policy had to change, because this was the very reason to go public, but it managed through various means to restrict financial market pressures. Its stock option program was quite short-lived, and profit goals were not introduced.

Siemens is the most complex case. Being the most exposed to financial market pressures, it shows the highest degree of change, compared to the other firms. Above all, it introduced stock options, profit goals, and a much higher transparency. In these areas, a higher investor orientation is obvious. However, Siemens's profit goals and its stock option

program are—compared to Anglo-Saxon practices—differently designed and provide lower-powered incentives for management to prioritize shareholder value. Due to the different design, the introduction of
these shareholder value instruments has not undermined the general
product market strategy and decision-making structures. Siemens undertook a major divestment, but this was not the beginning of an active
portfolio policy. That Siemens and Bosch divested divisions in which
they lacked competitive advantages and which were characterized by patterns of radical innovation indicates that these decisions are the result of
problems that German firms have competing in fast-changing high-tech
markets rather than of financial market pressures.

Regarding the commonalities among the three firms, the differences
in basic strategic behavior are small. All three followed a policy of internationalization and growth, they continued to incorporate the work
councils into decision-making, they restructured in a way that left their
basic structures and business areas intact, and they kept their traditional
product market strategy. The basic strategic orientation has not been of
the "downsize-and-distribute" type. The structure of the enterprises under
investigation remained intact with a commitment to existing markets and
with a focus on expansion as main strategic goal. The pronounced internationalization strategy has not led to networklike structures, but continues with the multidomestic orientation without threatening the corporate governance arrangements.

How can we explain this emerging pattern? Pressure from the financial markets seems primarily to affect transparency without significantly affecting the other features of business policy. The main difference between the firms lies in their transparency. Bosch, not faced
with shareholder demands, remained secretive, whereas DT and, to a
significantly higher degree, Siemens changed their information policy.
In comparison with DT, Siemens generally shows a higher responsive-
ness to shareholder value demands. Key to this difference is certainly
higher exposure of the firm to the capital markets due to its dispersed
ownership structure. Nevertheless, Siemens stops well short of Anglo-
Saxon practices and introduced at most a soft version of a shareholder
value approach. This finding indicates that piecemeal institutional
change is possible without jeopardizing the whole institutional configuration on the firm level. The introduction of a more open information policy has not resulted in breakdown or a simultaneous adjustment of other, and more basic, features of company strategy, such as
employee-management relations.

Continuity in the stakeholder orientation and internal decision-
making is consistent with the requirements of the DQP product market

strategies, incremental innovation patterns, and the leveraging of competitive advantages. Indeed, if product market strategies require certain institutional preconditions, then firms should not be expected to change them. Conversely, investors can be expected to accept these requirements of product markets, so that they do not push for a change of strategy, but rather support the existing strategy and the associated institutions, as long as transparency is provided. In summary, the shareholder value concept was filtered through existing institutions and associated negotiation processes; only those parts that did not provoke strong resistance on the part of stakeholders and that did not do damage to product market strategies were implemented.

Thus the adjustment paths and the restructuring patterns of the firms under investigation are still incremental and negotiated in character, undertaken in close cooperation with the work councils, and they have avoided the "asset-stripping, short-term planning, and social disruption"[3] with which Anglo-American restructuring is associated. The role of the work councils can even be said to increase during periods of restructuring. The preferences of investors received more attention than previously, but have been mediated by the German institutional context. The claims of other stakeholders, especially employees, have not been superseded by shareholder value demands; investor preferences have become an additional element of the complex bargaining that characterizes German firms. The focus on expansion indicates that profit and shareholder value maximization, which would mean downsizing, a hire-and-fire employment policy, and the distribution of cash flow mainly to shareholders, has not been pursued. The companies have rather followed the traditional restructuring path of stakeholder systems, stressing continuity and growth.[4]

Case Studies in Comparison

The following sections briefly investigate the developments in other large German firms throughout the 1990s in order to generalize the argument and make it applicable to German industry as a whole. The focus will be on the car and the chemical/pharmaceutical industries, because these are the industries that constitute a major part of the firms included in the DAX 30 index of the biggest German firms and are traditionally the most important industries in the German economy.

[3] Doremus, Keller, Pauly, Reich (1998), 33.
[4] De Jong (1997), 20.

Chemical/Pharmaceutical Industry

The three major chemical/pharmaceutical companies, Bayer, BASF, and Hoechst, are often seen to typify the "postwar 'German model' of stakeholder-oriented corporate governance and a productionist strategy focused more on investment and sales growth than on profitability."[5]

They were confronted with tremendous changes in the pharmaceutical industry over the last decades, which altered the dominant innovation paradigm as well as industry structure. Whereas pharmaceuticals traditionally were integrated into the broad chemical sector and innovation was largely achieved by screening a huge number of chemical compounds—hence the close connection between chemicals and pharmaceuticals—the rise of biotechnology and information technology turned the industry into a high-tech and also high-risk industry. The high-risk component has its roots in the blockbuster strategies of the largest pharmaceutical firms, which concentrate on developing drugs with huge worldwide sales potential. The research and development costs of these blockbuster drugs are enormous and so is the risk of failure. Thus the pharmaceutical industry developed from an incremental innovation paradigm into the showcase of a radically innovative industry. Congruent with this, the industry structure changed through massive merger activity, because minimum firm size increased and global marketing became imperative to earn the research and development costs.[6] Hence consolidation and portfolio restructuring became the main industry issues.

In terms of ownership, Hoechst, Bayer, and BASF belong to the German companies with the highest share of foreign investors. Throughout the postwar period, they pursued very similar strategies with similar structures, following an integrated chemical/pharmaceutical strategy. Their diversified businesses made them worldwide leaders in sales growth, but also the firms with the lowest level of profitability. Thus, they came under increasing pressure from the financial markets to increase profitability, define core businesses, and divest businesses with low profit margins. However, the strategies that have been adopted vary considerably.

Hoechst took the most radical approach. It was among the first firms to adopt a shareholder value rhetoric, starting with the appointment of a new CEO in the mid 1990s, and it followed the prescriptions of the shareholder value approach resolutely. Due to the assumed higher growth and profit potential of pharmaceuticals and agricultural products—the so-called life sciences—Hoechst decided to sell off its chemical

---

[5]Vitols (2003).
[6]See Casper, Matraves (1997), 9.

businesses, which accounted for three quarters of sales; its aim was to become a pure life science company.

The money from the selling of the chemical business was to be used for acquisitions in the life science business in order to achieve critical mass in pharmaceuticals, in which a merger wave was taking place in the 1990s. Hoechst found a merger partner in the French pharmaceutical/chemicals company Rhône-Poulenc. Following this merger, the new company gave itself a new name, Aventis, and the headquarters were moved to Strasbourg, so that the new company would be subject to French law, thereby evading German codetermination. This new strategy involved heavy job losses: about 45 percent of jobs were cut between 1993 and 1998.[7] This resulted in severe conflicts with the work councils and unions. Regular demonstrations took place to protest against the job losses as well as a new system of pay, which partly tied remuneration to the financial performance of the company and its business units. However, management stuck to its strategy. In this way, Hoechst can be seen as an example of a shareholder value company. It pursued an active and radical portfolio policy in line with a new product market strategy and according to the expectations of the financial markets and exited the German corporate governance system. Its exit might be due to the incompatibility of its strategy with the institutions of German corporate governance.

Bayer was confronted with the same challenges. Institutional investors hold 68 percent of total capital,[8] and it was thus faced with the same investor's expectations and product market changes. The company also appointed a new CEO in the mid 1990s, who, as in the case of the new Hoechst CEO, had a finance background. However, despite these almost identical initial conditions, strategic orientation differs widely between these two companies. Bayer's strategy involved a commitment to the strategy of an integrated chemical/pharmaceutical company and to consensual decision making with stakeholders as well as an incremental approach to change. It defined four main product areas as core businesses in order to achieve a gradual refocusing. These four pillars—polymers, chemicals, pharmaceuticals, and agrochemicals—have been strengthened through acquisitions, whereas product lines that do not fit into the four-pillar strategy have been divested.

The company came under pressure from institutional investors, who preferred to split up the company completely in order to concentrate either on chemicals or pharmaceuticals. Bayer rejected a split-up of the

---

[7]See Menz, Becker, Sablowski (1999), 145; for a general account of the development of the German chemical/pharmaceutical industry see Becker (2003).

[8]See Streeck (2001), 11.

company and undertook a less far-reaching step in 2004 by spinning off underperforming business lines. Parts of its chemical—the cyclical commodity chemicals—and polymers business were listed under the name Lanxess. Although a significant step in itself, it did not much change Bayer's structure as a conglomerate, a fact that institutional investors heavily criticized.[9] Bayer's agreements with the work councils, including the waiver of compulsory redundancies on the part of management until 2007, are also valid for the new firm. The remaining parts of chemicals and polymers were merged to the new business division material science. Thus gradual refocusing continued and portfolio restructuring remained partial, with the spin-off constituting the official end of portfolio restructuring. After the spin-off, the strategic focus of Bayer is now primarily on pharmaceuticals. However, its product market strategy in pharmaceuticals has not followed the blockbuster strategy, but has concentrated on over-the-counter drugs. This segment, in which Bayer belongs to the market leaders, contrary to the overall pharmaceutical market, involves less risks and less profit potential, but allows incremental innovation patterns by upgrading and diversifying known drugs.[10]

In industrial relations terms, cooperation with the work councils has continued. There is an agreement with the work councils that contains commitments to training and investment levels. The work councils prevented the inclusion of business unit performance in determining additional pay and blocked plans to set up a joint venture for pharmaceuticals with Bayer as the junior partner. Management compensation grew modestly at 7.3 percent between 1996 and 1999, compared to 45 percent at Hoechst.[11] Bayer further internationalized its business over the 1990s; whereas in 1991, the company made 64 percent of its sales abroad, in 2001, foreign sales made up 86 percent of turnover. Nevertheless, Bayer also employs disproportionately more employees in Germany, 43 percent.[12]

BASF has an institutional ownership of over two-thirds of its total capital. Its degree of diversification is the highest among the global chemical firms and therefore prone to downsizing demands on the part of institutional investors. The crucial feature of its strategy has been to follow a *Verbund* model, which means the ambition to produce high-quality products combined with cost leadership in core markets. This strategy has been implemented by the concentration of production at one site in

[9]See *Financial Times Deutschland*, "Bayer-Aktionäre kritisieren Mischstruktur des Konzerns," 3.5.2004.

[10]See *Manager-Magazin*, "Bayer: Die Chemiesparte wird verschenkt, das Pharmageschäft vergrößert," 23.7.2004.

[11]See Höpner (2001), table 5.

[12]See Bayer, *Annual Report 1991*, and Karsch (2002).

Ludwigshafen, which results in economies of scale and scope.[13] The importance of financial performance at BASF has been growing, but this has occurred in the context of its traditional strategy and does not affect the commitment to specific markets. Some under-performing business lines have been divested, and due to new research paradigms and the missing critical mass in pharmaceuticals, this business has been sold; this was balanced out by some major acquisitions in other businesses. However, BASF's main business lines, oil, gas, chemicals, and crop science, have not been affected; it continues to be a broad chemicals conglomerate with a stronger focus on chemicals than before. Industrial relations at BASF are cooperative. As in the case of Bayer, there is an agreement that commits management to training and investment levels. Management pay rose by 14.8 percent,[14] quite moderately in comparison to Hoechst. Similar to Bayer and the firms investigated in the case studies, BASF is a highly internationalized firm, whose foreign sales account for 78 percent of total turnover. Nevertheless, 55 percent of its employees are located in Germany.[15]

All in all, Bayer and BASF remain committed to the stakeholder system and have adjusted their traditional strategies and gradually refocused their business activities. They continue to be conglomerates while the diversification across industries has decreased. In these cases, portfolio restructuring has been modest and partial. This stands in line with their product market strategy, which focuses on businesses characterized by incremental innovation. In the case of BASF, it is the chemical business, whereas in the case of Bayer, it is a certain segment of the pharmaceutical market. Hoechst, on the other hand, has pursued a strategy of radical portfolio restructuring in order to become a life science company, and eventually exited the German corporate governance system. The radical changes at Hoechst followed the different requirements of the life science industry, which is characterized by radical innovation and high risks in the development of blockbuster drugs. Thus, even in firms with a very high proportion of institutional investors and very similar initial conditions at the beginning of the 1990s, we do not see convergence in strategies but divergence depending on the product market strategies chosen.

Automobile Industry

The car industry is the most important sector of German industry in terms of innovation, employment, and exports. In the early 1990s, it was

[13] See Vitols (2003).
[14] See Höpner (2001), table 5.
[15] See Karsch (2002).

heavily affected by a deep recession. As a consequence, employment levels dropped significantly and company structures were reorganized. Also in the car industry, global consolidation has been the major topic over the last years. Many car producers, such as Volvo, Saab, Jaguar, Nissan, Mazda, Suzuki, and Subaru lost their independence and were bought by global firms such as General Motors, Ford, or Renault.

It was in the car industry that the shareholder value concept made inroads into Germany. After the appointment of Jürgen Schrempp as CEO in 1995, Daimler-Benz announced that it would follow a shareholder value strategy. Daimler-Benz, now Daimler-Chrysler, has had no majority owner, but Deutsche Bank and the State of Kuwait have held considerable stakes in the company; Deutsche Bank currently holds 12 percent and the State of Kuwait 7.2 percent. The first moves in the shareholder value direction were the introduction of one of the first stock option plans in Germany and the listing of Daimler-Benz on the NYSE. The aim of the new management was to transform the company and give priority to shareholders' interests.[16] Management compensation grew enormously between 1996 and 1999—by 466 percent.[17] Simultaneously, the new management ended and reversed the diversification strategy into other fields of transport in order to focus on the automotive industry. Daimler-Benz was the first company to lower the continuation of payments for sick employees, from which it, however, retreated after heavy protests by its workforce.

Despite the official shareholder value strategy, downsizing was not on the agenda. On the contrary, Daimler-Benz pursued a strongly expansionist strategy. In terms of product market strategy, it tried to leverage its position in the premium segment toward many more segments of the automotive market; examples include the introduction of the A, B, and M classes, of the Smart compact car or the luxury brand Maybach. Its acquisition of Chrysler in 1998, then the largest industrial merger ever, and its stake in Mitsubishi were intended to make the firm a truly global company. Even after the merger with Chrysler, Daimler-Chrysler remained incorporated in Germany, and therefore subject to German law even though it could have exited easily to the United States or elsewhere. The work councils supported both the expansion and general strategies. Indeed, the support of the work councils and of Deutsche Bank as a major shareholder was critical for the survival of the CEO, who publicly supported codetermination in general. Industrial relations continued to be cooperative, and Daimler-Chrysler maintained a strong commitment to

---

[16]See O'Sullivan (2000), 285.
[17]See Höpner (2001), table 5.

investments in worker training.[18] In this sense, the shareholder value strategy has not been detrimental to industrial relations. However, although global consolidation has been legitimized with shareholder value and profit potential, the strategy has not been appreciated by the financial markets. Three years after the merger, Daimler-Chrysler was worth less than Daimler-Benz alone before the merger, with net profits halved by Chrysler's losses.[19]

Volkswagen (VW) tried to combine a shareholder and a workholder orientation.[20] VW's major shareholder is the state of Lower Saxony, which holds a 20 percent stake. Two factors contributed to an increased shareholder orientation. First, a capital increase in 1997 failed due to its traditionally closed business policy with a very low degree of transparency. Second, due to a very low stock market value, it would have been a potential takeover target, had it not enjoyed the stake held by Lower Saxony. However, the legality of this stake has been subject to considerable conflict between the European Commission and Lower Saxony, so that there was an ever-present risk that the stake had to be sold. Thus Volkswagen aimed at increasing both profits and share price. In collaboration with the work councils, it introduced the International Accounting Standards (IAS), segmental reporting, and higher priority for investor relations. It set profit goals and introduced a new incentive system with stock options offered to all employees, as well as other bonuses. Simultaneously, VW introduced the workholder concept, which sought to complement shareholder value with social responsibility and employment protection. Even in the acute crisis in the car industry, VW did not resort to mass dismissals. It distributed work among its employees by reducing weekly working hours, which secured twenty thousand jobs. Furthermore, it guaranteed a certain employment level. In terms of product market strategy, Volkswagen moved upward in its segments and acquired several luxury car brands, such as Bugatti, Lamborghini, and Bentley, in order to support this move. Furthermore, it increased product variety by introducing new models, for example in the minivan or sports utility vehicle (SUV) categories.

The profit goals were not met, although profits rose moderately. This had no strategic consequences. Even if the profit goals could have been met by reducing investments, VW refused to do this. There were no effects on investments, which are financed completely out of cash flow. Major divestments did not take place, but VW acquired several compa-

---

[18]See Foudy (2001), 40.
[19]See *The Economist*, "Schrempp's Repair Job," 3.3.2001.
[20]The following section draws on Jürgens (2002).

nies. Also research and development expenses as well as dividend policy were unaffected. The work of Ulrich Jürgens thus finds a continuing productionist orientation in the case of VW and sees no shift toward financialization or evidence for a fundamental change in VW's distinct corporate governance system due to capital market pressures. He argues that VW is "responding to capital market pressures and shareholder value demands while continuing a productionist orientation and emphasizing the need for long-term capability development."[21]

BMW and Porsche pursued strategies that follow the German corporate governance patterns even more closely and both explicitly reject shareholder value as a guideline. Both are family-owned enterprises. The Quandt family holds 46.6 percent of BMW's shares, and the Piech and Porsche families own 55 percent of Porsche's shares. BMW has always relied on high-quality production and technology with an "unflinching focus on engineering excellence"[22] for which it could charge a premium price. In the mid 1990s, the company ran into trouble when it tried to achieve economies of scale without damaging its brand name by acquiring British carmaker Rover. However, despite heavy investments, the Rover acquisition incurred major losses and was finally divested in 2000. This led to a severe crisis. The CEO and his potential successor were fired, and BMW became a potential takeover target; Ford, General Motors, Fiat, and VW were said to be interested. However, the commitment of the Quandt family as majority owner prevented a takeover.[23]

The new plan was a go-it-alone-strategy with a focus on the premium niches in all car segments. In order to differentiate its product range BMW acquired Rolls Royce and in the small car segment it introduced the Mini, which it retained from Rover. Furthermore, it has developed many more variants of its own models and targeted new niches, such as the SUV segment. This upscale strategy, with the introduction of many new models, which all "compete on quality, engine power, and ride— none on price,"[24] has been successful. Sales rose from €16 to €38.5 billion between 1992 and 2001, investments reached a new height with 9.1 percent of sales, research and development expenses are 7 percent of sales, and with ninety-seven thousand employees in 2001 BMW employs twenty-six thousand people more than in 1993.[25] Industrial relations remained cooperative: the influence of the work councils was visible in the appointment of the new CEO in 1999, when the work councils vetoed

---

[21] Ibid., 41.
[22] See *Fortune*, "Why Is BMW Driving Itself Crazy?" 26.6.2000.
[23] See *Manager-Magazin*, "Piech: BMW ist leider unverkäuflich," 9.3.2000.
[24] See *Business Week*, "BMW: Speeding into a Tight Turn," 29.10.2001.
[25] See BMW, *Annual Report 2001*, 104–5.

the appointment of the then number-two executive because of his radical plan concerning Rover. BMW has also been very successful in financial terms. It has significantly outperformed the DAX as well as the Euro STOXX 50. BMW was in 2004 the second most profitable carmaker worldwide, with margins of more than 9 percent, more than double the industry average and more than double Daimler-Chrysler's margins.[26] It achieved this without any stock option plan or other moves that are associated with a shareholder value strategy. Management compensation even decreased between 1996 and 1999 by 10 percent, probably due to the problems at Rover.[27]

The only carmaker worldwide that is more lucrative than BMW is Porsche, with a profit margin of 11.9 percent in 2001.[28] It is also the most respected German company, according to a survey among managers, followed by BMW.[29] However, this was not always the case. Porsche was severely hit by the automobile recession in the early 1990s. It sustained considerable losses; it had outdated models and production facilities and was widely seen as a likely takeover target. In 1992, a new CEO was appointed who significantly restructured the company, dismissing two thousand employees. Sales since then grew enormously, mainly abroad, from €980 million in 1993 to €4.5 billion in 2001. After the earlier dismissals, Porsche increased employment from almost seven thousand to about ten thousand between 1995 and 2001. Moreover, the Porsche employees have an employment guarantee through 2010. The cooperation with the work councils is praised in the firm's annual report as trusting and cooperative, and it is seen as a cause of Porsche's success.[30] It certainly contributes to such peaceful industrial relations that the company produces exclusively in Germany and exports its cars. A major new plant is being built in Leipzig. All investments are financed from cash flow.[31] Also Porsche enlarged product variety, indeed doubled it, by introducing a cheaper sports car—the Boxster—as well as a SUV model.

All in all, Porsche's turnaround has been extremely successful. Production rose fourfold, profits fivefold, and the share price twenty-five-

---

[26] See *Business Week*, "BMW: Speeding into a Tight Turn," 29.10.2001, as well as *Manager Magazin*, "Der weiß-blaue Himmel strahlt," 16.5.2002.

[27] See Höpner (2001), table 5.

[28] See *Fortune*, "Best Companies to Work for: 10 Companies in Europe: Porsche Combining Style and Substance," 4.3.2002.

[29] See http://www.manager-magazin.de/unternehmen/imageprofile/0,2828,282456,00 .html?Ranking=1&Branche=1&x=5&y=10. The rankings of Porsche and BMW were the same in 2002 and 2004.

[30] See Porsche, *Annual Report 2001*, 5.

[31] See *Die Zeit*, "Für ein paar Euro mehr," 19.10.2000.

fold, outperforming all indices.[32] Similar to BMW, there is no stock option program at Porsche, and the CEO does not hold a single Porsche share. The CEO furthermore publicly took a position against a shareholder value policy in general, which he thinks results in a short-term business policy.[33] This led to a conflict with the German stock exchange, whose new rules required quarterly reports for companies included in the DAX and the MDAX, which is an index for medium-sized enterprises. Porsche refuses to prepare quarterly reports and was excluded from the MDAX in 2001.

In sum, the major German car producers continued their strategies of DQP production. BMW and Porsche have been the most successful by focusing on premium niche markets. They have not introduced any instruments associated with shareholder value and their family ownership prevented them from a takeover in times of acute crisis. Volkswagen introduced some shareholder value instruments but combined that with a "workholder" orientation, which was intended to give employment security. Daimler-Chrysler publicly promoted the introduction of the shareholder value concept in Germany, but this has not resulted in downsizing or conflicting industrial relations. Despite these differences, all firms in the car industry tried to maintain their peaceful industrial relations arrangements and pursued an expansionist strategy by differentiating product range and expanding internationally. All four carmakers significantly increased their foreign sales. Whereas international business made up approximately 50 percent of sales for each firm in the beginning of the 1990s, in 2001 it contributed between 70 and 85 percent. At the same time, employees remain fairly concentrated in Germany; BMW has 75 percent of its employees in Germany, and Daimler-Chrysler as the most internationalized—or indeed binational—German car producer, 51 percent.[34]

These additional cases from two major German industries show that adjustment of large German firms has not resulted in shareholder-value-type strategies. This is because of the continuation of DQP product market strategies, which rely on preconditions such as cooperative industrial relations, a cautious approach to portfolio restructuring, and a highly expansionist instead of a downsizing strategy. The case of Hoechst confirms the importance of product market strategies for general firm behavior, because here changing product market strategies resulted in a far-reaching downsizing, conflicting approach to industrial relations, and finally to the exit from the German corporate governance system.

[32]See ibid., "Nicht alles so machen wie die Amerikaner," Interview with Porsche CEO Wiedeking, 12.7.2001.
[33]See ibid.
[34]See Karsch (2002).

Theoretical Implications

The evidence presented does neither unambiguously support the predictions of convergence theory nor those of the varieties of capitalism approach. The case studies suggest that there is an incremental adaptation of the German corporate governance system underway. What we see is the selective incorporation of some, but by no means all, elements of shareholder systems into the German corporate governance system. Change is limited to certain areas. Those elements of the German corporate governance system that are related to the transparency of firms are changing; certain instruments are imported from shareholder systems and accommodated, while the other elements of the corporate governance system remain unchanged and still fit the traditional logic of the system. What is important about the different depth and scope of changes is that the improved transparency and the import of some shareholder value instruments have not transformed the fundamental structures of decision-making within companies; because of the absence of a market for corporate control, these changes have not replaced internal through external market control.

Thus the prediction of convergence theory that stakeholder systems must converge toward shareholder systems in their entirety has not materialized. True, there was a shift toward stock options and higher transparency. But the introduction of these changes required accommodating these imported institutions to the prevailing corporate governance system while other institutions were not affected. Thus German firms continue to look fairly different in comparison to their competitors from shareholder systems in such important areas as decision making, product market strategy, portfolio policy, and industrial relations.

Whereas the changes observed are not far-reaching enough to support convergence theory, they are far-reaching enough to pose a problem for the varieties of capitalism approach. The varieties of capitalism approach is very good at explaining the continuities in corporate governance and business policy—especially noteworthy is the deepening of product market policy. The empirical evidence supports one of the key insights of the varieties of capitalism approach, namely, that firms need several institutional preconditions to pursue DQP strategies, which they are unlikely to abandon. Furthermore, the different speed and the different depth of measures taken in the three dimensions of restructuring are to a large degree an outcome of the institutional framework, its constraints and incentives.

However, the selective incorporation of elements from stakeholder systems, even if limited to certain areas of business policy, questions the existence of tight complementarities and therefore notions of change associated with them. Tight complementarities allow only one pattern of change. Either small changes have large effects, that is, lead to the breakdown of the system, or they have no effect at all, because actors stick to their behavior. Thus change either happens in an abrupt and very wideranging manner, or the system remains stable.[35]

As the case studies demonstrate, complementarities allow for more change than is commonly assumed in the varieties of capitalism literature, without leading to a fundamental transformation or breakdown of the model. It rather seems to be the case that institutions are not tightly, but more loosely coupled, so that change in one institution will not necessarily lead to a chain reaction and to convergence. It will lead to different outcomes than in other corporate governance systems and to a modified configuration. Generally, the institutional features that the varieties of capitalism approach assigns to the German model have not been stable in the sense that no change took place: "Only in the 1970s, then, did the system as such exhibit all the characteristics we now attribute to it."[36] Thus the stability of these systems can easily be exaggerated when seeing them as static models. As a consequence, the threat to the model when change occurs may also be exaggerated.

Corporate governance and economic systems as a whole must not necessarily be coherent in all of their subsystems; there is the real possibility that subsystems with a different logic coexist, that they complement each other in different ways under different conditions, or that they are loosely integrated so that change in one subsystem does not affect the rest of the system.[37] Thus partial adaptations are quite possible. In favor of the complementarities perspective it should be added that even if institutions are selectively imported, the imported institutions will be accommodated to the institutional framework and will therefore provide different incentives than in the original setting. Hence the institutional framework shapes the adjustment paths by influencing which institutions are imported and how these institutions are designed. In this sense, a certain degree of coherence and fit is created, even if the institutions do not seem to fit at first glance.

The possibility of importing institutions from shareholder systems, however, indicates that company behavior is not determined by national institutions. Firms have higher degrees of freedom than the varieties of capitalism approach would predict. National institutions shape the general parameters within which companies operate, but they cannot fully explain company behavior. To do this, the actual behavior of firms and how they

---

[35] See Hackethal, Schmidt (2000), 31.
[36] Schmidt (2002), 166.
[37] Deeg (2005), Mayer, Whittington (1999).

respond to new pressures must be studied. The problems of explaining the empirical evidence with the theoretical models is a consequence of their setup. Both convergence theory and the varieties of capitalism approach are essentially macrolevel theories. Convergence theory uses standard microeconomic reasoning to deduce the consequences of globalization on the system level, whereas the varieties of capitalism approach applies institutional economics to the macroeconomic level to predict the persistence of institutional structures. The reasoning is in both cases based on comparative statics and therefore leaves adjustment processes and firm behavior in different areas underspecified.

Future Challenges for German Corporate Governance

To repeat the general argument of the book, institutional change in German corporate governance has been happening, but it has been limited to certain aspects that left the fundamental structures of corporate governance intact. The process and the outcome of restructuring in German firms differ from the patterns found in shareholder systems because of preexisting institutions and the resulting negotiation processes among stakeholders, the different components of the shareholder value concept with their different consequences for employees and managers, and the institutional preconditions of the product market strategies pursued. The changes affected subinstitutions and a critical mass of changes has not been reached. However, this argument must be sensitive to developments that have the potential to shift this pattern of adjustment toward more radical change. Hence, the question is, *where do we go from here?*

There are three political and economic developments that might accelerate the change in German corporate governance and possibly lead to large-scale change in the future: the cumulative effects of incremental changes; a deepening of financial markets, especially through pension reform; and the emergence of a market for corporate control.[38]

On a theoretical level it is quite possible that it is "precisely on the margins that the new shows first."[39] Thus convergence theory may under-

---

[38] A weakening of codetermination and labor more generally might be added as a fourth possible development. However, as this book and several other studies have shown, codetermination has proven a valuable institution for management, especially during periods of restructuring. Therefore, the interest of management to abandon codetermination and thereby give up valuable coordination mechanisms will likely be fairly limited. Besides that, codetermination has been strengthened on a regulatory level, not weakened and no party in the parliament aims at abolishing codetermination; the only party that wants to weaken codetermination to a certain degree is the Free Democratic Party.

[39] Streeck, Yamamura (2004), 26.

estimate the time needed to transform German corporate governance and stakeholder systems more generally. But further piecemeal changes may gradually accumulate over the long run and will finally result in a fundamental transformation toward a shareholder system. In this sense, the process of convergence may be less spectacular than envisaged by convergence theory, but incremental change will slowly transform the dominant logic of action.[40] However, whether the process of small-scale changes will continue is an open and basically empirical question. There is an inherent danger in simply extrapolating from current trends in some areas of company behavior. As this book has tried to show, the adjustment strategies of companies are to a considerable degree dependent on their product market and innovation strategies; therefore, they are unlikely to change the core institutional preconditions of these strategies.

Apart from that, the shareholder value instruments German firms introduced in the 1990s have come under attack on several fronts, which also speaks against extrapolating this trend. The main reason for the introduction of these instruments was that the management of German enterprises—filled with the "new economy" euphoria of the late 1990s, the stock market boom, and the pressure from institutional investors—aimed at introducing those institutions that were seen to encapsulate the success of American firms, mainly stock options and higher investor-orientation. Not surprisingly, managers were self-interested enough to be keen on getting stock options in order to participate in a bullish stock exchange.

However, the current trend is not favorable for stock options. Owing to diverse scandals, the dubious connection between stock options and company performance, and most important, to new international regulations, management compensation through stock options has fallen out of fashion. The new International Financial Reporting Standards foresee that firms must expense stock options, so that they have to charge the cost of options on their income statements. This obviously decreases the attractiveness of stock options and is the main reason for the move away from them as a means for compensating management. Firms such as Deutsche Telekom and Daimler-Chrysler have already abandoned their stock option programs.[41] What will replace stock options is uncertain; however, it is likely that the rush toward stock options was a phenomenon of the bull market of the 1990s.[42]

[40] Streeck, Thelen (2005).
[41] Deutsche Telekom replaced them with a variable bonus, which is tied to personal goals, firm performance, and share performance; thus share performance is now only one of several benchmarks.
[42] Similarly, there are even indications that investors are beginning to appreciate conglomerates once again. Rating agencies recently started to give them a bonus in their rat-

The same is true for U.S. listings. After the end of the new economy boom, the attractiveness of a listing in the United States decreased considerably and the already listed German firms have been trying to withdraw from the U.S. exchanges; Siemens was the first firm to publicly state that plan. This new preference of German firms—seventeen are listed in the United States—is due to the high costs of a listing, the limited impact of a U.S. listing in terms of trading volume and U.S. shareholder base, as well as the liability rules for managers. However, U.S. regulations set high hurdles for a withdrawal.[43] Thus German firms with a listing in the United States lobby intensively via the EU commission and their national government for softer delisting rules.[44]

A second development that might transform German corporate governance would be a substantial deepening of financial markets, especially by a reform of the pension system toward funded schemes. The underdevelopment of German financial markets is to a large degree caused by the pay-as-you-go pension system. Considering the demographic problems of Germany and industrialized countries more generally, private pension assets are likely to grow significantly in the medium term, resulting in more liquid and highly capitalized financial markets. However, it is too early to make any predictions about the consequences of this development on corporate governance. Much more research is needed on the preferences of and the differences between institutional investors: for example, between pension and mutual funds, their regulation, and their strategies.[45] For example, whether institutional investors seek an active governance role with the capacity to influence corporate strategies directly or whether they remain largely passive investors will be crucial for German corporate governance.

One insight follows from cross-country comparison. Expansion of the financial markets alone may not necessarily lead to a transformation of the whole corporate governance system. Research on changes in stakeholder systems has concentrated on the German case. Often overlooked is the fact that other stakeholder systems manage to combine more highly developed financial markets and a large role for institutional in-

ings due to their better diversification of business risks, which eases the raising of capital. See *Financial Times Deutschland*, "Mischkonzerne stoßen wieder auf mehr Toleranz am Markt," 16.11.2004.

[43] The most important regulation in this context is that even after a delisting the firms have to comply with U.S. reporting standards given that they have more than 300 shareholders permanently residing in the United States.

[44] In the case of insurance company Allianz, the costs for a listing in the United States add up to $30 million a year. Costs increased since also foreign firms have to implement the regulations of the Sarbanes-Oxley act. At the same time, Siemens's daily turnover at the NYSE is only 3 percent of that in Germany. See *Financial Times Deutschland*, "Firmen unterstützen Delisting-Vorstoß," 22.10.2004.

[45] For an account on the differences of institutional investing in Germany and France see Goyer (2006).

vestors with labor influence and patterns of stakeholder governance. Sweden, the Netherlands, and Switzerland, for example, have much higher stock market capitalizations than Germany and the role of institutional investors in these economies, in terms of their assets, is much closer to the Anglo-Saxon pattern.[46] Nevertheless, they show clear characteristics of stakeholder governance in other subsystems. There is obviously more than one coherent configuration of economic institutions for coordinated market economies and stakeholder systems, which reinforces the point made earlier about more loosely coupled institutions.[47] This opens up the possibility that even if we witness further changes in German financial markets, the outcome may not be a shareholder system, but rather a different variant of a stakeholder system. If we abandon the assumption that there are only two stable equilibria for corporate governance and economic systems as a whole, other coherent combinations are possible.

A third challenge for the persistence of the structures of German corporate governance would be the emergence of a market for corporate control. Some commentators have postulated that the missing market for corporate control in Germany has stabilized some of the crucial elements of corporate governance and business strategy: for example, higher spending on research and development and investments, the pursuit of higher market shares, and focus on segments with lower returns and lower risk.[48] In other words, it is the absence of a market for corporate control that crucially contributes to strategic coordination patterns in stakeholder systems, because its absence allows firms to enter into longer-term commitments with their employees and other stakeholders. Hence, an active market for corporate control would set a dynamic in motion whose logic would probably not be consistent with the other core principles of the system. It would likely push firms to introduce a very strict share price orientation, which would come into severe conflict with consensus orientation, commitment to markets, and generally most implicit long-term contracts. Thus, it is not financial development per se that might unravel the German corporate governance system but the emergence of a market for corporate control.

After the takeover of Mannesmann by Vodafone in 2000, many scholars and analysts were convinced that this hostile takeover marked the be-

---

[46]See OECD (1998a), 18, and OECD (2001b), 46. In 2001, the financial assets of institutional investors (as percent of GDP) were 81 percent in Germany, 153 in Sweden, 233 percent in Switzerland, and 191 percent in the Netherlands. The figures for the United Kingdom and the United States were both 191. See OECD Institutional Investor Database.

[47]For a comparison between Swiss and German corporate governance see Börsch (2006).

[48]See Höpner, Jackson (2001), 12.

ginning of a market for corporate control in Germany and the beginning of the end of stakeholder governance. However, Mannesmann has
been the only major hostile takeover to date; the expected wave of hostile takeovers failed to appear and so did a market for corporate control.
Considering the concentrated ownership structures in Germany, to
which Mannesmann was an exception, this should not be surprising.
The concentration of ownership, which is persisting in the aggregate,
makes it very likely that in the future a market for corporate control will
be of marginal importance and that merger and acquisitions will be bargained. This is reinforced by political attempts, supported by the unions
and employers, to prevent the emergence of this market, as was evident
in the rejection of the liberal EU takeover directive by the European parliament in 2001 and the German Takeover Act of 2002 with strong protection for management. Thus the main actors seem to be aware of the
potentially wide-ranging consequences of a market for corporate control
and they have attempted to prevent its emergence. If they succeed, the
fundamental structures of the stakeholder system and the capacities of
actors to coordinate among themselves are likely to remain intact.

The institutions of German corporate governance proved more resilient
than convergence theory would expect, but they also proved more open
and adaptive to small-scale changes and a layering of institutions than
the varieties of capitalism approach predicts. Change in German corporate governance took place not by transforming and replacing the institutional framework; change was mediated and accommodated by existing
institutions. These institutions shaped the direction of change as well as
the depth and the scope of restructuring.

Even if institutional change and its consequences is difficult to cap-
ture for institutional theories, especially for those of a systemic nature,
its occurrence is actually good news. It is evidence that institutions are
flexible enough to allow experimentation on the part of actors. Without
some degree of experimentation and adaptation, stability in corporate
governance systems may develop into inefficient inertia; such a development might then indeed threaten the whole system and its logic by increasing the need for radical changes. For the future, the findings of this
book lead us to expect that incremental and small-scale changes will
continue, but which direction they will take is uncertain. In any case,
they may not necessarily or inevitably result in a shareholder system. On
the contrary, the links between corporate governance, innovation patterns, and product market strategies make this an unlikely scenario.

One key finding of this book is that institutional diversity in corporate
governance systems does not preclude change and adjustment. It would
have been surprising to find no change in German corporate gover-

nance given the changes in the world economy. However, how companies respond to these pressures is highly dependent on the corporate governance arrangements in place and the product market strategies pursued. Globalization does not erode the competitive advantages of stakeholder arrangements of corporate governance; global competition rather requires leveraging them. Companies such as Porsche or BMW even demonstrate that stakeholder governance can be associated with superior profits. Further evidence for the competitiveness of stakeholder governance is provided by the recent export performance of German firms. Between 1994 and 2004 German merchandise exports more than doubled. Between 2000 and 2004 exports rose by 65 percent, whereas those of the United Kingdom increased by 22 percent and those of the United States by 5 percent. In the same period the growth of German exports in absolute terms was even higher than that of China, the new star in the global economy.[49] This shows two things that have been central to the argument of this book. First, companies from stakeholder systems of corporate governance can be highly competitive in the global economy. Second, the selective import of shareholder-value instruments does not necessarily destroy their fundamental structures and corresponding capabilities.

The discussion about corporate governance, the relative efficiency of different systems, and their distributional consequences is likely to continue in the foreseeable future. This in itself is a sign that globalization has had an effect: namely, to highlight the importance of firms as entities on which political economies are based. Not so long ago, firms, their organization, and their strategies were of no interest to political economists. The new interest in the organizational properties of firms and their relationship with national political economies in many disciplines opens up possibilities for interdisciplinary research. The issues in question are important and complex enough to deserve this attention. In this book, I have tried to underline that it is not national structures alone that determine the behavior of firms, but the interplay between those institutions and the structure and strategy on the firm level. Thus, I hope future researchers will acknowledge that firms are at least partly autonomous actors and deserve to be studied as actors in their own right.

[49] Author's own calculations based on WTO (2005), Appendix table A6.

References

Achleitner, Ann-Kristin, and Alexander Bassen. 2002. "Entwicklungsstand des Shareholder-Value-Ansatzes in Deutschland—Empirische Befunde." In *Corporate Governance, Shareholder Value, and Finance*, ed. Markus Ruffner. Munich: Vahlen Verlag, 611–35.

Alchian, Armen, and Harold Demsetz. 1972. "Production, Information Costs, and Economic Organization." *American Economic Review* 62: 777–95.

Allen, Franklin, and Douglas Gale. 2000. "Corporate Governance and Competition." In *Corporate Governance: Theoretical and Empirical Perspectives*, ed. Xavier Vives. Cambridge: Cambridge University Press, 23–85.

Amable, Bruno. 1999. *Institutional Complementarity and Diversity of Social Systems of Innovation and Production*. Wissenschaftszentrum Berlin Discussion Paper FS I 99–309.

Aoki, Masahiko. 1996. "Towards a Comparative Institutional Analysis: Motivations and Some Tentative Theorizing." *The Japanese Economic Review* 47: 1–19.

——. 2000. *Information, Corporate Governance, and Institutional Diversity: Competitiveness in Japan, the USA and the Transitional Economies*. Oxford: Oxford University Press.

Bartlett, Christopher A., and Sumantra Ghoshal. 1987a. "Managing across Borders: New Strategic Requirements." *Sloan Management Review* 28: 7–17.

——. 1987b. "Management across Border: New Organizational Responses." *Sloan Management Review* 29: 43–53.

Bassanini, Andrea, and Ekkehard Ernst. 2002. "Labour Market Regulation, Industrial Relations, and Technological Regimes: A Tale of Comparative Advantage." *Industrial and Corporate Change* 11: 391–426.

Baums, Theodor. 1995. *Universal Banks and Investment Companies in Germany*. Institute for Commercial and Business Law, University of Osnabrück, Working Paper No. 26.

Bayer AG. *Annual Report*. Various years.

Becht, Marco, Patrick Bolton, and Ailsa Röell. 2003. "Corporate Governance and Control." In *Handbook of the Economics of Finance*, ed. George Constantinides, Milton Harris, and Rene Stulz. Amsterdam: North Holland, 1–109.

Becht, Marco, and Colin Mayer. 2001. "Introduction." In *The Control of Corporate Europe*, ed. Fabrizio Barca and Marco Becht. Oxford: Oxford University Press.

Becker, Steffen. 2003. "Sachzwang Shareholder Value? Die Chemie- and Pharmaindustrie." In *Alle Macht dem Markt? Fallstudien zur Abwicklung der Deutschland AG*, ed. Wolfgang Streeck and Martin Höpner. Frankfurt: Campus, 222–49.

Berle, Adolf, and Gardiner Means. 1932. *The Modern Corporation and Private Property*. New York: Macmillan.

Biggart, Nicole, and Mauro Guillen. 1999. "Developing Difference: Social Organization and the Rise of the Auto Industries in South Korea, Taiwan, Spain, Argentina." *American Sociological Review* 64: 722–47.

Blair, Margaret. 1995. *Ownership and Control: Rethinking Corporate Ownership for the Twenty-First Century*. Washington: Brookings.

Blommestein, Hans. 1998. "The New Financial Landscape and Its Impact on Corporate Governance." In *Corporate Governance, Financial Markets, and Global Convergence*, ed. Morten Balling, Elizabeth Hennessy, and Richard O'Brien. Dordrecht: Kluwer Academic, 41–70.

BMW. *Annual Report*. Various Years.

Boehmer, Ekkehart. 2000. "Business Groups, Large Shareholders, and Bank Control: An Analysis of German Takeovers." *Journal of Financial Intermediation* 9: 117–48.

Börsch, Alexander. 2006. "Institutional Variation and Coordination Patterns in CMEs: Swiss and German Corporate Governance in Comparison." In *Beyond Varieties of Capitalism: Conflict, Contradiction and Complementarities in the European Economy*, ed. Bob Hancké, Martin Rhodes, and Mark Thatcher. Oxford: Oxford University Press.

Bosch. *Annual Report*. Various years.

Bratton, William, and Joseph McCahery. 2000. *Comparative Corporate Governance and the Theory of the Firm: The Case against Global Cross Reference*. George Washington Law School, Public Law and Legal Theory, Working Paper 007.

Bühner, Rolf, Abdul Rasheed, and Joseph Rosenstein. 1997. "Corporate Restructuring Patterns in the US and Germany: A Comparative Empirical Investigation." *Management International Review* 37: 319–38.

Bühner, Rolf, Abdul Rasheed, Joseph Rosenstein, and Toru Yoshikawa. 1998. "Research on Corporate Governance: A Comparison of Germany, Japan, and United States." *Advances in International Comparative Management* 12: 121–55.

Bursee, Michael, and Ramona Schawilye. 2003. "Stock Options—und was kommt danach?" *Frankfurter Allgemeine Zeitung*, 24.3.2003.

Casper, Steven. 1999. *High Technology Governance and Institutional Adaptiveness*. Wissenschaftszentrum Berlin für Sozialforschung, Working Paper FS I 99–307.

Casper, Steven, Mark Lehrer, and David Soskice. 1999. "Can High-Technology Industries Prosper in Germany?" *Industry and Innovation* 6: 5–24.

Casper, Steven, and Catherine Matraves. 1997. *Corporate Governance and Firm Strategy in the Pharmaceutical Industry.* Wissenschaftszentrum Berlin für Sozialforschung, Discussion Paper FS IV 97–20.

Chandler, Alfred, Jr. 1990. *Scale and Scope: The Dynamics of Industrial Capitalism.* Cambridge, MA: Belknap Press.

Coffee, John C., Jr. 1999. *The Future as History: The Prospects for Global Convergence in Corporate Governance and Its Implications.* The Center for Law and Economic Studies, Columbia Law School, Working Paper No. 144.

Corbett, Jenny, and Tim Jenkinson. 1998. "German Investment Financing: An International Comparison." In *Competition and Convergence in Financial Markets. The German and Anglo-American Models,* ed. Stanley Black and Matthias Moersch. Amsterdam: Elsevier, 101–23.

Darbishire, Owen. 1997. "Germany." In *Telecommunications: Restructuring Work and Employment Relations Worldwide,* ed. Harry C. Katz. Ithaca: Cornell University Press, 189–227.

Davis, Gerald F., and Michael Useem. 2002. "Top Management, Company Directors, and Corporate Control." In *Handbook of Strategy and Management,* ed. Andrew Pettigrew, Howard Thomas, and Richard Whittington. London: Sage, 233–59.

Decker, Hans, and Arvid Lukauskas. 2000. *Is Corporate Governance Converging across Countries? Recent Trends in Germany.* School of International and Public Affairs, Columbia University, manuscript.

Deeg, Richard. 1996. *German Banks and Industrial Finance in the 1990s.* Wissenschaftszentrum Berlin für Sozialforschung, Discussion Paper FSI 96–323.

———. 1999. *Finance Capital Unveiled: Banks and the German Political Economy.* Ann Arbor: University of Michigan Press.

———. 2001. *Institutional Change and the Uses and Limits of Path Dependency: The Case of German Finance.* Max-Planck-Institute for the Study of Societies, Discussion Paper 01/6.

———. 2005. "Path Dependency, Institutional Complementarity, and Change in National Business Systems." In *Changing Capitalisms? Complementarities, Contradictions and Capability Development in an International Context,* ed. Glenn Morgan, Richard Whitley, and Eli Moen. Oxford: Oxford University Press, 21–52.

De Jong, Henk Wouter. 1997. "The Governance Structure and Performance of Large European Corporations." *Journal of Management and Governance* 1: 5–27.

Deutsche Bank Research. 2002. "Corporate Governance in Germany—Perspectives from Economics and Finance." *Research Notes in Economics and Statistics,* 02–3.

Deutsche Bundesbank. 1999. *Corporate Finance in Germany and France: A Comparative Analysis.* Monthly Report October, Frankfurt.

———. 2004a. *Monatsbericht Juni.* Frankfurt.

———. 2004b. *Financial Accounts for Germany 1991–2003.* Special Statistical Publications 4, Frankfurt.

Deutsche Telekom. *Annual report.* Various years.

———. 2000. *IPO prospectus.* 26.5.2000.

Deutscher Bundestag. 2005. *Bericht des Bundeskartellamtes über seine Tätigkeit in den Jahren 2003/2004 sowie über die Lage und Entwicklung auf seinem Aufgabengebiet und Stellungnahme der Bundesregierung*. Drucksache 15/5790, 15. Wahlperiode, http://dip.bundestag.de/btd/15/057/1505790.pdf.

Deutsches Aktieninstitut. 2001. *Corporate Governance—Nutzen und Umsetzung*, Studien des Deutschen Aktieninstituts No. 15, Frankfurt.

——. 2005. *DAI Factbook*. Frankfurt.

Doremus, Paul, William Keller, Louis Pauly, and Simon Reich. 1998. *The Myth of the Global Corporation*. Princeton: Princeton University Press.

Dörrenbacher, Christoph. 1999. *Vom Hoflieferanten zum Global Player. Unternehmensorganisation und nationale Politik in der Welttelekommunikationsindustrie*. Berlin: Edition Sigma.

Dufey, Gunter, Ulrich Hommel, and Petra Riemer-Hommel. 1998. "Corporate Governance: European vs. U.S. Perspectives in a Global Capital Market." In *Strategisches Euro-Management*, ed. Christian Scholz and Joachim Zentes. Stuttgart: Schäffer Poeschel, 45–65.

DWS. 2001. *European Corporate Governance Ranking Report—Euro Stoxx 50*. downloadable from www.managermagazin.de.

Eberwein, Wilhelm, and Jochen Tholen. 1993. *Euro-Manager or Splendid Isolation? International Management—An Anglo-German Comparison*. Berlin: Walter de Gruyter.

Edwards, Jeremy, and Klaus Fischer. 1994. *Banks, Finance, and Investment in Germany*. Cambridge: Cambridge University Press.

Edwards, Jeremy, and Marcus Nibler. 1999. *Corporate Governance in Germany: The Influence of Banks and Large Equity Holders*. Center for Economic Studies, University of Munich, Working Paper No. 180.

Fligstein, Neil. 2001. *The Architecture of Markets: An Economic Sociology of Twenty-First-Century Capitalist Societies*. Princeton: Princeton University Press.

Förschle, Gerhart, and Martin Glaum. 1998. *Kapitalmarktorientierung deutscher Unternehmen. Ergebnisse einer empirischen Untersuchung*. Frankfurt: Verlag Moderne Wirtschaft.

Foudy, Joseph. 2001. *Shareholder Value and the German and Japanese Models: A Case Study of the Automobile Sector*. Paper presented at Comparative Political Economy of Developed and Less Developed Countries conference, Yale University, May 4–5, 2001.

Franks, Julian, and Colin Mayer. 1995. "Ownership and Control." in *Trends in Business Organization: Do Participation and Cooperation Increase Competitiveness?* ed. Horst Siebert. Tübingen: Mohr, 171–95.

——. 1997. "Corporate Ownership and Control in the UK, Germany, and France." In *Studies in International Corporate Finance and Governance Systems*, ed. Donald H. Chew. Oxford: Oxford University Press, 281–96.

German Federal Ministry of Education and Research. 2005. *Bericht zur technologischen Leistungsfähigkeit Deutschlands 2005*. Berlin.

——. 2006. *Bericht zur technologischen Leistungsfähigkeit Deutschlands 2006*. Berlin.

Gerpott, Torsten J. 1998. *Wettbewerbsstrategien im Telekommunikationsmarkt*. 3rd ed. Stuttgart: Schäffer-Poeschel.

Gerschenkron, Alexander. 1962. *Economic Backwardness in Historical Perspective*. Cambridge, MA: Harvard University Press.

Gilson, Ronald J. 2000. *The Globalization of Corporate Governance: Convergence of Form or Function.* Center for Law and Economic Studies, Columbia Law School, Working Paper 192.

Glotz, Peter. 2001. *Ron Sommer: Der Weg der Telekom.* Hamburg: Hoffmann und Campe.

Gordon, Jeffrey N. 2000. *Pathways to Corporate Convergence? Two Steps on the Road to Shareholder Capitalism in Germany: Deutsche Telekom and DaimlerChrysler.* Center for Law and Economic Studies, Columbia Law School, Working Paper No. 161.

Goth, Günther. 1999. "Veränderungen in der unternehmerischen Personal- und Beschäftigungspolitik am Beispiel der Siemens AG." In *Wandel der Arbeitswelt— Folgerungen für die Sozialpolitik,* ed. Winfried Schmähl and Herbert Rische. Baden-Baden: Nomos Verlagsgesellschaft, 83–105.

Gourevitch, Peter, and James Shinn. 2005. *Political Power and Corporate Control: The New Global Politics of Corporate Governance.* Princeton: Princeton University Press.

Goyer, Michel. 2006. "Capital Mobility: Varieties of Institutional Investors and the Transforming Stability of Corporate Governance in France and Germany." In *Beyond Varieties of Capitalism: Conflict, Contradiction and Complementarities in the European Economy,* ed. Bob Hancké, Martin Rhodes, and Mark Thatcher. Oxford: Oxford University Press.

Guillen, Mauro. 2000a. "Corporate Governance and Globalization: Is There Convergence across Countries?" *Advances in International and Comparative Management* 13: 175–204.

———. 2000b. *Comparative Economic Sociology: Blending Social Stratification, Organizational Theory, and the Sociology of Development.* Paper prepared for the Latin American Studies Association, Miami.

———. 2003. *The Limits of Convergence.* Princeton: Princeton University Press.

Hackethal, Andreas. 2000. *Banken, Unternehmensfinanzierung und Finanzsysteme.* Frankfurt: Peter Lang.

Hackethal, Andreas, and Reinhart Schmidt. 2000. *Finanzsystem und Komplementarität.* Johann Wolfgang Goethe University, Frankfurt, Working Paper Series Finance and Accounting No. 50.

Hall, Peter. 1986. *Governing the Economy: The Politics of State Intervention in Britain and France.* Oxford: Oxford University Press.

———. 1997. "The Political Economy of Adjustment in Germany." In *Ökonomische Leistungsfähigkeit und institutionelle Innovation. Das deutsche Produktions- und Politikregime im globalen Wettbewerb,* ed. Frieder Nachold, David Soskice, Bob Hancke, and Ulrich Jürgens. Berlin: edition sigma, 293–317.

———. 1999. "The Political Economy of Europe in an Era of Interdependence." In *Continuity and Change in Contemporary Capitalism,* ed. Herbert Kitschelt, Peter Lange, Gary Marks, and John D. Stephens. Cambridge: Cambridge University Press, 135–63.

Hall, Peter, and Daniel Gingerich. 2001. *Varieties of Capitalism and Institutional Complementarities in the Macroeconomy: An Empirical Analysis.* Draft Paper for the Annual Meeting of the American Political Science Association, San Francisco, August 30, 2001.

Hall, Peter, and David Soskice. 2001. "Introduction." In *Varieties of Capitalism: The Institutional Foundations of Comparative Institutional Advantage*, ed. Hall and Soskice. Oxford: Oxford University Press, 1–68.

Hancké, Bob, and Michel Goyer. 2005. "Degrees of Freedom: Rethinking the Institutional Analysis of Economic Change." In *Changing Capitalisms? Complementarities, Contradictions and Capability Development in an International Context*, ed. Glenn Morgan, Richard Whitley, and Eli Moen. Oxford: Oxford University Press, 53–77.

Hassel, Anke, Martin Höpner, Antje Kurdelbusch, Britta Rehder, and Rainer Zugehör. 2000. *Dimensionen der Internationalisierung: Ergebnisse der Unternehmensdatenbank Internationalisierung der 100 größten Unternehmen in Deutschland*. Max-Planck-Institute for the Study of Societies, Working Paper 2000/1.

Hedlund, Gunnar, and Dag Rolander. 1990. "Action in Heterarchies—New Approaches to Managing the MNC." In *Managing the Global Firm*, ed. Christopher A. Bartlett, Yves Doz, and Gunnar Hedlund. London: Routledge, 15–45.

Hellwig, Martin. 2000a. "On the Economics and Politics of Corporate Finance and Corporate Control." In *Corporate Governance: Theoretical and Empirical Perspectives*, ed. Xavier Vives. Cambridge: Cambridge University Press, 95–124.

———. 2000b. *Corporate Governance and the Financing of Investment for Structural Change*. Paper presented at the Bundesbank Spring Conference, Investing Today for the World of Tomorrow, Frankfurt.

Herdt, Hans Konradin. 1986. *Bosch 1986—1986. Porträt eines Unternehmens*. Stuttgart: Deutsche Verlags Anstalt.

Hilferding, Rudolf. 1981. *Finance Capital*. London: Routledge and Kegan Paul.

Holmström, Bengt, and Steven N. Kaplan. 2001. *Corporate Governance and Merger Activity in the United States: Making Sense of the 1980s and 1990s*. National Bureau of Economic Research, Working Paper 8220.

Holmström, Bengt, and John Roberts. 1998. "The Boundaries of the Firm Revisited." *Journal of Economic Perspectives* 12: 73–94.

Höpner, Martin. 2001. *Corporate Governance in Transition: Ten Empirical Findings on Shareholder Value and Industrial Relations in Germany*. Max-Planck-Institute for the Study of Societies, Discussion Paper 01/5.

Höpner, Martin, and Gregory Jackson. 2001. *An Emerging Market for Corporate Control? The Mannesmann Takeover and German Corporate Governance*. Max-Planck-Institute for the Study of Societies, Discussion Paper 01/4.

Hoskisson, Robert E., Daphne Yiu, and Hincheon Kim. 2000. "Capital and Labour Market Congruence and Corporate Governance: Effects on Corporate Innovation and Global Competitiveness." In *Corporate Governance and Globalization. Long Range Planning Issues*, ed. Stephen S. Cohen, and Gavin Boyd. Cheltenham: Edward Elgar, 129–54.

Jenkinson, Thomas, and Colin Mayer. 1992. "The Assessment: Corporate Governance and Corporate Control." *Oxford Review of Economic Policy* 8: 1–10.

Jensen, Michael. 1989. "The Eclipse of the Public Corporation." *Harvard Business Review* 67: 61–74.

Junne, Gerd. 1989. "Competitiveness and the Impact of Change: Application of 'High Technologies.'" In *Industry and Politics in West Germany*, ed. Peter Katzenstein. Ithaca: Cornell University Press, 249–74.

Jürgens, Ulrich. 2002. *CGEP—Industry Studies: The German Car Industry.* Manuscript for the project Corporate Governance, Innovation, and Economic Performance in the EU, INSEAD, Fountainebleau.

Jürgens, Ulrich, Joachim Rupp, and Katrin Vitols. 2000a. "Shareholder Value in an Adverse Environment: The German Case." *Economy and Society* 29: 54–79.

——. 2000b. *Corporate Governance and Shareholder Value in Deutschland. Nach dem Fall von Mannesmann—Paper Revisited.* Wissenschaftszentrum Berlin für Sozialforschung, Discussion Paper FS II 00—202.

Kaplan, Steven. 1994a. "Top Executives Turnover and Firm Performance in Germany." *Journal of Law, Economics, and Organization* 10: 142–59.

——. 1994b. "Top Executive Rewards and Firm Performance: A Comparison of the Japan and the United States." *Journal of Political Economy* 102: 510–46.

Karsch, Werner. 2002. "Der Dax unter der Lupe: Unternehmensstrukturen im Zeichen der Globalisierung." *Die Bank* 12: 818–22.

Katz, Harry, and Owen Darbishire. 2000. *Converging Divergences: Worldwide Changes in Employment Systems.* Ithaca: Cornell University Press.

Köke, Jens. 1999. *New Evidence on Ownership Structures in Germany.* Zentrum für Europäische Wirtschaftsforschung, Discussion Paper 99–60.

Lane, Christel. 1998. "European Companies between Globalization and Localization—A Comparison of Internationalization Strategies of British and German MNCs." *Economy and Society* 27: 462–85.

——. 2000a. "Globalization and the German Model of Capitalism—Erosion or Survival?" *British Journal of Sociology* 51: 207–34.

——. 2000b. "Understanding the Globalization Strategies of German and British Multinational Companies." In *Embedding Organizations: Societal Analysis of Actors, Organizations and Socio-Economic Context,* ed. Marc Maurice and Arndt Sorge. Amsterdam: John Benjamins, 189–208.

La Porta, Rafael, Florencio Lopez-de-Silanes, and Andrei Shleifer. 1998. "Corporate Ownership around the World." *Journal of Finance* 54: 471–517.

Lawrence, Peter. 1980. *Managers and Management in West Germany.* London: Croomhelm.

Lazonick, William, and Mary O'Sullivan. 2000a. *Perspectives on Corporate Governance, Innovation, and Economic Performance.* Report to the European Commission (DGXII) under the TSER programme.

——. 2000b. "Maximising Shareholder Value: A New Ideology for Corporate Governance." *Economy and Society* 29: 13–35.

Leuz, Christian, and Jens Wüstemann. 2004. "The Role of Accounting in the German Financial System." In *The German Financial System,* ed. Jan Krahnen and Reinhard Schmidt. Oxford: Oxford University Press, 450–82.

Maher, Maria, and Thomas Andersson. 1999. *Corporate Governance: Effects on Firm Performance and Economic Growth.* Paris: OECD.

Matthes, Jürgen. 2000. *Das deutsche Corporate Governance-System. Wandel von der Stakeholder Orientierung zum Shareholder-Value-Denken.* Institut der deutschen Wirtschaft, Beiträge zur Wirtschafts-und Sozialpolitik No. 259.

Mayer, Michael, and Richard Whittington. 1999. "Strategy, Structure and Systemness: National Institutions and Corporate Change in France, Germany, and the UK, 1950–1993." *Organization Studies* 20: 933–59.

Menz, Wolfgang, Steffan Becker, and Thomas Sablowski. 1999. *Shareholder-Value gegen Belegschaftsinteressen. Der Weg der Hoechst-AG zum 'Life-Sciences' –Konzern.* Hamburg: VSA-Verlag.

Milgrom, Paul, and John Roberts. 1992. *Economics, Organization, and Management.* New Jersey: Prentice Hall.

Naschold, Frieder. 1997. *Die Siemens AG: Inkrementale Anpassung oder Unternehmenstransformation? Eine Fallstudie über Kontinuität und Wandel eines Konzerns.* Wissenschaftszentrum Berlin für Sozialforschung, Working Paper FS II 97–201.

North, Douglass. 1994. "Economic Performance through Time." *American Economic Review* 84: 359–68.

Nürk, Bettina. 1998. "Institutional Investors and Their Implications for Financial Markets in Germany." In *Institutional Investors in the New Financial Landscape.* OECD: Paris, 179–95.

OECD. Institutional Investor Database. http://cs4hq.oecd.org/oecd/eng/TableViewer/Wdsview/dispviewp.asp?ReportId=1879&bReportOnly=True, accessed May 2005.

——. 1998a. "Shareholder Value and the Market in Corporate Control in OECD Countries." *Financial Market Trends* 69: 15–37.

——. 1998b. "Structural and Regulatory Development in OECD countries." *Financial Market Trends* 71: 21–25.

——. 2001a. *New Patterns of Industrial Globalisation: Cross-Border Mergers and Acquisitions and Strategic Alliances.* Paris: OECD.

——. 2001b. "Recent Trends: Institutional Investors Statistics." *Financial Market Trends* 80: 46–52.

——. 2001c. *Communications Outlook 2001.* Paris: OECD.

——. 2004. *Employment Outlook.* Paris: OECD.

O'Sullivan, Mary. 2000. *Contests for Corporate Control: Corporate Governance and Economic Performance in the United States and Germany.* Oxford: Oxford University Press.

——. 2001. *A Revolution in European Corporate Governance? The Extent and Implications of Recent Developments in the Role of the Stock Market in Five European Economies.* Synthesis Report on National Systems of Corporate Governance, INSEAD, Fountainebleau.

Pierer, Heinrich von. 1996. *Langfristige Ausrichtung des Unternehmens.* Supervisory board presentation, 11.12.1996, internal Siemens document.

Porsche. *Annual Report.* Various Years.

Porter, Michael. 1980. *Competitive Strategy: Techniques for Analyzing Industries and Competitors.* New York: The Free Press.

——. 1990. *The Competitive Advantage of Nations.* New York: The Free Press.

Prahalad, C. K. 1994. "Corporate Governance or Corporate Value Added? Rethinking the Primacy of Shareholder Value." *Journal of Applied Corporate Finance* 6: 40–50.

Prigge, Stefan. 1998. "A Survey of German Corporate Governance." In *Comparative Corporate Governance—The State of the Art and Emerging Research,* ed. Klaus Hopt, Hideki Kanda, Mark Roe, Eddy Wymeersch, and Stefan Prigge. Oxford: Clarendon Press, 943–1044.

Prowse, Stephen. 1998. "Atlantic Systems of Corporate Finance and Governance." In *The Struggle for World Markets: Competition and Cooperation between NAFTA and the European Union,* ed. Gavin Boyd. Cheltenham: Edward Elgar, 80–109.

Rappaport, Alfred. 1986. *Creating Shareholder Value: The New Standard for Business Performance.* New York: The Free Press.

Rathe, Klaus, and Ulrich Witt. 2001. "The Nature of the Firm—Static versus Developmental Interpretations." *Journal of Management and Governance* 5: 331–51.

Roe, Mark. 2003. *Political Determinants of Corporate Governance.* Oxford: Oxford University Press.

——. 2004. *The Institutions of Corporate Governance.* Harvard Law School, Discussion Paper No. 488.

Rothblum, David. 1996. "IR: Zweigleisige Kommunikation entscheidend." *Börsen-Zeitung,* 7.11.1996.

Rugman, Alan, and Alain Verbeke. 2000. "Six Cases of Corporate Strategic Responses to Environmental Regulation." *European Management Journal* 18: 377–85.

Ruigrok, Winfried, Andrew Pettigrew, Simon Peck, and Richard Whittington. 1999. "Corporate Restructuring and New Forms of Organizing: Evidence from Europe." *Management International Review* 39: 41–64.

Sablowski, Thomas, and Joachim Rupp. 2001. "Die neue Ökonomie des Shareholder Value: Corporate Governance im Wandel." *Prokla* 31: 47–78.

Schmid, Frank, and Mark Wahrenburg. 2004. "Mergers and Acquisitions in Germany: Social Setting and Regulatory Framework." In *The German Financial System,* ed. Jan Krahnen and Reinhard Schmidt. Oxford: Oxford University Press, 261–87.

Schmidt, Reinhard. 1999. *Differences between Financial Systems in European Countries: Consequences for EMU.* Paper prepared for the Monetary Transmission Process conference organized by the Deutsche Bundesbank, March 26/27, Frankfurt.

——. 2004. "Corporate Governance in Germany: An Economic Perspective." In *The German Financial System,* ed. Jan Krahnen and Reinhard Schmidt. Oxford: Oxford University Press, 386–424.

Schmidt, Reinhard, and Stefanie Grohs. 1999. *Angleichung der Wirtschaftsverfassung in Europa—ein Forschungsprogramm.* Johann Wolfgang Goethe University Frankfurt, Working Paper Series, Finance and Accounting No. 43.

Schmidt, Reinhard, Andreas Hackethal, and Marcel Tyrell. 1999. "Disintermediation and the Role of Banks in Europe: An International Comparison." *Journal of Financial Intermediation* 8: 36–67.

Schmidt, Reinhard, and Jens Maßmann. 1999. *Drei Mißverständnisse zum Thema 'Shareholder Value.'* Johann Wolfgang Goethe University Frankfurt, Working Paper Series, Finance and Accounting No. 31.

Schmidt, Reinhard, and Gerald Spindler. 1999. *Path Dependence, Corporate Governance, and Complementarity—A Comment on Bebchuk and Roe.* Johann Wolfgang Goethe University Frankfurt, Working Paper Series, Finance and Accounting, No. 27.

Schmidt, Vivien A. 2002. *The Futures of European Capitalism.* Oxford: Oxford University Press.

Seibert, Ulrich. 1999. "Control and Transparency in Business." *European Business Law Review* 10: 70–75.

Shleifer, Andrei, and Robert Vishny. 1997. "A Survey of Corporate Governance." *The Journal of Finance* 52: 737–83.

Shonfield, Andrew. 1965. *Modern Capitalism.* New York: Oxford University Press.

Siebert, Horst. 2004. *Germany's Capital Market and Corporate Governance.* Kiel Institute for World Economics, Working Paper No. 1206.

Siemens. *Annual Report.* Various years.

——. 1984. *Die Siemens Aktie: Finanzierungsinstrument, Kapitalanlage.* 3rd edition. Siemens Archives.

——. 2005. *Corporate Technology.* http://w4.siemens.de/ct/de/about/anlagen/besucher2005_d.pdf, accessed April 2006.

Sommer, Ron. *Speech at the General Annual Meeting of Deutsche Telekom.* Various Years.

Soskice, David. 1997. "Technologiepolitik, Innovation und nationale Institutionengefuege in Deutschland." In *Oekonomische Leistungsfaehigkeit und institutionelle Innovation: Das deutsche Produktions- und Politikregime im globalen Wettbewerb,* ed. Frieder Naschold, David Soskice, Bob Hancke, and Ulrich Juergens. Berlin: edition sigma, 319–48.

——. 1999. "Divergent Production Regimes: Coordinated and Uncoordinated Market Economies in 1980s and 1990s." In *Continuity and Change in Contemporary Capitalism,* ed. Herbert Kitschelt, Peter Lange, Gary Marks, and John D. Stephens. Cambridge: Cambridge University Press, 101–34.

——. 2000. "Explaining Changes in Institutional Frameworks: Societal Patterns of Business Coordination." In *Embedding Organizations: Societal Analysis of Actors, Organizations, and Socio-Economic Context,* ed. Marc Maurice and Arndt Sorge. Amsterdam: John Benjamins, 167–83.

Steiger, Max. 2000. *Institutionelle Investoren im Spannungsfeld zwischen Aktienmarktliquidität und Corporate Governance.* Baden-Baden: Nomos.

Steinherr, Alfred. 1998. "Universal versus Specialized Banks." In *Competition and Convergence in Financial Markets: The German and Anglo-American Models,* ed. Stanley W. Black and Mathias Moersch. Amsterdam: Elsevier, 181–94.

Streeck, Wolfgang. 1992. *Social Institutions and Economic Performance: Studies of Industrial Relations in Advanced Capitalist Economies.* London: Sage.

——. 1997. "German Capitalism: Does It Exist? Can It Survive?" In *Political Economy of Modern Capitalism: Mapping Convergence and Diversity,* ed. Colin Crouch and Wolfgang Streeck. London: Sage, 33–54.

——. 2001. *The Transformation of Corporate Organization in Europe: An Overview.* Max-Planck-Institute for the Study of Societies, Working Paper 01/8.

Streeck, Wolfgang, and Kathleen Thelen. 2005. "Introduction: Institutional Change in Advanced Political Economies." In *Beyond Continuity: Explorations in the Dynamics of Advanced Political Economies,* ed. Streeck and Thelen. Oxford: Oxford University Press, 1–39.

Streeck, Wolfgang, and Kozo Yamamura. 2004. "Introduction: Convergence or Diversity? Stability and Change in German and Japanese Capitalism." In *The End of Diversity? Prospects for German and Japanese Capitalism,* ed. Yamamura and Streeck. Ithaca: Cornell University Press, 1–50.

Teece, David, and Gary Pisano. 1994. "The Dynamic Capabilities of Firms: An Introduction." *Industrial and Corporate Change* 3: 537–56.

Teece, David, Gary Pisano, and Amy Shuen. 1997. "Dynamic Capabilities and Strategic Management." *Strategic Management Journal* 18: 509–33.

Thelen, Kathleen. 1999. "The Effects of Globalization on Labor Revisited: Lessons from Germany and Japan." *Politics and Society* 27: 477–505.

Tirole, Jean. 2001. "Corporate Governance." *Econometrica* 69: 1–35.

Towers Perrin. 2002. *Worldwide Total Remuneration 2001–2002.* http://towersper rin.com/hrservices/webcache/towers/Germany/publications/Reports/2001 _02_WorldwideRemun/WWTR_2001_German.pdf., accessed March 2005.

Useem, Michael. 1996. *Investor Capitalism: How Money Managers Are Changing the Face of Corporate America.* New York: Basic Books.

Vitols, Sigurt. 1995a. *Are German Banks Different?* Wissenschaftszentrum Berlin für Sozialforschung, Discussion Paper FS I 95–311.

——. 1995b. *Corporate Governance versus Economic Governance: Banks and Industrial Restructuring in the United States and Germany.* Wissenschaftszentrum Berlin für Sozialforschung, Discussion Paper FS I 95–312.

——. 2000. *The Reconstruction of German Corporate Governance: Reassessing the Role of Capital Market Pressures.* Paper presented at the first annual meeting of the Research Network on Corporate Governance, Wissenschaftszentrum Berlin für Sozialforschung, June 22–23.

——. 2003. "Many Roads to Rome? Corporate Governance, Production Regimes, and the Transformation of the German Chemical-Pharmaceutical Industry." In *Alle Macht dem Markt? Fallstudien zur Abwicklung der Deutschland AG*, ed. Wolfgang Streeck and Martin Höpner. Frankfurt: Campus, 197–221.

Warburg, M. M., & Co, Investment Research. 1998. *Aktie im Blickpunkt Siemens.* August 1998.

Windolf, Paul. 2002. *Corporate Networks in Europe and the United States.* Oxford: Oxford University Press.

Windolf, Paul, and Michael Nollert. 2001. "Institutionen, Interessen, Netzwerke: Unternehmensverflechtung im internationalen Vergleich." *Politische Vierteljahresschrift* 42: 51–78.

Wüstemann, Jens. 2001. "Mängel bei der Abschlußprüfung: Tatsachenberichte und Analysen aus betriebswirtschaftlicher Sicht." In *Der Wirtschaftsprüfer als Element der Corporate Governance*, ed Marcus Lutter. Düsseldorf: IDW-Verlag, 19–43.

Ziegler, Nicholas J. 1999. *Corporate Governance and the Politics of Property Rights in Germany.* Center for German and European Studies, University of California, Berkeley, Working Paper #5–90.

Zugehör, Rainer. 2003. "Kapitalmarktorientierung und Mitbestimmung: Veba und Siemens." In *Alle Macht dem Markt? Fallstudien zur Abwicklung der Deutschland AG*, ed. Wolfgang Streeck and Martin Höpner. Frankfurt: Campus, 249–71.

Zysman, John. 1983. *Governments, Markets, and Growth: Financial Systems and the Politics of Industrial Change.* Ithaca: Cornell University Press.

Index